THE KRAYS' FINAL YEARS

My Time with
London's Most
Iconic Gangsters

STEVE WRAITH
AND **STUART WHEATMAN**

First published in Great Britain by Percy Publishing in 2015

Second edition published in Great Britain by Gadfly Press in 2020

Copyright © Steve Wraith 2020

The right of Steve Wraith to be identified as the author of this work has been asserted by her in accordance with the Copyright, Designs and Patents Act 1988. All rights reserved

No part of this book may be reproduced, stored in a retrieval system or transmitted in any form or by any means (electronic, mechanical, photocopying, recording or otherwise) without the prior written permission of the author, except in cases of brief quotations embodied in reviews or articles. It may not be edited, amended, lent, resold, hired out, distributed or otherwise circulated without the publisher's written permission

Permission can be obtained from gadflypress@outlook.com

This book is a work of non-fiction based on research by the author

A catalogue record of this book is available from the British Library

Typeset and cover by Jane Dixon-Smith

SPELLING DIFFERENCES: UK V US

This book was written in British English, hence US readers may notice some spelling differences with American English: e.g. color = colour, meter = metre and = jewelry = jewellery

CONTENTS

Introduction	1
Chapter 1: East End Development	5
Chapter 2: Cockney Rebels	25
Chapter 3: Likely Lads	43
Chapter 4: Meeting the Krays	61
Chapter 5: Doing the Door	100
Chapter 6: Party Time	128
Chapter 7: Mr X	175
Chapter 8: The Final Curtain	233
Chapter 9: Looking Back	238
Other Books by Gadfly Press	246
Hard Time by Shaun Attwood	254
Prison Time by Shaun Attwood	261
About the Authors	266

INTRODUCTION

In 1982, I saw Ron and Reg Kray on the news. Sitting there with my parents, Celia and John, I watched the twins get bundled in and out of a prison van to their mother's funeral. It was one of those things that stick in your mind. For me, it almost has the same importance as knowing where you were when Kennedy was shot.

It was my first sighting of them. I'd never heard of these men before, but my parents certainly had. They were talking about the crowds of people who were there ... I mean, if not for the police and handcuffs, you would never know they were serving life sentences for murder. I was awestruck. Cuffed to huge officers ... *why*? Crowds of well-wishers ... *why*? Serving that amount of time? There were so many questions. The gist of what I was told was that they were gangsters from London who were locked away when my parents were in their teens. That was enough for me. I needed to find out more.

Later at school, I wrote an essay about the Kray twins, after reading their official biography, *The Profession of Violence* by John Pearson, and received a B+ for it. The book is awesome. Without having what I'd call a true academic interest in a lot of subjects, this was a minor miracle ... another encounter with the twins and this time it goes towards passing an exam.

The 'real' part of the Krays' story for me began as a teenager in 1990. This was when I went to see a film described by *The Mail on Sunday* as, 'Life at the cutting edge of the Sixties'. That film was the biopic called *The Krays*. I went with my best mate at the time, Matthew Gregory, paid £1.50, and armed with a family pack of salt and vinegar crisps and a large carton of Coke, began to reacquaint myself with the brothers grim.

The film seemed to be over in an instant, and as the credits rolled and the music began to fade, we found ourselves paying to watch the film again. I needed to see it again to believe it. To see Ron and Reg being played on the big screen was something special. How often are biopics made about people who are still alive? Not too often. It was great to see them up there. The Kemp brothers from Spandau Ballet played the twins convincingly ... I don't think that there was anyone around who could have done it so well.

Although a good film with high production values, certain events had been fabricated, and fact and fiction blended into one. As the credits rolled for the second time, I noticed an update: "Ronald Kray currently in Broadmoor Hospital, Reginald Kray H.M.P. (Her Majesty's Prison) Gartree."

I was hooked right there in that cinema. There had always been a mythology surrounding not just the twins, but all three Kray brothers. The release of this film gave it its second wind, turning it almost into a mania. No one can really pinpoint the fascination ... Are they heroes? Are they villains? Anti-heroes?

The truth is, they were all of that and a whole lot more. They had style, charisma and charm. Everyone who watched that film would come out with a different perspective. Their story struck a chord somehow. It certainly did with me, and I knew I had to do something about it. I'm not saying I came out of the cinema and wanted to *be* a gangster. For most lads at that age, the whole thing had appeal. Knowing they were still alive was the key to the whole thing and being told where they were at the end was the clincher.

I made my mind up to write to them. That was my perspective on it. The film rejuvenated my interest and I just knew I had to at least try. Of course, it sounded crazy, I knew that, but it was a decision I was going to stick by. Then came the questions in my mind ... Would they write back? Would they have time? Duuuuuuuh, Steve ... just a decade or so. What would my mam and dad think? Who cares! I was going to do it ... I was going to write to the Kray twins.

So how do you start writing a letter to someone who (a) does not know who you are, (b) is a convicted murderer and (c) is unlikely to be interested in you and will probably not even bother replying? By writing about yourself, of course, and by trying to make yourself sound as interesting as possible. It was kind of like writing a résumé – a selling document. I was selling an idea.

In a way, I suppose it was my first step into self-publicity. I set the ball rolling that day and little did I know the scale of what I'd started. That initial letter propelled me into a completely different world – one like the film I had just watched, a world in which all those teenagers could only dream about.

Over the years that followed, I became close to the three Kray brothers, and was invited by them to join a select circle of friends. I did a lot of growing up and learnt a hell of a lot in such a short space of time. I went from a Kray fan to being a Kray friend and Kray associate. I became one of the few people to visit all three brothers in prison, to be called a close friend, to oversee countless business ventures ranging from the outlandish to the mental.

Imagine being given the chance to walk around inside the pages of your favourite book ... to meet the main characters, meet their friends, become part of that book and to have a physical effect on it and change it in some way. In replying to my initial letter, that's what Reggie did for me. He handed me the opportunity to become a part of the mythological world that once seemed light years away.

In introducing myself, I'd like to start by saying I'm not a gangster. I don't try or pretend to be, never have been and never will be. There are certainly a lot of people I know as friends that you may say are gangsters. I've also met a hundred and one people who you would call plastic gangsters, cartoon gangsters, wannabes, hangers-on ... you name it.

It's the types who are acting the part that you learn to be wary of. They can damage you and others around you through sheer stupidity. Why? Because they *really are* playing the part in the gangster film, in their own eyes. They start to believe the hype and think that they are untouchable. In the real world, they are not De Niro, and Eliot Ness has been known to turn up and spoil one or two parties, I can tell you.

I'd also like to say that this is not another hardman book. To talk like that isn't my style, so to act like that would be alien. I used to work as a doorman and can handle myself when the situation calls for it.

To write a book has always been an ambition of mine. They say that there is a book within all of us waiting to be written. Well this is my book. There have been dozens of books written about them: rehashed, repackaged and redesigned, updated third edition, repriced ... and ... repetitive. All written for the same reason ... to cash in on the name Kray, and this book is no different.

Kray ... You know that there is something about the name, but you just can't put your finger on it. Much the same can be said about the three brothers: Ron, Reg and Charlie. Whenever I met them, they were always dressed immaculately, like any high-flying businessman, from any city, yet you knew something was unusual; they were different to me or you, and they knew it.

I have talked about a hypothetical 'journey' already. I'd say that this book is about journeys: mine and theirs. Different paths that crossed and then parted; paths that ran the same course for a bit, though I had the power to change the direction of mine.

This book gives you an insight into my life within the inner circle of the Krays' friends and family. It gives you a look into how they still made things tick from behind prison walls. It's true to say that their business only began to thrive once they were locked up. I know, because I was a part of it. I can tell you what they were really like, as a firm as well as individuals. This book is about how I became their 'Geordie Connection'.

I would like to think that Ron, Reg and Charlie could look at this book and say that I did them proud, but I know that deep down all they would want is their cut ... maybe that says it all. To me it's not about hero worship, it's about the truth.

CHAPTER 1

EAST END DEVELOPMENT

Many know the story of the Krays. Most know that the twins were incarcerated in the Sixties for murdering two people. They were born in a time when the UK was beginning to go through a huge transition, socially and economically.

The East End of London conjures up different images. It has changed a great deal since the Krays' era, but to go back just over 100 years, it was a different place altogether. London in the early nineteenth century was dark and dingy. East London became industrialised at around that time and a working-class population soon became established, as more people went to live there and start families.

The area saw a huge growth in size and population. Conditions were poor and soon became overcrowded. The narrow streets were filthy, neglected and barely even lit at night. Prostitutes, brothels, drunkenness, robbery and assaults … it's hard to imagine what the place was like unless you were there. There were slaughterhouses, rendering plants, glue factories, engineering works, loads of breweries … With all this in the East of London, the westerly winds would carry the stench away from the affluent West End.

Leather was another growth industry, so there were many tanning yards in the area. To darken the leather hides, 'pure' was used. The 'charvers' (wasters, scallies, losers, etc.) of their day would procure the pure of a night, which basically means they would supply the leather workers with dog shit found on the street. Now you are starting to get the picture. Dog turds on the streets and pollution in the air.

East London was also the stomping (or stabbing) ground of the first world-famous serial killer: Jack the Ripper. In 1888, between Friday, 31 August and Friday, 9 November, he murdered and mutilated five women so savagely that it caused fear throughout the city. The victims were prostitutes in or near Whitechapel. The crimes were known as the Whitechapel murders.

Once the newspapers picked up on the second and third victims, Jack the Ripper was born. He was no average serial killer – he was called that because of the way he would tear out their organs or rip them to pieces. He was never caught and has been the subject of much speculation and countless film adaptations, including *From Hell*, by the Hughes Brothers.

North of Whitechapel is Hoxton, or Shoreditch as it is now known. This is where another famous East End name would emerge. That name is Kray. Charles James Kray, the twins' older brother, was born in 1927 at the first family home in Gorsuch Street in Hackney.

Ronald and Reginald Kray were born on 24 October 1933 in Stene Street. They were identical twins, born within an hour of each other – Reginald first, then Ronald, at around 8 p.m. that night. Already with one special son, proud parents Violet and Charles Kray had unknowingly given birth to three sons that would soon etch the name 'Kray' into the British crime hall of fame. They went on to become Britain's most notorious gangsters, securing the East End's infamy for crime and violence.

It's hard to pinpoint when the 'gangster' as we know it came into being. The whole gangster 'image', as in the look, was borrowed from old American films and from infamous gangsters such as Al Capone. In London, gangsters had run protection rackets down at horse-racing tracks as far back as the 1930s, covered brilliantly in Graham Greene's novel *Brighton Rock*. In the racing game is where a lot of the names you hear about now stuck out – this is where the now 'retired' gangsters cut their teeth. These people were not fictional, they were real-life characters.

They started their careers by working for the racketeers in one way or another. Bookmakers were offered services they had no requirement for and would be persuaded that they did need the service after all. It was usually something like having someone come around and clean the chalkboards, but those who would not comply would be made an example of ... and the youngsters saw from an early age that crime could pay.

Most entered this long before their teens and grew up in a world of crime. Other than protection rackets, there were safe-crackers and smash 'n' grabbers, pickpockets, jump-uppers – robbers who would target delivery wagons – conmen, burglars ... most of which amounted to not much more that petty thievery. An adept thief could earn riches. A bad thief could go to prison for further education and training.

In those days, security was absent. Why should there be any? Society was unprepared for dishonesty, which enabled some astute villains to thrive. When you hear of people saying that 'the good old days' were safe, they were not really that safe at all. It was regularly said that, 'you could go out and leave your door open' – yes, that is true, but it's only because there was never anything worth stealing in those days. Go out and leave your front door open and someone will walk off with your televisions, computers, mobile phones and jewellery ... in 'the good old days', you could clear an entire house out for a few pence. The criminal is not a new phenomenon.

Pre-war underworld activities were not a patch on what was going on in America, but just like the Americanisation of many other cultures, the British criminal would soon catch on. Instead of 'cracking' a safe with tools, thieves learnt to (assume a Michael Caine accent here) blow the bloody doors off. That's when the big money started to come in.

Other changes taking place were in the police approach to solving these crimes, and now the media began to play a big part, with both TV and newspaper coverage. Still, at that time, guns were unheard of. They were available, but there were still certain rules to adhere to ... the police didn't carry guns, so criminals didn't – something that would change over time. Though there weren't that many professional criminals, they stuck together in the same drinking dens and were close-knit, just like all the other communities of the East End.

Mentally, Ronnie and Reggie were inseparable; they had a bond where if one of them was happy, the other one would feel it, and suffering corresponded, too. If one was around, it was assumed that the other would be not too far away, so they took on the name 'twins', becoming a single entity.

They would share *everything* – even illness. They both caught diphtheria and measles at an early stage in their lives, which, in those pre-vaccination times, put children at high risk, so they had to be separated for the first time, taken to different hospitals.

Reg recovered quickly, but Ronnie almost died of the infection. Ronnie was kept in hospital long after Reg was discharged, but Violet brought him home against the wishes of the doctors, saying he needed only her and Reg to put him back on track.

Just before the outbreak of World War Two, the Kray family moved to Vallance Road in Bethnal Green. They lived at number 178, which had the Liverpool Street Line running over the top of the backyard – perfect for a sleepless night. Violet wanted to be closer to her own parents. When she'd married at seventeen, she was basically outcast by her family. The birth of Charlie eased the tension a bit and put them back on speaking terms, but the birth of the twins was the clincher.

Vallance Road was quite typical of its time – overcrowded and slum. Houses had no bathrooms and toilets were always outside in the backyard. There were gambling dens, seedy pubs, billiard halls and brothels dotted all over. An area that was known for drinking, poor housing conditions, unemployment and a love for boxing.

After the twins had fully recovered from illness, Ronnie seemed slower and more socially reserved than Reggie, finding it harder to get on with other people. He would spend time on his own or with the family's pet Alsatian, roaming around the bomb sites of Bethnal Green.

Their illness was to play an important part in their early years because, from Violet's viewpoint, she noticed differences between them for the first time. In the family home, Ronnie would compete for his mother's attention. He felt disadvantaged in comparison to Reg ... physically seeming bigger and clumsier. They would often fight each other, but would never allow a third party to come between them ... squabbling but always sticking together.

In Bethnal Green, being identical twins gave them the edge over the other little tough kids. It unnerved the others and it was something that Ronnie and Reggie used to their advantage. They became known as the 'Terrible Twins' and were always fighting alongside their cousin Billy against others, against gangs, but nearly always against older boys ... and they were fast learning how to handle themselves.

When the war broke out, school was closed until they were eight years old, so this war-torn and derelict world provided the backdrop to their countless fights and vendettas with other kids. It was the perfect setting. Always following a fight, they would appear at home cleaned up as if nothing had happened, so as far as their mother knew, nothing had. They were experts at keeping this side of their lives from her. This is the side of them that their father was all too familiar with, though. He was streetwise and knew exactly what they were doing. The war and no school meant they could fight in their own wars. That was their education.

Without trying to sound too much like Uncle Albert from *Only Fools and Horses*, during the war was when crime really took off. The Blitz created many opportunities, making way for the Black Market. There were shortages and plenty of deserters from the war to do any dirty work for organised criminals. Rationing was introduced and this saw a big turnaround in people's attitudes. There was temptation – mothers wanting to provide that bit extra, people wanting cigarettes, clothes, coupons for this and that ... and the criminal could cash in on it all. They would supply anything and everything, and started to be viewed as heroes.

This is where we see similarities with the USA again. American gangsters were propelled into the big time through prohibition – they saw an opportunity at a time when many people were tempted to break the law. Never before the war would the housewives of Britain have even dreamt of breaking the law, but now they had to provide for their families by any means necessary. It was all about supply and demand.

Because of the call-up to war, there was not a great deal of policemen around, which created a freedom for criminals to operate. There were people like Eric Mason, who essentially invented ram raiding; Eddie Chapman, the safe-breaker from the North East (another Geordie Connection), once named as the most wanted man in Britain … but now criminals were starting to work as teams instead of as individuals.

Two men robbing a safe could get away with twice as much money; three or four men dressed as guards, casually stealing the contents from a shop window and loading up a smart (stolen) car looked more credible than one man in a mad panic. In some cases, the public even helped them load the cars up because they were *that* convincing. It was the birth of crime with more organisation behind it. The South East of Britain was the centre of the war, leading to a population increase with incoming service personnel, leading to an increased desire for drinking and prostitution.

Bethnal Green was bombed badly during the war. For a while, the brothers were evacuated to the country to avoid the devastation but missed Vallance Road too much and were soon reunited with the rest of the family to become even closer. They were an old-fashioned East End family. Soaked in tradition, they were close, devoted and self-sufficient as families were. They had to stick together and be tough to survive.

Their dad was either on the run from the law, having refused to join up for military service, or would be out earning a living. After going on the run from his service, he changed his name to continue his work. It wasn't that he was a coward. He was a product of the East End – a fighter. It just happened that he wanted to do what he was doing instead of going to war, which he had no interest in at all.

He was known as a 'pesterer' – a travelling trader – who would roam the country buying and selling silver, gold and clothing. He earned good money, so the family was able to live slightly above the standard of most others in Bethnal Green, though he himself was never cut out to be a 'family man'. He was well known and knew a lot of the East End villains.

He became notorious for a few other activities, drinking and gambling number one and two on his list. With this lifestyle, he was seldom at home and the brothers went a great deal of their lives without a proper father, so the twins' early lives were hidden behind their mother or 'under her feet'. They were brought up in an environment without any real male role model and were strongly influenced by their mother Violet, her two sisters and their grandmother.

This early nurturing in their lives moulded their way of thinking. When he was at home, their dad would often comment on their lack of respect towards him. He didn't agree with the way Violet had let them do as they wanted. His solution was to discipline them. This was the way for families everywhere, but not for Violet's family. She knew from her own strict upbringing what the result would be. They would have arguments about it with the twins close by, not missing a word.

Charles later blamed himself for the twins' behaviour. He said that he should have been more authoritative and taken them out of the area. Who knows what would have happened? You could look back now and see exactly what effect it would have had on the twins.

Their experiences with their part-time father increased their resentment towards authority. You can see the love for their mother, then their dad arriving on a weekend to make his mark. It was through him that they got their first taste of the underworld. Once he'd gone on the run, he would hide out with criminals and the twins would sometimes be sent with messages from their mother.

Violet held the family together in the war years. She was a warm and generous woman and looked after the three things that mattered to her the most: her sons. She taught them values and respect from an early age and instilled her strong sense of family values upon them. Her love for her twins was to practically smother them.

When she'd returned to Vallance Road with them as the prodigal daughter, she had an enormous sense of pride. She dressed them the same – just like little dolls in a pram. *Everyone* was interested in them. People were not used to identical twins. With this in mind, and with their mother's love, the twins had a sense that they were invincible. She would accept everything they did, in doing so destroying their ability to judge right from wrong.

Every area of London had a reputation with the police for the different crimes it was associated with. Villains were known to acquire money by any means and to have a total disregard for it once they had it. It was a means to an end … a night out and a chance to gamble and drink. They were known to live fast, die young and leave an ugly corpse. They had a complete disregard for the family way of life and were categorically selfish.

Crime-wise, it was the bank messengers (people who carried money from bank to bank) who were the target and violence was fast becoming a way of life for the robbers. To blow a safe took skill and patience. Messengers were easy pickings, as there was little protection and minimal resistance. They would always surrender without a struggle but would be given a few punches for authenticity. In time, protection increased and so robbing them was more of a risk. Bank robbery was the next step.

Jump-uppers were also seeing a logical progression. They used to follow the cigarette wagons and make off with a few hundred cartons; the next step for them was to hijack the entire wagon and make off with hundreds of thousands of cartons.

In those days, sentences for violence and robbery was by corporal punishment and a short prison term, usually twelve months maximum. Prison was different to what it is nowadays; it was a tough regime.

The twins met robbers, hijackers, fighters and racketeers through their dad, and through him they had their first encounters with the law. On more than one occasion, they were woken up at night by police searching for Charles senior. Scared at first, they soon learned how to deal with them but also picked up a fear and loathing of them. Vallance Road became known as 'Deserter's Corner', so with all these people coming and going, the twins were constantly on the lookout for the law. It became second nature, and conditioned them further with hatred towards authority.

Crime in its infancy was mainly a family concern. With close communities, there would always be the local families who had a reputation and stuck out from all the others. You could have people on your side, but if you came from a family with a few brothers, you immediately had a tight trust. That's how the Sabini brothers became the first real organised crime family in Britain; they made a name for themselves on the racetracks in the Forties.

Then there were the Nashes from North London, who paved the way for two other gangs: the Richardsons from South London, who both ran powerful and feared gangs; and of course, the Krays. They had firms made up of family and would stand by each other through anything.

Family firms would build up reputations through fear to gain power ... the power would lead to influence and so on. Brothers would start gangs or enter one as a member of the next generation. The Krays were already beginning to drift towards this way of life, though they probably didn't realise it. As children, they loved fighting and had a reputation amongst their peers ... it was a reputation that would undoubtedly grow. It seems natural for it to have happened now.

The Krays had rather unconventional influences in their early years, which was a major contribution to the business they entered. Other than their dad, older Kray family members were also well-known local characters in Bethnal Green. One of which was 'Mad' Jimmy Kray, their paternal grandfather. He was a stallholder in Petticoat Lane and was famed for his drinking abilities nearly as much as his bar brawling. Their maternal grandfather, Jimmy 'the Southpaw Cannonball' Lee, was another character. In his younger days, he'd been a bare-knuckle boxer and then a music hall entertainer. He was a one-off in more ways than one – a non-drinker – and loved to tell the twins stories of his fighting days.

Family influence led the Kray brothers towards the boxing world as well. The twins' first real taste came when they were at the Victoria Park fair in the boxing booth. Men could win money by going the distance with the 'in-house' boxers, but not that many of them were successful, and most would be half-cut to begin with and would run out of steam or be sick within a few seconds.

In the interval, the organisers allowed pairs of fighters to slug it out to keep the crowds hungry for more. Ronnie was quick to volunteer himself as a contender, but there was no one else of his weight division in the crowd for him to fight. The MC was about to refuse him a fight when Reg stepped forward. They climbed into the ring and gave a no holds barred boxing exhibition in front of the bloodthirsty crowd. Neither would back down ... they fought each other toe to toe as though they were sworn enemies. In the end, it was declared a draw, but the most important result for the twins was that the men – the fighters of the East End – were now made aware of who they were.

From then on, boxing took over their lives. It was all there was for them. Young Charlie had been the first to put the gloves on and the twins had watched as he sparred round after round in the backyard under the guidance of their grandfather. Although he was known as the gentler of the brothers, the training paid off for Charlie and he went on to win a few boxing titles as a welterweight during his stint in the Royal Navy, where he'd carried out his National Service. He was discharged from service because of severe migraine attacks, and the twins begged him to teach them the noble art. Charlie was becoming more involved in boxing and didn't need much persuading.

Once they had talked Violet into giving them some space in the house, Granddad Lee set up a punchbag (an old Navy kitbag filled with rags). As word spread, Violet found herself with a house full of young boxing hopefuls and more gym equipment than she'd imagined ... but she loved it.

The twins must have been around ten years old when they fought that first time, and then they met again in the Hackney Schoolboy's Boxing Championship 1948, where Reg won on points. This was only a year or so later and they had come such a long way in so little time. Their dad had encouraged them to take up boxing, thinking it would discipline them and steer them away from the only other career option in the area, hopefully. They went on to destroy everyone in their way.

Ronnie was good but was only considered to be a brawler. He would just steam in using brute force. He fought with heart and would never give up. Reg was the better of the two and was an accomplished boxer, with skill and a game plan. He studied it and saw it more as an art than an all-out punching competition. Local papers reported on the twins and they received rave reviews after each fight. A boxing career beckoned, though it looked like Reg would be the only one to make it.

They soon turned professional ... but it proved to have the opposite effect on them as to the kind one would imagine. Reg was Schoolboy Champion of London. He told me in later years that it was one of the proudest moments of his life, but it was the violence outside the ring that led to their downfall as boxers. They just could not help themselves. Managers would not touch a boxer with a reputation for street violence, but I don't suppose the twins saw it the same way. They were destroying everything they had worked so hard to build up.

They got into trouble with the police on several occasions for grievous bodily harm and other violent attacks. The stories about their fighting on the streets had become just as frequent as seeing them in the sports pages of the *East End Advertiser*. One attack even involved a police officer. Up until now, they had earned respect from people following their up-and-coming boxing careers, but now they were earning themselves a reputation as a couple of tearaways.

The older generation considered the act of hitting a policeman as crossing the line. The post-war years were still uncertain times and other than in the criminal community, this was a law-abiding area. Police were there to keep the peace and to protect – such behaviour was unknown. They were no longer known as the clean-living boxing hopefuls from the area; they had drifted into a world of violence. They narrowly escaped prison sentences each time they were on a charge, but they were lucky. For this to happen in their mid-teens, they thought they could get away with anything. Why should they believe anything different? Even with witnesses involved, evidence didn't stick, and their mother was always there to believe anything they told her.

Violet also looked to her family for support. Her sisters May and Rose lived on each side of her in Vallance Road; her brother Jimmy shared her home and slept on the settee; while Granddad Lee, his wife and son John lived across the road above the café. Violet and her parents doted on the twins. As too did her sisters – they all wanted to be seen with the twins because of their uniqueness in the community. Everyone has a favourite auntie and Auntie Rose was the twins'.

Famously, Aunt Rose told Ronnie his eyebrows were too close together; she told him that it was an omen. She said it was because he was 'born to be hanged'. She loved them, but apparently had a bit of a temper and would often fight with other women (or anyone, really) in the street. Years later, when she died, it was said to be the catalyst that finally tipped Ronnie over the edge, sending him into the world of madness that had been following him. Maybe this is true; it would certainly appear to be a contributing factor ... a sudden loss of a loved one can affect people in different ways and there may well have been other elements adding to his state of mind.

Charlie married his childhood sweetheart, Dorothy Moore, in 1948. They moved to number 178, which meant converting the gym back into a bedroom. The twins didn't get on well with their sister-in-law and as Charlie spent more time with her, a space between the brothers began to grow, but boxing would always be their bond. In December 1951, all three brothers appeared on the same fight card at a middleweight boxing championship held at the Royal Albert Hall. This was massive and attracted more attention to the brothers, though the results were not as they would have hoped. Charlie lost his fight, Ronnie got disqualified and Reg won.

On 2 March 1952, the twins were called up for National Service. Everyone had to do it. All fit men over eighteen were called up for two years. 'Fit' being a loose term – how do you think Mr Fraser became 'mad' Frank? Because he was 'unfit', of course. The twins were now Royal Fusiliers, for a day. They went AWOL to see their mam, only to be brought back the following day. Their service to their country meant (a) doing a runner whenever they could or (b) they were locked up for doing a runner. Military service was just another authority figure that they had no respect for. Part of their service included a nine-month stretch in Shepton Mallet Military Prison, where they were able to meet up with like-minded people.

For all they hated the army, though, it did teach them something. Without their 'service', they would not have been able to organise people and plan strategically for their own battles on Civvy Street. It also led to them meeting and working with various criminals while plotting their escapes and hanging around with them once they had escaped. This was the best networking they could have done.

It was their dad who made their first introduction, and it took off from there. On the run, they would go to a club called The Royal, where the local gangs would turn up in strength to show who was number one. Fights were almost compulsory. Again, this was the twins' means of paving the way for themselves once their time was up; they were proving themselves as a force to be reckoned with as well as having the balls to do so while on the run.

They were finally dishonourably discharged from the army and could now go about their business. Fighting was now a way of life. They enjoyed inflicting pain on their victims and would always take the fight to the extreme. They would use weapons without a second thought, and now owned their first gun. They leased a billiard hall called The Regal in Eric Street, off the Mile End Road in Bethnal Green. It was open all hours and became the meeting place for criminals whom the twins had built friendships with.

The lease was taken out for three years at £5 a week, and came about as a result of ridding the place of some unsavoury characters that had been hassling the previous owners. This may have been good fortune or good planning ... it was their first step into their new world, and it meant that they could now start to write their own set of rules. It seemed quite fitting that they had a place called The Regal. They now had their feet firmly on the first rungs of the criminal ladder.

Ronnie had now developed the image he'd been dreaming of and reading about for years. He started to dress *gangster-style*: The big chunky jewellery and wide-shouldered suits, crisp white shirts and tightly knotted ties. He was adapting to a lifestyle that went with the job, too. He'd sit in his own chair, soaking up the atmosphere at the club. To anyone now, it was obvious that the twins had big plans for themselves. They would fight anyone at any time and never lost ... always on the move ... and never seemed to rest or sleep.

Ronnie was now at the forefront as the dominant twin. He had a network of young boys who were his information service – keeping their ears to the ground on his behalf. This was where he got the nickname 'The Colonel' ... because of his ability to organise and lead people, building up his own arsenal of weaponry, which was kept hidden at Vallance Road. Ronnie would show no apparent weakness ... the only weakness he had was for young boys. He never showed an interest in women, but with boys he was gentle – a different person altogether.

One thing he could not be in this environment was a homosexual ... not openly. In such a world as the one they were entering, it was unheard of. Ronnie didn't really want for much and had what was basically a simple life; living at home meant cooking and ironing was done for him by Violet. He had manicures, massages ... you name it. It was his very perception of the gangster. He even started getting his hair cut at home, tailors brought in, started doing yoga ... why? Because that's how gangsters lived their lives, isn't it? He didn't really have any want for material possessions; after all, Reg was the one who could drive and who owned an American car. Ronnie could live out some of his childhood dreams. It was like a reinvention ... he had a new identity, a new persona ... he was The Colonel and now he could act like it.

Reg began to follow suit (no pun intended) and took on the gangster chic dress code. This has significance to the twins as a partnership. Where once it had seemed Reg was the dominant force, it was Ronnie who now emerged as the dominant twin. He was no longer reserved and awkward. Getting such a nickname as The Colonel was because of his drive, and now it seemed that Reg was in the back seat and was doing as Ronnie said.

Reg strived for what he'd call the 'good life', meaning that he didn't see this lifestyle as a true retirement package. He wanted the respect, a showpiece wife, a nice car, comfort – the same goals the working man strives for. He did not consider his 'job' as a long-term profession at all. In this instance, they were different. Maybe Reg was just in denial ... all this may have been because of his want to be different to his twin, to have his own identity and to prove that he was not dominated.

Different desires would be something else that set them apart from each other ... then in contradiction, Reg started dressing the same, so on the outside they appeared to be as identical as they were in the pram all those years ago. Those close to them knew they had many personal differences, but visually, it was important for them to look the same and to an extent to act in a similar manner. It was all about image and presentation. To see twins dressing differently could hint towards conflict, and any suspicion of conflict between the Krays would be seen as a weakness.

They now had a small team working for them, knock-off gear was stored in the club for money, little blags going on here and there – it was a small operation in a constant fight for recognition amongst the established underworld. By the time they were twenty-two, they were making good money through all kinds of activities, but it was always small time. They wanted bigger goals, and it was to happen possibly sooner than they anticipated.

The two major gangsters of the time were Billy Hill and Jack 'Spot' Comer. They had formed an alliance to control the whole of the city and even called themselves 'The Kings of the Underworld'. They had been ruling London for ten years as friends, but sure enough, they fell out and Spot had his face carved up in a vicious attack in what became known as 'the Battle of Frith Street'. The odds were stacked up against Jack and he needed someone to turn to … he turned to the Krays.

He offered them a pitch at what would be an historical gangland event – the 1955 Epsom race meeting. The twins could barely tolerate Spot anyway but took him up on his offer. The idea was that it would be a show of strength by Spot and would warn Hill off from trying anything. They may have been there as his 'ally' but showed contempt towards the gangs of both Hill and Spot. They were bored by the horse racing and showed no interest in the day, but at the same time showed no fear of anyone from either rival gang.

These were the top gangsters in the country and the twins' behaviour was insulting to them and implying that they were has-beens. It was the proverbial two-fingered salute to all of them. The Italian gang was also there to observe what was going on – if there was to be a war, they would certainly be interested in the outcome. Ronnie and Reggie took their cut for the day's outing and returned home. It was obvious to everyone that they had treated the day as a chance to show everyone who they were and that they feared no one.

Frankie Fraser was part of Hill's gang and was eager to fight it out with the Krays. If the twins wanted a war, then Hill's gang would be ready for them … a date was set, and The Colonel prepared his army and gathered weapons in anticipation. This was the confrontation he had been looking forward to for some time, and now it looked as though he was going to get his chance.

Both Hill and Spot heard about the battle and called it off. They had always exercised control without the use of violence and had an understanding with the police that if violence was kept off the streets, then they were okay to go about their business. It had been a good working relationship. Spot kept the twins at arm's length after that incident. He was put off by their ruthlessness and wanted nothing more to do with them but remained 'friends' with them rather reluctantly. They wanted to learn from him and to take over the West End, wiping out Hill and his gang along the way. Spot, however, was not about to give his secrets away to anyone.

The feud between Spot and Hill carried on, and around a year or so later, Spot was ambushed again, care of Frankie Fraser and Alf Warren. He called it a day soon after that, refusing the twins' help to rid the world of Hill's gang once and for all. Billy Hill also went into retirement ... and the coast was now clear for someone else to step in.

The Italians stepped up and the rumours were that they were not happy with the twins after they had favoured Spot in the power struggle. If they weren't happy with that, they would have been even less happy when Ronnie strolled into a club one night with The Firm in tow, took out a Mauser pistol and fired at them. No one was shot, but a few Italian suits would be at the dry cleaners the next day. They challenged the Italians on their own patch, and they backed down immediately. It was a wise move. This had been the break that the twins needed, and everything seemed to be falling into place. Along with their firm, the twins were convinced they could fill the gap that Jack Spot and Billy Hill had left empty ... it was now their chance to reign as kings.

Ronnie, on the inside now as well as the outside, had become a fully-fledged gangster. If the Italians were the main competition, he and Reg would be unstoppable. It was their graduation ceremony.

'Real villains' were now part of the gang ... and that gang became known as The Firm. Reason and calculated strategies would now need to come into play. They could not just fight for the hell of it anymore. In 1956, Ronnie shot someone for the first time. Knowing that he collected guns and had shot at people, it was certain that one day he would shoot someone for real. He was identified by his victim and charged with grievous bodily harm. The eleventh commandment, 'thou shalt not grass', was broken, but friends in high places and the powers of persuasion meant that Ronnie walked.

He could have been wearing Teflon suits at that time because no matter what was thrown at him, it would not stick. Ronnie loved it ... it was another victory in the battle against authority. If you keep getting away with wrongdoing, do you ever think about stopping? Not a chance. Neither did Ronnie, but he also never gave a second thought to the consequences.

The firm soon earned themselves the tag of 'the most dangerous mob in London', and were getting money from all over the place in protection rackets, thieves and villains in the area offering them a cut of their action. Ronnie felt he was above the law ... and in some ways he probably was ... though not for long.

In the same year, he led a revenge attack on a man and ended up doing time for it. He got three years for grievous bodily harm and found out first-hand that you can't get away with everything, certainly not all the time anyway. The commandment had been broken again, and it wouldn't be the last time as far as Ronnie's liberty was concerned.

Inside, Ronnie lived a comfortable prison life and Reg took care of business on the outside. This was the longest time to date they had been apart, which meant Reg could now be his own man and run The Firm in his own way. He had seen the dangers in Ronnie's battles, but up till now had gone along with them. Fighting and shooting were certain to lead only to one thing, and Reg wanted something different out of life. He took on a shop in Bow Road, Bethnal Green, which was turned into a club and became their new base ... a new drinking club ... the Double R, standing for Ronnie and Reggie.

So, he hadn't forgotten about Ronnie altogether, but while he was in prison, Reg could live his life as he wanted and go to work as a businessman. Helped by brother Charlie, the club was becoming a huge success. Charlie had a good head for business but would prefer to remain in the background as opposed to running with the gang. This way, he could get on with running the family business interests and not worry about the criminal side, which worried Reggie.

Ronnie's prison life soon took a turn for the worse, and he was heading for a breakdown. His constant mood swings and disruptive behaviour was doing him no favours ... but this all pointed to a medical condition that was much deeper than originally thought. This is the point that it is believed that the death of Auntie Rose led to a breakdown. He was sent to the psychiatric wing of Winchester Prison, where doctors declared him insane. Diagnosed as a paranoid schizophrenic and his health deteriorating, Ronnie was moved to Long Grove Mental Institution in Surrey.

At this point, he began to panic; he had seen his friend Frank Mitchell in a similar position, where he was to be held indefinitely because of his mental condition. Ronnie had begun to react well to his medication, but was still considered to be unstable for release, and so a plan was successfully hatched to get him out. The law back then stated that if someone escaped and was at large for more than six weeks, they would have to be re-examined upon capture and dealt with accordingly ... this is what they had in mind for Ronnie. They needed him out long enough to be re-examined, declared mentally stable and to serve the rest of his time in prison, knowing he would be released.

The twins concocted a ploy to beat the system, which was simple but effective. Reg visited Ronnie one day and they simply exchanged coats. Both were wearing the same suits, which meant Ronnie could just walk out whilst Reg sat at the table patiently.

Minutes later, Ronnie was on his way to freedom ... as the minutes ticked by, Reg sat in the visiting room waiting to reveal his identity. When he was asked where Reg had gone, the people at the institution were baffled when they heard the reply. One of their patients had just walked out to freedom so easily – it was their own stupid fault and had nothing to do with Reg, he told them, as he too walked out.

The plan didn't run as smoothly as expected, though. Ronnie's mental illness worsened after he was holed up in a caravan in the country after the escape. Reg moved him back to Vallance Road to be with Violet, but his mood swings and eventual suicide attempt gave the family no other choice but to surrender him back to the authorities. They didn't like to do it, but it was their only solution and was for his own good. Fate decreed that he should be returned to Long Grove and after a thorough examination, he was no longer certified insane. Bizarrely, the twins' plan had worked, and Ronnie was moved to Wandsworth Prison to serve out the rest of his sentence.

He was finally released in 1959. The mood swings were still there ... the paranoia ... he'd pace the floor like a caged lion, ready to snap at any second. He was put on medication to calm him down but there were side effects. His speech and walking slowed, and he put on weight. This 'calm' was just before the storm.

Following that, just to top it all off, Reg got an eighteen-month stretch in prison for his involvement in a protection racket. This left Ronnie with the reigns to the Kray Empire. Up till now, he was unpredictable, but Reg had been there to smooth problems over and look after him when it was needed. Now, Ronnie was dangerous, unpredictable, powerful ... and in charge of The Firm.

CHAPTER 2
COCKNEY REBELS

In the 1930s, Britain was in depression; in the Forties, we had the war; and rationing went on well into the Fifties. The East End had proved to be easy prey for the twins, and with London still vulnerable, they could move on to other enterprises. Reggie and Charlie had made some shrewd deals while Ronnie had been away, and things were picking up ... they had clubs, illicit gambling joints, were making a name for themselves, and the rich and famous flocked to have their photo taken with them.

There was a need for glitz and glamour at the end of the decade and the Krays filled the void with their clubs. Whilst Charlie and Reggie had built up and strived to operate on a more legitimate level, Ronnie had different ideas. Ronnie's philosophy was that of 'live by the sword' ... he was a loose cannon and at times was uncontrollable. Everything he saw, he wanted, and his way of getting what he wanted was by force. Ronnie knocked down relationships that had been built up with firms like the Italians with ease. He'd claim that people, i.e. Reggie, had been getting soft in his absence, and his way of declaring he was back was to declare war. He'd be more aggressive and spiteful than usual – there was a definite change.

By the end of the Fifties, a new lease of life had engulfed London – there was a party atmosphere that brought about new ideas. The 'Chelsea Set' met and socialised regularly to form the basis of a trendy new 'in-crowd' made up of clothes designers, writers, fashion icons and photographers. Lord John opened in Carnaby Street – a boutique that catered for men and set the scene for the growth of fashion central. David Bailey and Terence Donovan brought the models Twiggy and Jean 'The Shrimp' Shrimpton ... their faces defining an era.

Sixties London was the centre of the world for music, fashion, art ... a whole new freedom that wasn't around in the war years. All eyes were on the capital as it was now one of the trendiest places in the world. *Swinging London*. There were only really a few happening places; the whole 'swinging' mania was, as usual, a media creation and it took off from there.

Despite the media hype, there was still energy and creativity in the air. Go back just a few years and the mood was totally different. The youth of the country was realising they could have an identity and lifestyle different from their parents ... traditions and rules of generations past were thrown out the window. This was the first time the working classes had any money in their pockets, and they were spending it as quickly as they were making it. There was spending power and a complete liberation from Victorian and post-war taboos. Even *Lady Chatterley's Lover* by D.H. Lawrence was allowed on general release ... it was a great time to be young. As Paul Weller wrote later, "Life is a drink and you get drunk when you're young."

The devastation of the war had made way for development. If recent decades had been bomb times, then the Sixties was boom time ... in the form of a property and gambling boom.

The Krays' quest to conquer the West End led to the acquisition of clubs such as The Kentucky and Esmeralda's Barn, and an empire began to flourish. Esmeralda's Barn in Wilton Place was taken as part of a pay-off. Reggie was on bail after nine months, awaiting a review of his case at the time the deal was struck. He was proving himself as a businessman ... handling things with the help of Charlie meant money was being made, whereas Ronnie on his own would act on impulse and never quite made the right decisions. He was good at winning arguments, though, even if it meant arguing his way into a bad deal and loss of money.

At this point in time, there were not that many people who

knew the gaming business or knew about clubs and how to keep them 'safe' – the Krays were learning all the time and could see there was a market for this knowledge. There was a whole new nightlife culture centred on clubs and casinos – gambling was all the rage. London was the centre for gambling; with a huge illicit economy, the Krays controlling clubs meant it placed them in line for rich pickings. It was not all about gangland violence – they were savvy enough to know that it was a business.

Prior to The Betting and Gaming Act 1960, there were no casinos or bingo clubs in the country, and the law prohibited all commercial gaming of any significance. The idea behind the 1960 Act was to allow games of equal chance between friends and in clubs, but to prohibit the commercial exploitation of gaming. There were so many loopholes to the act ... all of which were exploited in one way or another by such people as the Krays.

Gaming, as it was known then, has always been associated with criminal activities, but prosecution was difficult, because the legislation was unclear. It was perfect for the criminal-minded of the time. By the late Sixties, there were over a thousand casinos in Britain, offering instant membership and live entertainment by highly paid stars as a means of attracting people and inducing them to game.

In 1968, the Government chose a system where commercial gaming could be properly regulated and controlled. The Gaming Act 1968 introduced a new test whereby prospective and existing casino operators needed to obtain the Gaming Board's approval and a gaming licence. Many candidates failed on one or both criteria and so were no longer able to hold casino gaming on their premises. There were plenty of ways around this, though; there would *always* be a front man.

Reggie had been enjoying his freedom in recent months, but it soon came to an end as the appeal against his conviction failed. He was sent to Wandsworth Prison for six months, but this was only a minor setback. Six months in that time of life didn't mean a great deal. Prison is always going to be a consequence for a career criminal, but the crimes that they were being locked up for were crimes that they should never have been doing in the first place. It was generally a result of Ronnie's hot-headed behaviour or some petty crime they just hadn't thought through. Reggie away for six months meant that Ronnie would be in charge again, and that would certainly give Reggie cause for concern.

Running operations by himself, Ronnie was *Gangster No. 1*, organising his troops into battle from 'Fort Vallance' ... he was The Colonel, after all, and he had a name to live up to. He'd be forever planning his strategies, determined to prove he was back with a vengeance, and no Reggie meant he was hassle-free ... Charlie, while Reggie was away, kept a low profile. Ronnie had a man called Leslie Payne working as an adviser for him in Reggie's absence, and he helped as Ronnie muscled in on various properties – gaming clubs were acquired with such ease it was frightening. He was also going through a phase where he would put his name to any venture; he would throw money into ludicrous schemes and wonder why there was no pay-off.

At the beginning of the Sixties, the twins were reunited once again. Ronnie had enjoyed his time at the helm with Reggie away, but with him back, it was business as (un)usual. Deals were going on all over London and they were beginning to branch out ... one deal was putting money into a seaside development in Nigeria. Leslie Payne and Ernest Shinwell (son of Manny Shinwell, Labour MP) helped set this up.

An introduction took place between Ronnie, Leslie Holt and Lord Boothby, a Peer of the Realm. The whole venture fell through and the money disappeared ... then by sheer coincidence, Holt died under strange circumstances. Ronnie had met Boothby at a gay party they'd both attended. Their friendship was even exposed by the *Sunday Mirror* under the headline 'The Gangster and the Peer'. It also alleged that the two were homosexuals. It wasn't that Ronnie went out of his way to hide the fact; it was more to do with the freedom of expression brought on by the Sixties that word got around. This, of course, was common knowledge to the underworld already, but now the rest of the world was beginning to find out.

Considering the twins' status ... the lifestyle, the clubs, the fame ... they may as well have had huge neon signs above their heads taunting the police to investigate their empire. They were now mixing with some influential people. Some thought that they were getting too powerful. The authorities were watching them constantly and one of the main reasons for this was their love of publicity. They weren't just courting publicity, they were engaged to it with big plans of marriage.

Ronnie was the worst culprit – he loved being photographed with celebrities and sports stars who came to the clubs. He longed to be famous and to have the lifestyle that went with it. He would present himself as the stereotypical *American Gangster* just like he'd seen in old George Raft films. Whilst American real-life gangsters would delegate their dirty work ... making sure that they couldn't be connected to crime, the Krays just couldn't seem to grasp the concept of keeping a low profile and letting others do their dirty work.

Maybe it was all down to trust and the belief that the only ones they could truly trust were themselves. They were not unique in this – the Nash brothers were another firm who could not resist doing their own dirty work. Leader Jimmy Nash made news early in 1960 for receiving a grievous bodily harm charge when he was blatantly guilty of murder ... jury and prosecution witnesses were terrified for their lives and Nash escaped the death penalty. Soon after that, they retired from gangland activities, leaving the other main name other than the Krays – the Richardsons – brothers Charlie and Eddie, scrap metal businessmen from South London.

The Richardsons ruled the South and were known as sadistic practitioners of torture to those who got on their wrong side. Frankie Fraser joined the Richardsons in 1963 as their number one enforcer after he was released from his prison sentence for the attack on Jack Spot, and along with George Cornell, they were a formidable force in the underworld.

With Fraser on board, the violence escalated at a dramatic pace and their business interests, like the Krays', were now beginning to prosper. Suppliers of one-armed bandits to most of the West End clubs, they also had friends in high places and found that certain crimes could be swept under the carpet. Another lucrative business venture at this time was known as 'long firm fraud', a market that the Richardsons also cornered. This was where legitimate 'fake' companies were set up, and goods such as electrical appliances, household items, leather goods – anything in fashion at the time – would be bought in from other companies.

There would be businessmen brought in to front the operation so, to anyone on the outside, it appeared a respectable wholesaler. They would pay for the goods up front and sell them on just as any other business would do and earn themselves the trust of the places they were dealing with. After paying these companies immediately, they would be given credit on their next purchase. That's when the long firm would get as much as they could on credit – and then disappear. It was such an easy scam to get away with. The goods would be sold on to market traders and huge profits made.

The Kray firm was also into long firm fraud, though did not enjoy the same level of success as the Richardsons. They were still heavily into protection rackets and were subsequently arrested for demanding money with menaces in 1965, by Detective Inspector Leonard 'Nipper' Read. They were demanding money from a club called The Hideaway and were remanded in custody to Brixton Prison.

At this point in time, their level of influence could be observed ... questions were asked in the House of Lords as to how long they were going to be kept locked up. The questions, asked by Lord Boothby, caused outrage. Boothby was not their only high-placed contact. When the case went to court, they walked out as free men and were cleared of all charges. They had used the threat of violence to scare witnesses into retracting their statements, and Nipper Read had to watch them slip through his fingers. A few weeks after leaving the courtroom, they owned The Hideaway club and changed its name to El Morocco. The more they got away with encouraged them further – just as it had in their childhood.

In the same year, Reggie married the love of his life, twenty-one-year-old Frances Shea, the sister of one of his friends. The marriage ended in complete disaster, lasting less than a year, and Reggie was hit hard by it. Frances could not handle such a lifestyle – it seemed to her that she was in direct competition with Ronnie all the time, and to Ronnie it *was* a competition. Reggie would still visit her, but Ronnie could now get his claws back into him and get his own way. He'd do his best to help Reggie forget all about her, make him immerse himself into their business and keep him out at night as long as possible. Maybe Ronnie was doing all this for the good of Ronnie ... he'd claim to be doing it for Reggie, but all the time, he would try to put a wedge between him and Frances.

The twins were now forming links with the American Mafia in New York. They knew the Americans were setting up gaming clubs in London and wanted to offer protection, which would be lucrative. Contact was made, though after an unsuccessful trip to forge further relations, Ronnie returned to the East End. Mafia talks were still ongoing, and they were optimistic that something could be salvaged. Ronnie had been introduced to all the wrong people courtesy of a friend he'd travelled over with. It was said that one reason he had not been introduced to the right people on his trip was that the Mafia thought the Krays' power was slipping ... they needed to prove otherwise.

They went on to provide protection for American celebrities visiting or performing in England on behalf of the Mafia. Frank Sinatra's son had been kidnapped while performing in London recently – another firm was supposed to have been protecting him and this was the perfect opportunity to jump in. Favours would let them know who was running things in England; it suited them down to the ground, as they could combine business with pleasure.

Performances were always in clubs ... clubs had gaming

facilities ... gaming facilities had the Krays. Perfect. They came up with more elaborate plans to prove themselves further, one of which involved murdering someone who had crossed the Mafia to put them in the Krays' debt. This never happened, though; it was another idea that fell at the first hurdle.

Complications between the Krays and the Richardsons were about to set in. Members of the Richardsons got into a fight with Eric Mason, a good friend of the Krays, who was out with two friends in The Astor Club. Insults were exchanged and one of Eric's friends knocked out one of the Richardsons. The police were called, and the gangs legged it round the back of the club, where Eric was overpowered by the Richardson gang and taken to a lock-up to be tortured.

Eric was savagely beaten with bats, knives and an axe ... they could not have touched him if it was a fist fight. Eric raised his hand as Fraser went for his head with an axe, leaving the hand stuck between the axe and his head, which it was imbedded into. He was lucky to survive. They also tried to cut his hands off in the torture session, saying he would never fight again. It was a sickening and cowardly attack, which to this day, Fraser dismisses as lies. In Fraser's story, he beat Mason in a one-on-one fight before kidnapping him. Other people had different versions of events.

There was no real reason for conflict, as both firms could quite easily co-exist and run profitable businesses. Both firms were already preparing to go into battle against each other before this incident. What happened to Eric was a result of the pent-up anger that had built up between the firms. It was through greed that they had fallen out in the first place. Ronnie and Reggie wanted a cut of the Richardsons' long firm fraud success but were told in no uncertain terms that they did not fit into their plans. Charlie and Eddie Richardson were also powerful and had no interest in sharing their fortunes. It was winner takes all and there was no room for losers.

Ronnie was livid ... it was a tremendous insult to him personally, and in true Ronnie Kray style, he wanted revenge. It looked like there would be another war ... but it was settled in a different way altogether. There was a successful drinking and gambling club in Lewisham run by a local thief called Billy Heywood, which was attracting a lot of attention. It was on the Richardsons' patch and they wanted a piece of the action – simple as that.

It was making a lot of money and they believed they were entitled to some. It was taken for granted that the gamblers, who were mainly all thieves (a club run by thieves *for* thieves), would not be as tough as a firm of gangsters, but the Richardsons greatly underestimated the resistance they faced. Eddie Richardson and Frankie Fraser paid the club a visit and were not given the answer they were looking for because the owners – Gardner and Heywood – stood their ground that night. As a result, they got a call informing them that the Richardson gang wanted to see them in a club called Mr Smiths.

On 8 March 1966, Gardner and Heywood's gang members went to Mr Smiths to settle the score once and for all. They were heavily outnumbered as the two gangs squared up to each other ... then the guns were drawn and all hell broke loose. Dickie Hart, part of Gardner and Heywood's gang, was shot dead. Eddie Richardson and Frankie Fraser ended up in hospital with gunshot wounds.

This was the end of the line for the Richardson firm – the police instantly had enough evidence to put their top henchmen, including Eddie and Fraser, away for five years apiece for affray. Fraser was originally charged with the murder of Dickie Hart but was found not guilty. It has been said that it was George Cornell who killed Dickie Hart, managing to escape before the police arrived, though no one can confirm this. Hart had been the only member of the Kray gang involved at Mr Smiths and murdering him was a liberty that would be avenged at any cost.

He may have evaded the police, but there was one person Cornell couldn't hide from. Ronnie Kray walked into The Blind Beggar public house the following night with Ian Barrie, armed with his Mauser pistol. Cornell was sitting on a stool at the far end of the room with his mate Alby Woods, and as Ronnie walked calmly over to him, he had only one thing on his mind. Cornell sneered for the last time as Ronnie levelled the gun to his head and pulled the trigger. 'The Sun Ain't Gonna Shine (Anymore)' by The Walker Brothers was playing on the jukebox ... and to Ronnie Kray this was poetic justice. But did he kill for revenge, or was it for the fact that Cornell had (famously) called Ronnie "that fat poof"?

Ronnie told me himself that he'd killed Cornell because he had killed someone close to him, but never would say who it was revenge for. It always sounded plausible that it was for Dickie Hart. Cornell was on Kray territory at the time, but it's not as though he was out to cause trouble. He was from the East End originally, so he wasn't invading Ronnie's turf. Another statement Ronnie later gave me was that if Cornell had been anywhere other than The Blind Beggar, he would have lived. Ronnie couldn't stand the Beggar, so he had no qualms about soiling it with Cornell's blood.

Ronnie would say so many different things about the killing when I knew him. He loved to discuss it – just as he'd done in the Sixties. Everyone knew he'd done it. He made no attempt to hide the fact; he went as far as to brag about it. It was his first kill and he revelled in the notoriety. This one-upmanship was something that he'd use in arguments with Reggie all the time. He'd use it to dominate further; to taunt him, sneering and saying he didn't have the guts to go as far as Ronnie did.

Within a year from being sentenced for affray, the Richardsons found themselves in the dock again. The evidence had been mounting up for some time – the first-hand accounts of hideous tortures and revenge beatings had caught up with them at last. At first, they were being investigated for their long firm frauds, but it was the extent of violence they had used in trying to silence people that led to their ultimate downfall.

Charlie Richardson continued to go about family business in Eddie's absence; he had hired new people and their firm were as strong as ever. The torture they administered on their victims made the fraud look like a high-street shoplifting outing and the police were hell-bent on making them pay. They would beat people who worked for them and who fronted fraudulent companies and torture people for information. More and more people were traced ... a contract killing investigated ... more tortures ... the evidence read like a horror novel. People were scared to come forward because the Richardsons knew so many in the police force that it was likely to get back to them.

One bloke in particular was Jimmy Taggart. He'd been subject to one of the worst torture sessions anyone is ever likely to go through and survive. He was prepared to make a statement only when Charlie was in custody. Charlie was remanded and the prosecution evidence gathered before he was given a twenty-five-year prison sentence, but it wasn't over there. Evidence was pouring in all the time still; he was linked to a contract killing in South Africa, where a man had mugged him off for a few grand and ended up paying with his life. Two hired killers were used. One of them disappeared but the other, Johnny Bradbury, was given ten years for his trouble.

Jimmy Taggart also ended up telling everything he knew about the Richardson organisation and subsequently Eddie Richardson and Frankie Fraser were given a further fifteen years each. The Krays now found themselves in pole position. The Richardsons had effectively self-destructed. They were no more and now London was rich pickings for the Kray firm ... all they had to do was stay out of real trouble. Just as in the era of Spot and Hill, the police were quite willing to let incidents go unseen provided they were not serious and did not upset the equilibrium of the community. By putting the Richardsons away, the police force sent signals that gangsters were no longer above the law. They could not get away with murder.

The twins were still trying to portray themselves as the local boys who had made good, but by now, they were known for what they were – violent criminals. They used the East End ideals and values to their advantage – giving to charity and being seen with stars was a route to papering over their bad boy image – but the underworld was not so easily swayed, as they knew Ronnie had murdered Cornell. They had immense power now, but the attacks kept happening and the use of sheer terror was used to extort money.

Big Albert Donoghue had even become a member of The Firm as the result of a Kray attack. He'd been shot in the leg and because he did not tell the police who had shot him, the firm put him on a 'pension' until he was fit enough to work for them. It was utter madness – they trusted him for not grassing them up, and he decided he could trust them after they had just shot him. The perfect working relationship.

It was their reputation that they were becoming a victim of. They could never let it slip, so the violence would escalate all the time; even members of The Firm were beginning to worry if they would be next. I've heard from different sources that there were plans to kill the twins by The Firm, as they were so unpredictable. No one felt safe and with Ronnie being trigger-happy, anything was possible.

At the end of 1966, the twins hatched a plot to free Frank Mitchell, the Mad Axeman, from Dartmoor Prison. Mitchell would be useful to The Firm if they could get him out, but the main idea behind it was to enhance their reputations by helping him campaign for a release date. Teddy Smith, an 'author' and Kray friend, had put the idea to them and they went for it. It sounded like some of the bizarre schemes that were put to them twenty-five years later, when they themselves were locked up.

Teddy was also known as a madman, a trait not uncommon in their circle of friends, and the plan sounded mad, too. All they had to do was get him out of prison, keep him out long enough for the newspapers to run the story of his plight and have the authorities forced to investigate his case – then he'd give himself up and return to prison.

Mitchell was a huge, strong, fit and good-looking man, who

had been certified insane. He was such a difficult customer even to the high-security environment that he was basically left alone in, if he did not cause disruption. He had never been given a release date – he was there indefinitely. Albert Donoghue and Teddy Smith drove to the only phone box at Dartmoor to wait for Mitchell ... all he had needed to do was walk over the moors to his freedom and into a car. It was that easy. They were in London before news of 'Britain's most violent criminal' escaping prison had broken.

The media interest was massive. Donoghue and Smith had greatly underestimated the impact the escape would have, and therefore were left with a big problem. They had a huge, uncontrollable madman holed up in a flat in London with an extreme dose of cabin fever. He wanted out. They arranged to have a club hostess called Lisa Prescott to be taken to the flat to entertain Mitchell and to keep his mind off his plight. This kept him occupied for a period, but he quickly fell in love with her, which then became an additional problem.

He wrote a letter to *The Times* highlighting his prison conditions. He paced the room like a caged lion – threatening to leave and take his woman with him and threatening anyone present at the same time. Everyone in the underworld knew the twins had sprung Mitchell and if he walked out of the flat, the world would find out who had sprung him, too. They could not let that happen.

Frank Mitchell was subsequently killed just before Christmas in 1966. He was taken out to a van where he was told they were going to move him abroad to start a new life. Inside the back of the van, two hit men opened fire on him, finally ending his life by a shot to the head. That was it – another problem sorted out the gangland way. His body was never found, and no one was convicted of his murder.

The downward spiral had begun with the first killing. Ronnie would have said it was the complete opposite, but once the killings started, the overall outcome was not too difficult to predict. Then in 1967, Reggie was hit hard by the suicide of Frances. At one point, things were promising and reconciliation between them looked certain. Frances was unwell and her mental stability crumbled. She had a breakdown, was hospitalised and soon after her release she committed suicide by taking a lethal dose of pills.

Reggie subsequently went into depression. He tore himself apart over her death and was drinking heavily to try to ease the pain. The drinking only made matters worse. It was too much for Reggie to take. He was a sad case – a pitiful drunk and easy prey for Ronnie. At the same time, they were faced with another problem. This one was called Jack 'The Hat' McVitie, and there are very limited solutions in gangland.

McVitie had been making a mug out of the twins for some time. He was a loose cannon. He had no fear of the twins, and was a drug user and a woman beater. He had taken certain liberties – was disrespectful to them in public, was said to have taken a shotgun to a club once drunk out of his mind, looking to kill them. McVitie had been given money by the Krays to murder their one-time associate Lesley Payne. Lesley Payne was a business manager for the Krays and would be instrumental on the long firm frauds.

The Krays were right not to trust Lesley Payne, as years later he would be giving Queen's evidence against them in court and at the time was also supplying information to the police officer Nipper Read, but after a failed attempt, McVitie just kept the money. He'd had plenty of warnings but had refused to listen. It was decided that he was becoming a liability and had to be disposed of.

Ronnie was the worst person in the world to be anywhere near Reggie now. Reg was drunk, vulnerable and in need of 'belonging'. This was the perfect chance Ron could have hoped for – he could literally play the part of the devil. Reggie was putty in Ron's hands and Ron was quick to take advantage, goading his brother further – "You can't kill anyone, you, you're useless." He would not let it pass. It was the twins against the world now and Reggie Kray had to prove himself against some petty thief who was making a mockery of everything that they had built.

McVitie was lured to a party in Evering Road, Stoke Newington, where Reggie Kray stabbed him to death in a frenzied attack. The Lambrianou brothers, Tony and Chris, had taken him from a club where they had already plied him with drink. They had wanted to become a part of The Firm for so long, and now was their chance to prove their worth. It was all calculated murder, though I doubt those present at the time thought it would evolve to be so.

As they had entered the room, Reggie had tried to shoot McVitie, but the gun had failed. His motive now clear to a panicking McVitie, Reg could not just let him off with a warning. McVitie begged for his life. He was desperate and pleading for mercy. Most watching the scene just thought they were observing a bit of a joke. Ron was close at hand to wind Reg up further. One way or another, McVitie was going to die that night ... it had gone too far.

More taunting from Ron and soon Reg went too far. He grabbed a kitchen knife and stabbed McVitie through the face before finishing him off. That night, Reggie Kray finally achieved the same status as his twin. The entertainment over, they were both murderers. It was not necessary for them to kill McVitie. In the scheme of things, he was a nobody. It was bad timing – McVitie was in the wrong place at the wrong time.

He did more damage to them dead than he ever could have done alive. The body was disposed of and the flat cleaned up immediately ... more mystery, more cover-ups and more people to be silenced. The police were not aware of the murder until several months later, and it took a year to arrest the suspects. Nearly thirty people in total were arrested as the police moved in on The Firm. Nipper Read arrested the twins and The Firm on 8 May 1968.

The reason for this was that the Krays had seemingly become untouchable and difficult for the police to deal with. They had been called in for demanding money with menaces at the Hideaway club in Soho, which had been subsequently thrown out of court. There had also been an exposé of Ronnie Kray's liaison with Tory Peer 'Lord Boothby' in the *Sunday Mirror*. The *Mirror* ran the story of 'The Gangster and The Peer.' The Krays had made friends in high places and this had put the police on the back foot, which meant that the police had to move carefully on their activities to close down the Krays.

Both were defiant and confident, believing that their name alone was enough to stop anyone coming forward and talking. The Richardson case had been a good learning exercise for the police, though, and they too were confident this time. With The Firm locked up, the fear was no longer instilled upon the community, and the East End code of silence was ready to be broken. They didn't want the Krays anymore.

Amongst other charges, they were tried for the murders of George Cornell and Jack McVitie. They had lost their grip. Members of The Firm were willing to turn Queen's evidence in order to save their own skin. They had been ordered to take the rap for the twins but refused, making them instant enemies. All of those arrested pleaded not guilty apart from Albert Donoghue. He was tried separately and was imprisoned for two years. Ronnie had ordered him to take the blame for the murder of Frank Mitchell, but he had refused. His only way out was to become a grass.

The downward spiral continued … January 1969 saw the Kray trial begin, which turned out to be one of the most expensive in British history. Of the ten men who stood in front of the jury, only Tony Barry was acquitted as an accessory to the murder of McVitie. The remaining nine members of The Firm were charged with and convicted of the crime, and sentenced by Mr Justice Melford Stevenson at the Old Bailey on 8 March that year, who said, "I am not going to waste words on you. In my view, society has earned a rest from your activities. I sentence you to life imprisonment, which I recommend should not be less than thirty years."

The Firm was sentenced as follows:

Ronnie Kray, aged thirty-five, was found guilty of both the murders of George Cornell and Jack McVitie. He was sentenced to life imprisonment with a recommendation to serve at least thirty years.

Reggie Kray, aged thirty-five, was found guilty of murdering Jack McVitie and for being an accessory to the murder of George Cornell. Like Ron, he was also sentenced to life imprisonment with a recommendation to serve at least thirty years.

Charlie Kray, aged forty-one, was sentenced for being an accessory to the murder of Jack McVitie. He was sentenced to ten years in prison.

John 'Ian' Barrie, aged thirty-one, was found guilty for the murder of George Cornell. He was sentenced to life imprisonment with a recommendation to serve at least twenty years.

Tony Lambrianou, aged twenty-six, and Christopher Lambrianou, aged twenty-nine, were found guilty for the murder of Jack McVitie, and were sentenced to life imprisonment with a recommendation that they serve at least fifteen years.

Ronnie Bender, aged thirty, was sentenced to life imprisonment with a recommendation to serve at least twenty years for the murder of Jack McVitie.

Freddie Foreman, aged thirty-six, received ten years for being an accessory to the murder of Jack McVitie.

Cornelius 'Connie' Whitehead, aged thirty, was charged with carrying a gun and complicity in the murder of McVitie. He received two years for the gun and seven years for the Complicity charge.

There was more to come; Ronnie Kray was charged with the murder of Frank Mitchell and was found not guilty. Freddie Foreman was also charged and found not guilty. The charge of murder against Charlie Kray was dropped. Reggie Kray, however, received five years for freeing Frank Mitchell from Dartmoor and another nine months for harbouring him. This was to run concurrently with his other sentences.

There was never any remorse shown by the twins. They were selfish and defiant to the end. It was partly because they thought they were untouchable that led to their downfall. Instead of playing it cool and making a good living, they began to believe the hype – they thought they could get away with murder. Simple as that.

CHAPTER 3
LIKELY LADS

The Sixties in Tyneside were a big time for change, too. We always talk of a North–South divide, but youth all over the world are never that different. Newcastle had a massive music and fashion scene in those explosive times, along with other Northern cities. Clubland and gambling was fast becoming big business. The Newcastle scene echoed that of the capital … a lot of the pubs were still traditional, but it was the clubs and the music that made it different.

We had one of the biggest bands of the time, The Animals, who joined the likes of The Hollies, Herman's Hermits, Gerry and the Pacemakers and, of course, The Beatles and The Rolling Stones in the Brit invasion of America. Whether it was because there was youth employment, football or the quality of beer – at long last there was an optimism that the city had not seen in a long while.

We had clubs like The Bird Cage, The Piccadilly, The 69 Club and the A Go-go, where you could go and see the likes of Shirley Bassey, Tony Bennett or Tom Jones. It was amazing … a modern world with a new breed of stylish young modernists pioneering what is now a world-famous Geordie nightlife. With the increased spending power that the youth of the region were enjoying, clubs like those mentioned became the in places to be seen.

There was a huge gaming industry, too – casinos and slot machines were pulling the punters in and there was a lot of cash to be made. Along with clubs and gaming, there were other respects that made Tyneside and London similar … organised crime. It was going on in all cities, but most of the time, people were only alerted to it when it made the headlines. There was no reason why the public should be aware of any organisation; it was something new and only those involved knew the full extent to the crime behind it. Clubs, casinos, gambling – the entertainment industry – went hand in hand with extortion, violence, protection and other criminal activities.

The Krays made numerous trips to Newcastle in the early 1960s. In 2010, I worked alongside filmmaker Neil Jackson from a company called Media Arts to try and lift the lid on why they came to Tyneside and what they did while they were here. We met many of the old faces, such as John 'Mario' Cunningham, Dennis Stafford, Kenny 'Panda' Anderson and Ted 'Machine Gun' Kelly, who gave us a fascinating insight into Newcastle at the time.

The tales about the twins arriving in Tyneside have become folklore, with so many variations as to what happened, the basics being that they came up mob-handed to take over and were kicked out by *someone*. It's hard to find out which tales are true and which are false; *everyone* has their own version of events.

One of the Newcastle myths is that Superintendent Jack Vinton was dining in the same restaurant as them and sent the waiter over with a train timetable with the trains to London highlighted, but again, where this happens varies from practically every hotel to every nightclub and venue in the city. It needs to be noted that every big city in England has the same story or versions of, "The Krays came to [insert city name] and were met from the train by [insert the local crime family name]. They were told to get on the next train back to London and left immediately." Another one is that the police were there to meet them from the train and put them on the next one bound for London.

The Krays were so notorious that their names could be used to enhance the reputation of the local villains. They or the police would be the ones who sent the Krays packing. On a larger scale, though, it is not about the locals or the police, it's saying *our city* sent the Krays packing. I think that all these stories just prove that the Krays had such a reputation that it would precede them anywhere they went. It shows the level of overestimation attributed to them and their physical capabilities.

The Krays visiting a city would send it into panic – the city would think that they were coming to take over! They could not even visit a place for a few days on a social basis now. They were too well known. Every culture needs a bogeyman or a Keyser Söze ... the Krays fitted in nicely as modern-day Britain's most notorious monsters.

From this point on, there are conflicting stories as to what happened when the Krays were in town, other than they *were* in town at *some point* in the Sixties. I have heard so many of these stories, from Kray associates and people who were there or who claim to have been there. It all builds up an interesting picture.

To me, the intrigue lies in the fact you can never categorically say that they came to Newcastle and this is *exactly* what happened. Maybe all the stories are true or maybe none of them are. There are always going to be people who disagree with what went on during those visits, but hopefully they are represented fairly within these pages.

One story is as follows ... they arrived sometime between late 1963 and March 1964; singer Billy Daniels was performing in the city and the twins were asked to look after him. His agent had phoned and asked if the twins could do it – they were told it was in a suburb of London, which would be handy ... which then turned out to be Newcastle ... a few hundred miles away.

This was the protection they were offering for the American stars, which I mentioned earlier, though usually it was in the capital. It was the Mafia that they were ultimately working for by providing security. Many stars in those days had mob connections, and with relations between the Mafia and The Firm being forged, it was in the twins' interests to look after them.

Reggie phoned Eric Mason and asked if they knew anyone up there. Eric was probably closer to Reggie than he was to Ronnie. It was Eric who set about organising the Newcastle trip; he made a few calls to Henry and Jimmy Young, who he'd met in prison, and pretty soon it was arranged for nine members of The Firm to make their way to Newcastle: Ronnie, Reggie, Charlie, Johnny Squibb, Sammy Lederman, Mickey Fawcett with his mate Peter, Johnny Davis and Eric.

Mickey had also been up to Newcastle for a social night after a prison visit in Durham and where he bumped into two locals by the name of 'Blow' Shotton and Frankie Sayers. He was also suitably impressed with the Geordie hospitality and a club by the name of the Dolce Vita, which Fawcett described as a piece of Las Vegas on Tyne.

On their train journey, the gang had been discussing various business deals, Ronnie and Reggie never seeming to take time off from it. The long firm frauds were a going concern at the time and discussions were conducted with enough slang words and phrases so that no eavesdropping passengers would know what they were talking about. It was business, after all, and no one else's business.

Names became 'the other fella', places became 'that club' and events were 'that thing in that geezer's place'. Even though the restaurant car had closed, a generous tip ensured that they could still enjoy a meal – they were typical East End lads enjoying the fruits of what money can buy but were never arrogant with it. Eric Mason was great at organising such perks. He still lives by the same code: do things nice and with a smile, and people will like you and do what they can to help you. Do it wrong and try to bully people, and you'll get nowhere. The respect he commands everywhere he goes even today is testimony to that code.

The Levy brothers – Marcus, Norman and David – owned the Dolce Vita nightclub where Billy Daniels was to be performing. They met the Krays et al. from their train at Newcastle Central with a chauffeur-driven Rolls-Royce. Not a bad welcome ... it was a gesture they appreciated.

They were taken to the Royal Turks Head Hotel on Grey Street, which is where Legends nightclub now stands. At the hotel, they checked in and Eric began making calls to people they knew in Newcastle to meet up for drinks.

That night, they enjoyed an evening at the Dolce Vita where, amongst others, they were introduced to Angus Sibbet and Vince Lander. Angus Sibbet worked for Vince Lander and both were well-known faces in Newcastle. One theory behind this visit is that Lander had taken a thousand quid from gaming machines in London and fled to Newcastle using the money as capital to start his own business, which had flourished into the empire he now controlled.

The gaming machines were said to have belonged to the Krays and they were unhappy about it; they wanted their cut. If this had happened, then yes, they would have been looking for their cut. They were the Krays, after all. Maybe it did or did not happen ... in the eyes of the public, anyone at that time who was in power and with a reputation was immediately linked to the Krays. Lander pulling such a stroke sounds more interesting than a man coming up from London, spotting a gap in the market and making good money from it.

That theory aside, the twins, Lander and Sibbet were all in the same business, they enjoyed a spot of networking that night and kept in contact with each other. The Levy brothers were the perfect hosts that evening and the club was exactly what The Firm were used to, so they felt at home from the start.

On their second night, they took the party back to the hotel. They were all socialising and enjoying drinks from the bar ... the entire room was full of cigar and cigarette smoke as they exchanged stories and shared a few jokes. It must have felt even more like home for them with Ronnie sat amongst all the smoke, lapping up the atmosphere and holding court just like in the London clubs.

Billy Daniels, always the entertainer, began to recite poetry. He'd stood up and took to the floor as the room full of gangsters and hangers-on fell silent. They listened intently, which must have been a surreal sight. Before long, the party was bored and restless from it ... they were East End blokes out to have fun and had no interest whatsoever in poetry. Ronnie did, though. He made them sit through each rendition, hanging onto Billy's every word. Johnny Davis had enough. He got up to leave, saying, "What are we sat here listening to this prat for?" and was told by Ronnie to sit back down and listen, who added that the poems were good and to show some respect.

Billy asked Davis if he liked the poems. "Can't stand them. Sing a song and I'll stay here all night, but your poems, you can keep them, mate," Davis answered. Perhaps he was a little too honest. Ronnie had a go at him but Johnny stood his ground. Johnny was also a fighter and allegedly carried the guns for the twins, and could be as stubborn as Ronnie if he wanted to. Now, if the sight of the gang watching a poetry recital wasn't surreal enough, then Ronnie Kray enjoying it and forcing others to enjoy it too would have been the icing on the cake.

As things cooled down, it was soon time for a different form of entertainment. Eric Mason had been seeing one of the girls from the Dolce Vita called Theresa (who later became friendly with Eddie Richardson on a visit), and had a contact in there who could supply girls for them, if they wanted. This seemed an interesting prospect, but of course Ronnie was a homosexual. Squibby gestured to Ronnie, and said, "What about him? He's into poofs." (Johnny Squibb would always joke on with Ronnie in this way and it drove him crazy! In the times of pre-political correctness, the word 'poof' was always used and caused no offence.)

It turned out that the kitchen porter was homosexual and was paraded in front of Ronnie, who looked on approvingly. He eagerly took him upstairs to his room – I don't know whether the boy had much of a say – but they were soon interrupted when the manager barged in on them. Disgusted by the sight that greeted him, he threw the eight members of The Firm out immediately. On their way out, Eric ripped the page out of the reservation book that had his name on it, destroying the evidence and any association with the incident.

From then on, they stayed at The Imperial Hotel in Jesmond, and enjoyed the hospitality of a bloke called Joe Lyle, a club owner and another well-known face in the city. On their third night, they were taken around Newcastle, courtesy of Joe, who took them to his clubs The Piccadilly and The 69 Club, and introduced them to everyone worth knowing. They were introduced to the manager of every bar they went to and enjoyed another good night out.

Contacts were being made all the time, but not with sinister intentions. They were all in a profession where they needed contacts all over the country, and that's exactly what they were doing – making contacts. I don't know if the police had been alerted to the presence of gangland's most famous brothers arriving in the city, but it was certainly a secret that couldn't be kept for long, so maybe the police did have someone watching them as a precaution.

The twins had respect for the Levy brothers and Joe Lyle; collectively, they had shown great hospitality and put themselves in good favour. They were well-known faces in Newcastle and the North East, but as businessmen. Sure, they were in clubland, but saw no reason why it should include gangland. They certainly talked business with the Krays because it was their common ground, but that was where the similarities stopped. Reg and I discussed them on a visit one time, and he told me, "They were straight people who saw nothing wrong with hanging around with people such as ourselves when we were there. They wouldn't have wanted to get involved with anything criminal we were doing. Vince Lander would have, though."

Of the people they met in Newcastle, Reg described Lander as one of the only blokes who seemed to be a crook with good skills. He said it was probable that the police were following him and were most likely alarmed by them meeting each other.

There were no takeover plots going on as far as the Krays were concerned. As hard as it may be to accept, this is what I'd heard from people present on that visit and from the Krays themselves. I do know that they were interested in starting up a clip-joint in Jesmond, but that's as far as it ever got. They were there for Billy Daniels' protection and to socialise.

Of course, they wanted to meet up with the influential people while they were here – they would have wanted to in any city. Memories will always be selective and can become hazy over the years, though. I doubt there was any major conspiracy going on. It certainly puts the record straight about any gangs waiting for them and any police officers sending them back home. If they had forged any real links for business, I think they would have started making regular trips to the North East. As it was, their next visit was some three years later.

The next visit was a different story altogether. Angus Sibbet was infamous in Newcastle ... known as the one-armed bandit king of the region; he worked for a man called Vince Lander (formerly Vince Luvaglio). They were getting rich from one-armed bandits, supplying to around 400 clubs. The deal was that the clubs got 40 per cent of the takings and the rest went to Lander, who paid Sibbet his cut from it.

On 5 January 1967, Angus Stuart Sibbet was found shot dead in the back seat of his Mark 10 Jaguar under a railway bridge in a place called South Hetton in County Durham. He had been shot three times. Dennis Stafford, then thirty-three, and Michael Luvaglio (Vince's brother), then twenty-nine, were both arrested and charged with the murder on 15 March the same year at Newcastle Assizes. Michael Luvaglio was Sibbet's best friend and has always protested his innocence; Stafford was a career criminal who barely knew Sibbet and has also always protested his innocence.

The jury disagreed. They both received life sentences. *The one-armed bandit murder* even inspired the Mike Hodges classic, *Get Carter*, starring Michael Caine. It was something that went on to define an era in Tyneside's criminal history. Gangland Newcastle was about to be exposed through the murder of Angus Sibbet. It was an eye opener to the people of the North East. Up until then, it was assumed that gangsters were just confined to London, and any killing in London attributed to the Krays. Killings only took place in the capital and were ten a penny. Even today, killings are unusual, but the circumstances become more and more familiar each time. The Sibbet murder was shocking because he was well known and any criminal connections, though possible, were originally just rumours and idle gossip from green-eyed sceptics.

Gangland was alien to Newcastle in the Sixties, and even more alien to the pit village in County Durham where the body was found. It was alien to us because we'd never been exposed to it in such a dramatic way. Now, those businessmen who dressed in immaculate and expensive suits like their cockney counterparts would be looked at differently.

There is always speculation about people until they hit the headlines for all the wrong reasons. Lander was running Social Club Services Ltd and had Sibbet, Stafford and Luvaglio working for him. They supplied fruit machines, live entertainment and furnishings to clubs throughout the region, and pretty much had it sewn up. The Krays, though indirectly, played a part in the goings on surrounding the situation, but not in the actual murder itself.

Sibbet's body was found at 5.15 a.m. on 5 January in South Hetton by Tom Leak, a miner returning home from a night shift, and so began the investigation into Sibbet's flamboyant lifestyle. He was known as a womaniser (having two mistresses who were sisters) and was also married. He had enjoyed the fruits of his money, mixing with stars and entertaining friends in the clubs and restaurants of Newcastle. Years earlier, ex-soldier Sibbet had owned a Chinese restaurant with his brother James, where he had fallen in with bad company. At that time, he was given a one-year prison sentence for receiving stolen goods. The door to 'the other world' was opened and it appeared he put his foot through it.

The case itself is a curious one. Stafford and Luvaglio were together on the night of the murder and have never denied it. They left Stafford's house in Westmorland Rise, Peterlee, at around eleven o'clock in a red E-Type Jaguar, which belonged to Vince Lander. Twenty minutes after that, Sibbet was seen leaving the Dolce Vita in Newcastle. He'd been there for two hours with a group of friends, sitting at his favourite table in front of the cabaret stage. He had settled the bill and left the others, who stayed on till two in the morning. He was seen getting into his Mark 10 Jaguar.

The next hour in all their lives and what happened in it was the basis for the trial. It was argued that Luvaglio and Stafford murdered Sibbet in this hour, as prior to and afterwards they had watertight alibis. The police put it to the jury as this: at around 11.45 p.m., the E-Type smashed into the Mark ten and both cars stopped on the A181, just outside South Hetton. Sibbet was shot three times, with two other shots taking out the driver's side window, then bundled into the back of his car and driven back into South Hetton, where the car was dumped. Stafford and Luvaglio then drove to Newcastle and were spotted together in The Birdcage Club, now the Stage Door, on Stowell Street, at 12.20 a.m. The police had to link the damage to both cars, which was caused in the collision, and prove that the murder happened before midnight. They were both arrested the next day as a formality to help the police with their enquiries.

This is where the 'stitch up' is said to have come into play. Luvaglio had never been in trouble with the law before, whilst Stafford, on the other hand, had a string of convictions to his credit stretching back to 1956, when he was sentenced to seven years for housebreaking, and receiving and possessing a handgun. He escaped prison twice before being locked up again, this time for conspiracy to defraud and obtaining goods by false pretences, then onto car theft and possessing a pistol (he has indeed been in and out of prison most of his life, serving a six-year jail term in 1994 for forgery, released in 1998). He certainly had a criminal past and had a history of carrying guns, though it does not prove he did this crime.

By coincidence, Eric Mason had got to know Stafford when they were both locked up in Dartmoor. Eric was already made aware of Stafford – Reggie told him that Stafford had given evidence against them when they were seventeen years old. They became acquaintances and Stafford had even asked Eric to come up to Newcastle to work with him prior to the murder. He said it was all for the taking, but it would have to be just these two, as the twins were too high profile. Eric refused the offer ... if Stafford had given evidence once, it meant he was weak and therefore could not be trusted 100 per cent.

Stafford was linked from his past alone and because Luvaglio had been with him, he was in the frame, too, but there seemed to be a way out for him. During questioning, Luvaglio was asked to sign a statement where he would be saying he was away from Stafford long enough for a murder to have taken place. In other words, they were saying they only wanted Stafford for the murder.

He refused to do so, saying he was with Stafford from around 11.45 p.m. until 2.30 a.m., and was subsequently charged along with Stafford. This was reinforced when Luvaglio's solicitor went on record to say the police had told him to put the idea to his client – they knew he was innocent, but if he didn't say Stafford had left him for an hour and a half that night, then he would also be charged with murder. Ronald Kell, leading the investigation, denies this ever happened. It was the first of many conflicting stories to emerge from a sensational trial.

Both men served twelve years of their life sentences, having three appeals rejected in that time. Stafford maintains to this day that at the time of Sibbet's murder, he and Luvaglio were at his house in Chelsea Grove in the West End of Newcastle, along with the red Jag, which was parked outside. This puts the time at around midnight; a neighbour has since come forward to say she saw Luvaglio in his house talking on the phone and they even waved to one another through the window. This was apparently a call from Luvaglio's brother, Vince Lander, from Majorca, where he was on holiday.

From Chelsea Grove, they drove to The Birdcage to meet up with Sibbet for a drink. They both have said that it was here that the red Jag was damaged, not in South Hetton, and the club doorman came out with Stafford to assess the extent of it. Stafford went out to the car to get some cigarettes, which is where this damage was spotted – maybe this was just part of the plan to make it look like the damage happened in Newcastle and not in County Durham. Stafford and Luvaglio then had a meal at the club before going home. Sibbet never showed up for their meeting. That, they say, is what happened that night. They had no knowledge of the murder.

During the trial, there was no motive for the killing established, no confession and no murder weapon to link them to it. It seems odd to me how they can still end up on a murder charge in that respect. Photographs of debris from both cars at the scene of the crime were shown to the jury, as too were photographs of bullet cartridges, as well as Sibbet's glasses. There was nothing to suggest that Luvaglio and Stafford had *definitely* been at the crime scene – there were no eyewitness reports, nor was there any forensic evidence, which one would expect.

It proved that the Jag had not been damaged outside The Birdcage, though, as experts pieced together broken plastics from reflectors, and fragments of number plate – all of which suggested a collision on that road between both cars. This, it was said at the time, was the foundation the prosecution had produced, but they failed to lay a single brick on it. The rest of the case was made up of circumstantial evidence. It has since been discovered that witness statements in direct conflict with the police version of what happened that night were suppressed.

The police said that the car, with the body in it, had been abandoned at around midnight and lay unnoticed until 5.15 a.m. the next morning. However, at 12.55 a.m., another driver passed the Jag and noticed it was undamaged. One witness said that he passed the car at approximately 1.15 a.m. The lights of the car were on at the rear to indicate it had stopped, and as he approached in his car to pass, an arm extended from the driver's side to wave him on.

One miner has said he saw the car (undamaged) and investigated it. He said there was no dead body on the back seat. Then, at 2.25 a.m., three more witnesses passed and noticed no damage to the car. People were noticing the car because it was striking and unusual to the area. Ronald Kell denies that any of these statements were 'buried', but the fact remains that none of them were heard at the trial, and forty people said they had seen the undamaged car. But the Jaguar with Sibbet's body slumped inside was found damaged.

The police were pinning their case on the fact that the killing took place leading up to midnight, but the pathologist confirmed that the time of death was between midnight and 4 a.m. They went as far as doing the same journey in the same make of car to prove it could be done. It started at 11.45 p.m., where they gave generous pauses for murder and moving a body, and they arrived in Newcastle at 12.31 a.m.

A 7.65mm Walther PPK automatic had been determined as the weapon. Shots were fired from around three feet away, from one inch away and once with the muzzle of the gun touching the victim. Also, traces of blood were found in Sibbet's car, which belonged to neither of the three men. This indicated that there must have been someone else there.

Further down the road, blood was found in a phone box with blood that matched that of Sibbet's – this evidence suggested that someone had killed Sibbet, got his blood on their clothes and went to use the telephone. Neither of the accused had Sibbet's blood on them. Though upon Stafford's arrest, the suit he'd been wearing that night had been dry cleaned at 9 a.m. the following morning, and still contained tiny fragments of evidence from the car damage. At 10 a.m., he took the E-Type Jag to a garage to be repaired.

There have been further explanations linked to the killing. A one-time thief in Newcastle confirmed the theory that another man was involved in the killing. John Tumblety says he received a call, picked up and drove the killer from South Hetton to The Birdcage on the night. He said the man had a broad cockney accent and his clothes were covered in blood. He claimed the man had an injured leg, which would explain the blood in the car, and was determined to get to the club. The next night, Tumblety was approached by someone and told to forget what had happened that night in South Hetton; otherwise he would face a beating.

There have been other theories, too; one being a crime of passion, where it was said that one of his women was unhappy with him; and another one being that the Krays were coming to take over (as usual).

Luvaglio and Stafford continue in their quest to have the verdict overturned many years on. They are desperate to clear their names. Stafford even confessed to it in one newspaper but said he just did the confession for the money. They want the evidence that the jury did not hear to be heard, believing that if this is granted, they will finally be recognised as innocent.

It has also been said that Vince Lander had been linked to the murder. Lander was making millions, and if he were in the frame for the murder and put in prison, then there would be a spot to be filled at the top of the ladder. After the trial, Lander's firm ran into financial difficulties and he disappeared for several years.

During the Eighties, Lander sank £150,000 into a pub called the Castle Inn, in Durham, and later was ordered to pay £6,000 in unpaid fees to his financial adviser. In the early Nineties, the police investigated an arson attack at his home, The Lodge, attached to Stanhope Castle in Weardale. Declared bankrupt in 1992, he accused Dennis Stafford of burning down his house and threatening to kill his wife and children. Now in his early seventies, he is apparently living in the Daytona Beach area of Florida and is facing a legal challenge for various debts.

The whole case is fascinating; it was the first real taste of gangland activity in the region. It held the public's interest, as it was reported each day in the local papers and on the news. I think it shows that the role of the gangster was now becoming recognised and associated with the club and gaming industry. It showed that Newcastle was catching up with the capital in criminal stakes.

Violent crime is controversial enough and more so when it is on your own doorstep – it raises the stakes immediately. A gangland killing creates speculation, and with such inconclusive evidence sealing the convictions of two men, it becomes even more thought-provoking. Many in the North East have their own opinions as to who murdered Angus Sibbet that night. Many have said that the evidence for murder was far from conclusive and many have said it proved the two were guilty. The fact remains that they were convicted of murder, and until it is proved otherwise, it will always remain.

There is a subplot to the one-armed bandit murder. In this subplot, three more characters enter the story – Irishman Thomas Patrick Hallett, known as Paddy Hallett … and Ronald and Reginald Kray. Paddy moved to London in the late Forties, and after doing his National Service, returned to London looking for a way to make money. He was a hardman, a good boxer, and soon began working as a minder for the illegal street gamblers of the East End.

If you are good at something, you will always get recognised for it, and Paddy was no different. The Kray twins approached him and soon enough he was making a living by collecting protection money for them. He got involved in a few 'heavier' jobs, and as a result he spent some time inside. In true Kray style, Paddy's family was well looked after while he was away and, on his return, he was generously rewarded for keeping quiet.

Not long after his release, he met a girl from Newcastle, married her and decided to move up to become an adopted Geordie. He parted company with the twins, but it was not on bad terms. They still owed him for not grassing on them and they reassuringly offered their help to him any time he needed it.

In Newcastle, it was easy for a man like Paddy to find work. He had 'worked for the Krays' on his résumé, which helped him secure a job working for Angus Sibbet. He was earning £300 a week as Sibbet's bodyguard, which was a tidy sum in those days. So, Hallett was now working for Sibbet, who in turn was working for Vince Lander. Lander had nightclubs, gaming clubs, was supplying the fruit machines to working men's clubs and was making a fortune from it with his brother, Michael Luvaglio.

Sibbet was killed in a gangland-style shooting. This part of the story suggests it was a contract killing, and most fingers have been pointed at Vince Lander being behind it. There are certainly people around on Tyneside who know who ordered the hit on Sibbet and why it was ordered. It has been suggested that it was a 'Mr Big' from the city. It is not possible to say who ordered it. It is clear that *someone* ordered it.

Ronnie and Reggie were reportedly asked to carry out the killing on behalf of this 'someone'. They knew Hallett was connected to Sibbet, so they met up with him to discuss what was going on. Again, they made promises of loyalty to Hallett and decided not to get involved because they didn't want to rock the boat for their friend; end of story as far as they were concerned.

Another means of killing Sibbet was employed successfully. Hallett appeared as a witness at the resulting murder trial, which did not go down well with whoever had ordered the hit. His boss had been killed and Paddy had been sworn in to tell his version of events on the night of the murder. There was no way he could get out of it. We must remember here that Hallett was Sibbet's bodyguard and Sibbet was killed whilst under his protection. Naturally, a jury would want to know how that could happen.

Hallett told the court that he thought Sibbet had gone to see one of his mistresses that night. This was plausible and would explain why he went alone. Subsequent threats were made after Hallett's testimony, before he was attacked and had his face slashed. After hospital treatment, he phoned the twins, who came up immediately to show their support. They had relied on other people's loyalty in the past and now it was their chance to prove it was a two-way street.

Within a few hours, they were in Newcastle and looking for revenge. They wanted the bloke who had ordered the attack on their mate Paddy. The killing of Sibbet was by the by – the Krays had no interest in it – but the killer had messed with the twins by messing with Hallett, and they took that personally.

A firm was quickly assembled, which went from club to club,

scanning the dance floors and gaming rooms until they found who they were looking for. It was about to kick off in a big way until the police arrived. Inspector Jack Vinton bounded up with officers in tow and introduced himself to Ronnie and Reggie. He nodded an acknowledgement to the man the Krays had come to settle their differences with and suggested to all concerned that it would be an idea to settle those differences elsewhere and in private. It was a polite warning that did the trick – the last thing the city needed was a gang war in the middle of a murder trial. They took it to a hotel.

The Krays outnumbered the other gang by far and it was easy for them to take control. With them, they had Patsy Gallagher, a Glaswegian who was known to have a fondness for shotguns. As they filed into a room, Patsy lined the rival gang up against a wall and told them in no uncertain terms that if anything happened to Paddy Hallett again, those responsible for it would be killed. He added that compensation to Paddy was overdue and that the twins would be expecting expenses for their trip as well. The money was paid on the spot, the score settled.

I know the Krays came to Newcastle on more than two occasions – the first being to protect Billy Daniels, and the second time in 1967, where Ronnie was in the city with boxer Joe Louis. He was the only member of The Firm to travel up and was looked after by the same people he had made friends with on his earlier visit.

So, is the Paddy Hallett story true or another myth? Personally, I don't see any reason why it would be untrue. We know the other two trips happened because they are documented and there were photographs taken both times. In the Paddy Hallett story, they came up with haste for one night and for one reason only. It was not publicised. It would also tie in with other theories that Jack Vinton 'sent them packing', because technically he did. They were in a bar and he told them to get out. Anyone witnessing that would immediately infer that Vinton had run them out of town.

The Krays' visits to Newcastle are a perfect example of their notoriety. The fact that there are so many different stories – all of them true, of course – has managed to keep their legend alive. The fact that there are photographs that I've seen of the twins in the Dolce Vita and on a US Navy ship just fuel the fire and your imagination can run wild. I bet if each story were pieced together and believed, the twins would have been in Newcastle for six years in total.

I know that after reading this, people will approach me to tell them what *really* happened. Ron, Reg and Charlie have discussed Newcastle with me in the past. Reg was interested in moving here if he ever got out of prison – I know this because he asked me to look for properties. Ron came here by himself that time with Joe Louis, so he obviously felt comfortable to be here without backup. Charlie enjoyed many nights out in the city and loved the place.

Getting them to discuss Sibbet or Hallett was another matter. They could be vague and ambiguous when they wanted, and they could suddenly forget how to name-drop. The last thing they would wish to do would be to dispel the stories and myths, revealing their trips up North to be just a few social weekends. Such stories have kept the legend going … and stories are something that will keep the Krays going for a long time yet. Of course, there's a DVD about the whole thing out these days, with a starring role from a familiar-faced Geordie: http://kraysintown.com/

CHAPTER 4
MEETING THE KRAYS

Reg was the first brother I had contact with. I had sent a letter to both twins after the end credits of *The Krays* revealed where they were being held. I still remember that day the return letter arrived ... it was a self-addressed envelope, so I knew where it was from immediately. I opened it carefully so I wouldn't rip anything inside ... unfolding the piece of paper carefully; then there it was: a letter from Reg Kray.

In the top left corner was a photocopied newspaper cutting about Reg's forthcoming book, *Born Fighter*, and beneath that was a childlike scrawl which at first appeared to read, 'From B Cell Reg Kray'. After re-reading it, it took the form of 'Steve, God bless. Reg Kray', and beneath that it said I could publicise *Born Fighter* in my magazine if I so wished.

The magazine in question was *The Mighty Quinn* (named after Newcastle United's centre forward at the time, Micky Quinn), which I started up with my mate Steve Cross from Scunthorpe. We were both passionate about the Mags (Newcastle play in black and white stripes and have a mascot of a Magpie, hence the Mags), and the magazine evolved from our love for the team.

After three months in production, our very own soapbox was ready to hit the streets at forty pence a pop, undercutting our rivals by ten pence. Five hundred issues were sold in an hour and a half and we made a profit of £160! After that, we enlisted some helpers – my dad, brother Rob and mate Rob Blaylock. The next issue did a lot better and *The Mighty Quinn* began to grow in popularity. As far as I was concerned, I was just like Robert Maxwell ... well, after a decade on Slim Fast, that is.

I received Reg's first letter on 14 November 1990. I was ecstatic. I read the letter again and again, hoping for it all to sink in. Then my friends and family read it again and again. Then I did again, for good measure. I doubt Reg was thinking along the same lines when he was writing; I mean, God knows how many letters he must have received day in, day out, but to me it meant something.

I had not anticipated how I would feel if he wrote back, but a big part of my feelings that day was nervousness. I think. I hadn't really prepared for a reply. My head was spinning; I had a huge adrenaline rush as I poured over the signature again. Reg had bothered to write back ... he'd written to *me*.

It was like the impossible had happened. It was surreal. Now that I had a reply, I wanted more. I wanted a visit. Straight away, I began another: Dear Reg, Thanks for the letter ...

Within two days, I received another letter from Reg in an envelope he had addressed himself. How it arrived I will never know; it's surprising how mail gets to your door at the best of times, but miracles like this tend to restore your faith in the postal service. Again, the adrenaline took hold of me ... shaking, I opened it with care. Then the initial joy turned to disappointment. The second letter was almost identical to the first. It was just a run-of-the-mill mailshot he sent out to everyone. My hopes of a friendship with Reg Kray were beginning to fade before my eyes.

A day later, my reply from Ronnie arrived with a clear message, 'I will not be able to keep up a correspondence, God bless. Your friend, Ron Kray.' Again, this was a standard reply; it was typed with Ron's barely legible signature at the bottom. Two days later, there was another letter from Reg saying the same thing, in what appeared to be a new form of hieroglyphics. They were both pleased I was thinking of them, supporting them even, but that would be the extent of our contact.

I was gutted. After such a promising start, it was a let-down to get such news. I could see that my parents were relieved, so I decided not to dwell on it and to get on with my own life. I'd had some form of contact, brief though it was. There wasn't much I could say about either of them at that point. I was a bit surprised at Reg's handwriting, but that was about it. Maybe there are handwriting specialists who could use it to decipher his personality. At least they had both had the decency to say they could not continue writing, instead of just leaving it. So, there were no hard feelings from me, as I was sure they had to send dozens of these letters out every week.

Three months passed until the name Kray found its way into the Wraith household again. My mother handed me a copy of a magazine, *Take a Break*, with an article about a schoolboy who was hoping to become Reg Kray's adopted son. This lad, Brad Lane, had visited Reg after a pen-pal relationship ... and lived not too far from Scunthorpe, where my friend Steve Cross lived.

Time to put plan B into effect (you *always* need a plan B), I wrote to Brad and asked about his 'dad', and sent some copies of *The Mighty Quinn* down. Then it was the waiting game again. A long waiting game. A *four-month* waiting game! A letter arrived along with apologies, and my quest continued.

I know I have just said that I decided to get on with my life, but the curiosity was still there. If there was still a *slight* chance, then I wanted to take it. I had got so far and wanted to have another crack at meeting the twins. I have no idea what was spurring me on at that point; what is it that makes a nineteen-year-old want to meet two convicted murderers? In a way, I did see them as heroes. I was fascinated by their notoriety, the way they dressed, the cars, the celebrity status ... I suppose this was something I wanted for myself. Some may say I was obsessed. If I wanted something badly, I made sure I gave it my best shot.

* * *

My next step was to visit Steve and time it with a trip to see Brad and his mother, Kim. Brad was eleven when I met him, and his mother was in her thirties. She was no looker and in those days the twins had numerous middle-aged women contacting them in prison. These women used to want to pull a Kray, even though they were in jail. To get close to one of the twins, they would use their children as the hook, as the Krays were looking for someone to hand down to. Unable to have children of their own now, Brad was Reggie's informally adopted son.

This was the first week of April 1991. I called them from Steve's and was told by Kim that they were going to visit Reg. "Come tomorrow and we might be able to get you on a visit to see him." I nearly dropped the phone; unable to contain myself ... those were the words I'd wanted to hear.

The next day, I left Steve's and headed for Doncaster. Brad and Kim met me off the train, though I could see Brad had reservations about me turning up. I was probably seen as a threat who was there to 'take' Reg away from him. I think Kim was a bit embarrassed at his behaviour, but he became a bit more at ease as the day progressed.

We went back to their place, where Brad took me up to his room – or shrine – to look through some of his Kray memorabilia. He had a large oil painting by Paul Lake signed, 'To Brad from Dad and Uncle Ron.' Paul Lake was the only artist that had ever been commissioned to paint the twins. He visited the twins separately in prison; the prison service prevented him doing a formal sitting with them, so he painted the picture from memory and their official prison photographs. I was green with envy.

It was excellent to see all this, but at the back of my mind, I was thinking, *This is all well and good, but I want to meet him.* Kim said he'd be phoning soon and that he'd been asking about me. It felt eerie ... not in a scary way, though, just the fact that Reg had been asking about me ... what did he want to know? I was sitting on edge till he phoned, then it happened: The phone rang, and I could feel my heart thumping against my chest. "That'll be Dad," said Brad, and as Kim answered, I was straining to hear the conversation above the Edgar Allan Poe-esque heartbeat inside me. Everything was a blur till she turned to me, saying he wanted a quick word.

I must admit that I was shaking when I took the receiver from Kim. I said, "Hello, Reg," into the mouthpiece.

"Hello, who's that? Is that you, Steve?" he asked.

"Yes, Reg. It's Steve from Newcastle."

"Newcastle, eh? How far is that? About 300 miles, is it ... that's a long way, was it a long journey?"

"Yes, Reg, but it was worth it." I seemed to be gaining my confidence now.

"Good, good. Well, you look after Brad, he's a smashing kid, be like a brother to him, okay, and I'll see you soon, okay. God bless."

I handed the receiver back to Kim. That was it – my first conversation with Reg Kray. My first impression? His voice was a lot easier to understand than his handwriting. He was softly spoken, with his unmistakable cockney accent. I was trembling with excitement. Kim hung up the phone and told me I had clearance to visit him the following day.

There was speculation of a move, but my first visit to Reg was when he was still at HMP Gartree in Leicestershire. I had an overwhelming sense of fear entering the prison. The sheer enormity of the place ... you are in a different world immediately, reassured only by the fact that if you can get to look out of a window, you still share the same sky, and you know you are a visitor. It is too easy to forget yourself in such a short space of time. I can't imagine what it must be like to be locked up in a prison – people say there are tough prisons and easy prisons, but I think any situation where your liberty is taken away is tough.

Kim was asked for the visiting order, then I had to record my personal details. Why a nineteen-year-old would be married and have a long string of convictions was beyond me, but those were the type of questions I needed to answer before we could sit in the waiting room; soon after, we were led out by an officer to see Reg. We were taken through a series of what can only be described as contenders for the biggest, widest iron doors in history, each one of them thumping shut to send a rattling awareness of doom through you. I'm sure they probably *do* shut quietly, but the officers are not there to make visitors feel at ease. Quite the opposite, as I was now beginning to realise.

Through another iron gate and we were there. I wasn't quite sure what to expect but was surprised by what I saw in the visiting room. Four straight lines of six tables each, with four chairs around them. I suppose it was the openness of it all … after the contrast to seeing too many films with thick glass partitions and telephone headsets to communicate. Brad and Kim made for a table that was slap bang in the middle of the room. Brad said that "Dad likes to sit here"; I was bemused that he'd prefer to be in the middle, but this was all new to me. I was expecting to be sitting in a far corner, backs to the wall, a clear view of the door, and the entire room.

The other visits were in full swing now and there was no sign of Reg. Now, I was beginning to shuffle in my seat – anticipation … nerves … the lot. It seemed to have happened that quickly that I'd had no time to think about the situation. The contact I'd made already, meeting Brad and Kim, had been a long process – but now I'd spoken to Reg one day and was meeting him the next.

I trained my eyes on a small door at the far end of the room, and as I stared, a well-built, grey-haired man appeared. At first, it didn't register that it was him. Kim and Brad stood up to greet him, but I was fixed to my seat. I'd made the effort in a suit and tie, but etiquette-wise, the situation was so surreal I just couldn't react. Reg wasn't bothered … he extended his bony white hand from his prison shirt, shaking my hand in what was a vice-like grip.

"Pleased to meet you, Steve, glad you could make it. How are you? Did you have a good journey?" he asked, as he looked me in the eyes. I regained my composure and greeted him. The first thing I was aware of looking into Reg's eyes was power. He had a self-assured look, with piercing eyes.

As he sat, it struck me how small he was. I was just over six feet tall at the time, a few inches taller than Reg. I suppose that is what *everyone* thinks when they meet someone like this for the first time, 'you can't be Reg Kray. Reg Kray is seven feet tall' ... it is expected from mythological characters. Still in my mind was that black and white picture of the twins by David Bailey, both looking like towering giants, staring down at everyone, which I suppose was the effect they wanted.

For a man on the wrong side of fifty, he was an awesome sight ... physically fit, having never missed a training session since being locked up. He asked how I was getting on with Brad and what I did in Newcastle, or *Newcarsel* as his accent pronounced it. I hate it being pronounced like that, but this time I kept it to myself. I was explaining to him that I ran a post office and a magazine for Newcastle United fans when he stopped me mid-sentence. "That's it! I knew I had something to ask you. I'll write to you about it."

With that, he turned his attention to Brad, who was sat on his knee. He turned away and left me thinking, *Eh? Reg Kray is interested in my post office job? Wait a minute ... post office job? No way.*

Throughout the next two hours, Kim made her way back and forward to the canteen, collecting cartons of orange squash for Reg ... he'd take a drink before Brad would produce a small bottle from his pocket and top it up. I later found out that it was being topped up with Scotch, although the way he began slurring and repeating himself was a dead giveaway that it was some sort of alcohol.

He also acquired a nice colour to his face in this state of merriment, which was compounded by the fact that Kim was quite subdued throughout the visit. Even though drunk, he still asked what was wrong with her ... Kim just shrugged each time, silent. As I got to know her better, these sorts of mood swings were commonplace, so I didn't pay them much attention.

I knew a lot of women used to write to Reg with wild ideas of forming romantic relations with him – whether it was because they liked him or the notoriety, I don't know. As time went on,

I often wondered if Kim had similar feelings. Maybe Brad was a way of getting to know Reg ... I'll never know ... I used to think about it sometimes when she was in a mood, thinking that she was like that because I was there and was jealous because I was becoming friends with him. True or not, I wasn't bothered.

During that visit (and others), Reg spent a lot of his time elsewhere – literally. He was like a sideshow ... shaking hands with everyone ... having a quick word with someone ... leaving the three of us in an uncomfortable silence till his return.

With around fifteen minutes of the visit remaining, a familiar face approached our table. Paddy 'Joe' Hill, one of the Birmingham Six, came over and greeted us. He shook Reg's hand firmly, saying he'd be praying for him to get out. Paddy himself was about to be released after a severe miscarriage of justice had meant he'd spent the best part of his life in jail. Reg was visibly lifted by Paddy's words and this meant that my first visit was left on a high. Paddy had been locked away for sixteen years after confessing under torture ... he was finally awarded £1 million in 2002 for what he went through, but a million pounds does not come close as compensation for such a loss of time to an innocent man.

As we got up to leave, I shook hands with Reg again, and he said, "You must visit my brother, Ron. I'll try to sort something out. Thanks for the smashing visit, look after Brad and have a safe journey home. I'll be in touch." Then he hugged me just like he was Brando in *The Godfather*. This demonstration of affection made me feel important, not just that he had done it, but that everyone in that room saw it, too. The last of his 'squash' was then swigged back and he made his way back to the far end of the room, pausing for a second to wave at us, then was gone.

As we waited to be escorted out, I had time to think about what had just happened. He was a middle-aged man, as physically and mentally fit as I was. He was not bitter about being held there, though neither was he remorseful for why he was there, either. I was quite sad to leave him but at the same time it was not like he was begging us to take him with us. He was established there, he was a survivor, and that meant he had adapted to his environment. Though in this case, it looked like the environment was adapting to him.

I knew he was no stranger to prison, but I felt the length of such a sentence would have been enough to crush any man's soul. Not this man. I can look back on it now and know that it's not sympathy he wanted; sure, you can feel for his plight, but to him it was just about serving time. It wasn't the situation where you could say, "Poor Reg, locked up like that." He did his crime and he was doing his time … fair cop and all that. He knew he had a lot of time to serve, so he made the best of it.

At first, when he'd been locked up with Ron and The Firm, he was an angry young man. He'd get into fights with cons as well as officers, and was letting everyone know who controlled the inside – the two who had controlled the outside. There were newer kids on the block now, though, and fighting is a young man's game. Reg had done enough to ensure he was respected wherever he was; he didn't have to prove himself anymore.

Once I got home, I put pen to paper again, wanting to strike while the iron was hot. The next day, I received two more letters from him telling me to keep an eye on Brad, and insisting I visit Ron as soon as I could. After the first visit, local newspapers ran stories on my Kray friendship, and it became a bit of a novelty in the area. Media interest was something I could use to my advantage, and I made sure to mention the magazine in interviews, which helped to shift a few copies.

I could sense from that visit that we'd hit it off, then a few days later, Reg asked me to look out for a large house or a mansion for him in Newcastle with plenty of land. He had told me he'd been interested in an affluent area of the city on their infamous visit in the Sixties but hadn't done anything about it. Now he was thinking long-term about the future. It wasn't the first time he did this. Years on, I'd even put down a large deposit on a house for him, which he later lost interest in. The deposit was the sort of sum that would buy a comfortable house at the time.

* * *

It was round about two weeks after I had visited Reg that Kim phoned me to say I'd been given a visit to see Ron in Broadmoor, an institution which was built to house the type of criminals that normal prisons and hospitals couldn't handle. It was originally called Broadmoor Criminal Lunatic Asylum, changing from prison to hospital in 1948. It still resembles a prison rather than a hospital, though. My mam had already prepared me for what the place would be like, but deep down I was a bit uncertain. It was daunting to say the least; I was visiting a mental hospital … visiting him in a psychiatric visiting area.

I was glad that my mam could tell me a bit about what to expect, as she'd been in and out of them over the years, and glad too that I would not be alone on my first visit. Oh, by the way, my mam is a nurse … that's how she knows … I could tell you were wondering.

I went to Brad and Kim's the day before the visit to find there were a few problems. Brat – I mean, Brad – had been going slightly off the rails of late, and while down there, he dragged me into a situation that I didn't appreciate. He got drunk, acted stupid and let his mouth run wild with all kinds of 'beer talk'. The worst part was that he started saying he would get his dad to sort me out. His 'dad' being Reg Kray, of course. I didn't feel threatened by it … but the fact that some little kid started going on like that was a disappointment.

Now, I was on the eve of my first visit to Ron with this stroppy kid trying to threaten me because he couldn't get his own way. Over the years, I've heard enough 'I know Reg Kray and he won't be happy' stories to last a few lifetimes; to hear it come from a stroppy kid was just the start of it.

Friday, 19 April 1991 was the day of the visit. Armed with 200 John Player Specials (Ron's brand of cigarette), we drove through the Berkshire countryside and arrived at Broadmoor with half an hour to spare. The approach to it is something else … dense woodlands surrounding it with trees looming over the narrow winding roads till you reach the dark and imposing Victorian building. Immediately, your mind starts playing tricks on you … you double check the petrol gauge … you see movements in the shadows … you lock your door … stop for no one … it's the sort of place Stephen King would award five stars to if he ever went into the hotel and leisure industry.

Although I knew what to expect, I was still taken aback by the place. It could easily have been mistaken for a stately home, but the bars on the windows certainly gave me the feeling that there were some people in there that society was better off protected from.

We headed towards a part of the building that had obviously just been modernised. We entered through an automatic door, where behind a reinforced glass 'reception' area, two officers sat reading newspapers without so much as looking up as we approached. Kim explained to them that we were there to visit Ron Kray, and after filling out a form, I was in. Kim had to sign to leave the cigarettes for Ron, so there was a bit of a hold-up before an officer led us through the secure doors, gates, courtyard and corridors to an original Victorian part of the building.

All the time, I was noticing the colour scheme … light blues and pale yellows … calming colours … something that is essential in such an institution. Pale yellow is associated with the feeling of harmony and stability, and blue with feelings of tranquillity and the resolution of conflict. Green is also supposed to be a calming colour – apparently, when Blackfriars Bridge in London was painted green, suicide jumps dropped by 34 per cent. I was slightly cynical about the whole concept, as my post office interior was also of a 'calming' colour scheme, which never really had that effect on me.

From there, it was down another calming corridor and through to a large sunlit room containing around twenty tables, each with four chairs around them. There was a large stage to the left of the room where theatrical productions must have taken place. We dropped anchor at a table in the middle of the room. I found it strange that both twins preferred the middle; maybe it was something to do with wanting to be the centre of attention.

Brad and I were barely speaking by that point, so the long wait took even longer. There were ten or so nurses positioned at different vantage points around the room, which was unnerving at first but, considering where we were, it was another essential.

As we sat in silence, I noticed that most of the other visits were going on around us and still there was no Ron Kray. It was also at this point that I noticed something else, something inside myself. Up until now, I had been told about what to expect the institution to be like and the general environment and atmosphere of the place.

I had not thought much about the reason why I was in that environment ... to meet Ron Kray. What did I expect from Ron? Did I expect anything at all? What preparation had I done? What should I do and not do? What should I say? I didn't go in there with a game plan and I wasn't quite sure what to expect. I didn't think it right to preconceive anything about him. I had read plenty of books and articles, and now it seemed logical that I would meet Ron after meeting his twin brother. I was just going to go with the flow ... I was dressed well, he knew of me, I'd known about him for years ... let's see what happens.

Eventually, he appeared at the same door we had entered through and made his way over to us. He was immaculately dressed in a blue suit tailored from Savile Row, a crisp white shirt, silk tie and solid gold tie pin. He was wearing polished Gucci shoes and gold-tinted spectacles to complete the look. Here we were, sitting in the visiting room of a hospital for the criminally insane, and the man we were visiting was the best-dressed person you were ever likely to see for years. The sight of him amazed me as he approached us.

Charismatic, he stood out from everyone else in the place. He could easily have been mistaken for a wealthy businessman there on a visit himself. This time, I made no mistakes, I greeted him properly. I stood along with Brad and Kim. He was barely audible as he greeted them, and I decided to introduce myself to him and shake his hand. His grip was firm and cold, and he said, "Good to see you, Steve, Reg has told me a lot about you."

We all sat down, with Ron taking the seat next to me. The second thing to strike me about this man was his eyes – small, dark and piercing, like Reggie's, but there was something more here. I got the impression that this stare could turn a man to stone in an instant ... there was something menacing beneath the surface, but I couldn't quite put my finger on it.

He took out a pack of John Players and clicked his fingers. Immediately, his cigarette was lit by one of the nurses, and while he was there, Ron ordered him to bring us some tea and 'the usual' for him. It turned out that his order was non-alcoholic lager – four cans' worth, so at least he wasn't going to be as tired and emotional as I remembered Reg being.

The nurse returned with the drinks and Ron stood up and did the honours by adding milk and sugar to the teas. Brad and Kim were sitting there like it was nothing, and there was me with my eyes practically popping out! I had seen every photo and read every book on the twins; to have Ron Kray pouring tea for me just as he'd done for Reg in a picture taken at Vallance Road ... well, it was heart-stopping.

I was still savouring the moment during the small talk when Ron leaned forward and put his hand on my knee, asking, "You don't mind that I'm bisexual, do you, Steve?" I wish he had waited till I didn't have a mouthful of tea before he asked. Composing myself, I told him I wasn't bothered so long as he didn't fancy me. I just came out with it ... and luckily, he saw the funny side as he removed his hand and whispered, "Good, good." I could always see that I'd have to be alert.

It was always a strain to make out what Ron was saying, but as time went by, I could see that this was how he spoke normally. Probably another misconception about the twins – I suppose you just assume that with such a stature comes a bellowing voice. Ron spoke just like any other polite middle-aged bloke on the street. He was keen to know what was going on in the outside world and Kim passed on different messages from friends and associates. His reply was mainly the same each time, "Good, good."

Every now and again, he would turn to Brad and me and ask if we were all right, conscious of the fact that we were still there. Sitting there in an awkward silence, we would nod and say we were okay before he turned back to Kim to catch up on business, repeating, "Good, good."

He started to talk about a book he was reading that was all about world cruises. One thing you'd need in a place like that, I thought, would be escapism and something to look forward to. I imagine that's why so many prisoners take to painting, as a way of visiting other places inside the mind. It's a well-known fact that such activities are therapeutic, and with mental illness these forms of expression are encouraged.

He talked of how he'd go on a world cruise when he was released and how he'd love to take Brad and myself along with him. I could see his face light up as he told me; it was like he could taste the fresh sea air right there, and then he came back to earth, still with a slight sparkle in his eye. He promised to send me a brochure. I found this slightly unusual, as I'd only just met him. I mean, I just couldn't tell if he was being serious or not, but it was a gesture I appreciated.

Fresh air was something I would have killed for on a Ron Kray visit. On that first time I met him, he must have chain-smoked an average of around thirty John Players. He would smoke half of it, then stub it out, clicking his fingers for another one to be lit immediately. It seemed to say that he was in a hurry – quick movements, not enough time to finish, moving on from one thing to another, eager to get to the end – but time was one thing he did have.

It seemed to me like it was mimicking his thinking, with a certain restlessness and always needing to be on the move, almost agitated. He talked to me quite a lot for a first time visit and

I felt more at ease in his company than I did in Reggie's. Ron seemed to have a genuine interest in what I had to say and would listen to me, that was quite a big difference ... you can always tell when someone is listening and when someone is talking *at* you as opposed to talking *to* you.

On subsequent visits, he would enquire about things in my personal life that we'd discussed weeks earlier – he listened and remembered details like my mother's name or where I'd been on a night out and who I was with. Ron seemed interested in the fact that I liked to keep fit through football, circuit training and boxing. The gym I went to was run by former cruiserweight champion and friend, Glenn McCrory, so we talked about boxing for a bit and he asked if I had any pictures of me weight training. I said I could sort some out and send them on. I was quite chuffed that he was keen to find out things about me.

After an hour and a half, Ron made his way back. He liked to get back to his ward early to avoid the rush. One thing that never happened in there was a rush, but each to their own. We shook hands and said we'd keep in touch. As we walked back through the tranquil corridors, I went over some of the things we'd discussed. The world cruise; the photographs of me all sweaty in my training gear ... I dare say it was naivety on my behalf. I now know the true reason for him wanting such pictures and why he'd want to take younger men on a cruise with him, but that was Ron just being Ron. I wasn't angry with him at all. At least he was honest about who he was.

As we were leaving, one of the officers called Kim over. He had something that Ron had left for her. She signed for it and Brad carried it to the car; it was a box. Inside, it was opened, and we found it contained a huge collection of A4-sized black and white photographs of the twins in their heyday; a lot of them from Reg and Frances Shea's wedding day, and had remained unseen by anyone outside the family (I'm lucky enough to own some of the originals now).

As we looked through them on the journey back, another thing that struck me was the similarity between Ron Kray *then* and Ron Kray *now*. Obviously, they were the same person, but the way he dressed then compared to now was the same. The way he'd held court with his soft voice, a voice that was just quiet enough to make you pay close attention, always active and on the move ... but definitely the way he was dressed – nothing had changed. He was the same, only he was older. He was living as Ron Kray, the well-dressed archetype of London gangland, because for him, he still was that same person. It was as though he'd been frozen in the late Sixties and then thawed out later in life. His suits and mannerisms were all intact, but he'd aged with time.

What did I make of all this? To be honest, I wasn't too sure myself. It could be unhealthy to live in the past, but he was certainly in control of his faculties. I didn't necessarily think it was sad to see him like that; the only Ron Kray I'd seen before then was the exact image of what I'd seen now. Psychologically, it could have gone a lot deeper due to his illness. In dressing the same and trying hard to appear the same, it may have been some form of denial. He was still The Colonel, no matter where he was ... he was still active and trying to relive his better days.

A few days later, I received a letter from him dated the day after that first visit. In it he said he'd be sending me £200 to cover my expenses, and again he asked if I could send him any pictures of myself weight training. I didn't send any because now I knew why he wanted them. I also received a brochure through the post days later from him. It was full of different cruises like he'd mentioned on the visit.

This, I learned, was quite a normal thing for Ron to do when visited by a new boy or man. I didn't agree with it, but as I say, each to their own. Each time I hear people saying they visited Ron and they were that close that he offered to take them on a cruise, I have a chuckle to myself. It was standard procedure whether you looked like Johnny Depp or Johnny Merrick. Ron was upfront from the beginning; he didn't hide anything like this and was not backward in coming forward. He was always honest with me, or as honest as a convicted murderer in a mental institution could be.

* * *

Early on during my visits to Reg was when the requests and favours started. They were subtle at first ... on 25 April 1991, Reg told me to tell Ron that he disliked Kate (Ron's wife) and not to trust her. In September 1991, he asked if I had heard any news on Charlie Kray, as they weren't speaking ... every visit I can remember since I started 'working' for them began with, "Any news?"

I kept up regular correspondence with the twins. I could see that I'd made an impression and I also started to visit frequently. Reg was a Category B prisoner, and that meant he was only allowed two visitors a week, so I felt honoured to be invited round about once a month to see him. Ronnie in Broadmoor could have two visitors a day. The only problem I had was the travelling. As I don't drive, I had to catch the train to visit him, but it was worth it.

Then the visits began to change slightly ... I was visiting Reg on my own, and my friendship was independent of Kim and Brad. It also meant that there was not someone else there to fill the uncomfortable silences ... not that there were any. We got along fine as friends and he was intrigued by the fact that I was running a post office and editing the magazine at such an early age. He could see that I was entrepreneurial and took a chance ... he told me he had a warehouse full of merchandise and wanted me to help advertise and sell it – for a share of the profits, of course.

He gave me the number of a bloke called Pete Gillett, who would 'supply me'. Pete was a former cellmate of Reg's. It was one buzz after another in Kray World. It seemed like no time had passed since my first visit, and here I was talking openly with Reg and now being asked to do favours. I didn't really have to think about it ... it wasn't that I was bullied into anything or felt pressured, it just progressed that way.

I phoned Pete Gillett as Reg had suggested. I didn't feel out of my depth, but this was all new to me and I suppose I wanted to make a good impression. It was the rush of being part of something that made me feel a bit edgier than usual. Reg had trusted me enough to do this and I didn't want to let him down. It would look bad for him to befriend someone who would mess up first time, and it wouldn't do my confidence much good to know I had ruined a friendship in such a way. Pete had shared a cell with Reg and was a close friend of his. I told him what Reg had said. He seemed a nice enough bloke and said he'd sort something out.

Now, there's sorting out, and there's *sorting out* ... his impression of sorting out meant sending six huge boxes of merchandise to my door. I couldn't believe it. I took the boxes in and had a good rummage through them. I was like a kid on Christmas morning. There were hundreds of copies of the twins' autobiography, *Our Story*, T-shirts with Reg's face on and the words 'Enough is Enough' printed beneath, and some copies of an artist's impression of the twins that were selling at £250 each. There was a note with the pictures in Pete's handwriting: 'Steve. Keep up the good work. One of the prints is for you from the twins. Be lucky, Pete Gillett.

I made the post office my base and began advertising my new stock from there. At first, the response was slow, but once word spread, I was snowed under with orders and phone calls. It just needed to be rejuvenated slightly to get the ball rolling. I bought some sticky labels, sending half each to Reg and Ron to sign, then stuck them on the books. Now, the demand for limited edition signed copies of Kray books is a lot higher than your common or garden Kray book, isn't it? And that's what everyone else thought, as they were quite prepared to pay extra for them as well. They went for twenty quid each – it was amazing.

The twins were over the moon and so was I. I knew I was pretty clued up on making fast money like this, but I also learned something else that day: The twins may have been behind bars, but it was business as usual for them. It took time to realise exactly what I was doing – I mean, it was a favour I was doing. Reg asked me to do him a favour, right? So, I did him a favour. It was little favours like this that kept Reg's mind busy behind bars. A lot of people doing such favours would amount to quite a tidy little sum.

'Favours', as he would put it, were business, and people prepared to do favours for the twins meant they never went out of business. That first venture netted them a four-figure sum, and true to their word, I was given my cut, which was a tidy sum in those days. Reg suggested that it might be useful to advertise in my magazine, which was still called *The Mighty Quinn* at that point – a suggestion that I took on board, but I wanted something in return. I wanted him to write an article on football for it. He was a bit hesitant at first, but two days later, I received *My Football Recollections*, reproduced here in entirety:

Though I have never been a fanatical football fan, I have had the pleasure of seeing some of the great players. My earliest introduction to a football match was when I was about ten years old and an uncle of mine took Ron and I to Tottenham Hotspur's football ground to watch them play. There were thousands of people present on this day, packed together, and my first impression was that such a gathering of people could be dangerous for the sake of their safety, if they were not controlled properly. Those days there were not the same seating facilities as there are today. The other thing I noticed was that the footballers wore very long and baggy shorts and I wondered to myself why they did not wear neat shorts the same as boxers. At the same time I was fanatical about the sport of boxing and so would read all the boxing magazines, and so saw all the boxing photographs and how the fighters dressed in their shorts and boots for their bouts. One of the greatest footballers I ever saw was the great Stanley Matthews. I remember how he would dribble past each player on the right wing until he was in a position to pass across the goalmouth. His dribbling was uncanny, and the way he would swerve was a pleasure to watch. Another great player that I saw was the late Frank Swift. He was obviously one of the world's greatest goalkeepers. I remember how he would pick up the ball with one hand and throw it towards one of his side. Around about that time, I witnessed the great playing of Tommy Lawton, who could head a ball better than any other player I have seen. He was the best centre forward that I ever did see. I was also fortunate in that I saw the Compton brothers Denis and Leslie. I recall either one or both of them were associated with the hair cream Brylcreem, in that it was said that they used Brylcreem daily. Many years later I met Malcolm Allison the player manager at the Astor drinking club just off Berkeley Square in the West End of London. In one of the books I have written there is a photograph of Malcolm and I, along with others, taken on this occasion. Sometime in the Sixties, I met Dave Mackay and used to go to his shirt and tie shop to buy ties. When I was first convicted, I spent some time in Leicester Prison and there I met Frank O'Farrell. He came to Leicester Prison to give a lecture on football to the inmates, which he did on a regular basis, and I know that he gave his fee to charity. Frank is one of the nicest people it has been my pleasure to have met and we became firm friends to this day. Frank has been one of the best player managers in the game. Sad to say, some years later, after my first introduction to football and my perception of the crowd dangers, there was a disaster at one of the stadiums when the crowd got out of control. On reflection, I feel that if a ten-year-old could foresee a crowd control problem then the safety people at the time should have seen the same. On a happier note, I was pleased to say that my fashion consciousness did come into effect, by the wearing of shorter shorts and better all-round attire. I seem to recall that it was mainly down to the Italian teams that footballers did become smarter in general, because they copied the Italian teams. About five years ago my friend Pete Gillett influenced me into becoming an Arsenal fan, so I will be rooting for the Gunners, and wish them a successful season. Last but not least, I would like to take this opportunity to wish all football fans, regardless of which team they support, an enjoyable end to the season. God bless, Reg Kray.

Reginald Kray, May 1991

I couldn't thank him enough. It showed that he was not just on the take and that he could return a favour to me. That again was an important sign. I did receive a bit of criticism from the local press for my association with the twins, but sales of *The Mighty Quinn* increased following the article, and that's what counted. I don't believe in bad publicity, never have done.

Something was bugging me about the Reg T-shirts that Pete had sent me along with the other stuff. I couldn't put my finger on the reason, other than I just wasn't that impressed by them. I knew they could be better and that there was a demand for Kray merchandise. I suggested to him that I knocked up some designs for a new T-shirt and to see how they sold. The cut would be seventy-thirty in their favour, and I started as soon as I could.

A month later, we not only had a new T-shirt design but also shopping bags, tea towels, calendars and mirrors – a whole range which once approved, was snapped up almost immediately. A fanatic will buy just about anything, but I had to draw the line on a few items out of respect. For example, Kray condoms ... a pack of three personalised by each brother – the ultimate protection racket.

Reg supplied me with lists and lists of names and addresses he'd collected over the duration of his sentence and told me to mailshot them. I used freebie post office envelopes (thank you, your Highness) and received excellent feedback. It was amazing how much interest there was, and that people would feel they needed these things because they carried the Kray name on them. The T-shirts were popular, and I got a lot of praise from satisfied customers.

It wasn't long into our working relationship when I received a call from Reg. He would only tell me that it was urgent that I went to see him, so putting it like that, I didn't really have much choice. He'd just been moved from Gartree to Nottingham Prison, so it was a bit easier to get to.

The atmosphere in Nottingham was relaxed as we shook hands and embraced. Something was on his mind. Still in contact with Brad and Kim Lane, Reg was concerned for Brad and it seemed that he was really beginning to go off the rails. Reg put it down to not having a distinct father figure, something that Brad needed in his life.

I couldn't agree more, that is until he went on, "I can't be Brad's father cos I'm a lifer. I'd like you to move in with Brad and Kim and be a father to him."

I couldn't have disagreed more.

I was gobsmacked ... you could have knocked me down with a feather and then invented a few more clichés to express what was going through my head. Put yourself in that position for a second ... I was looking right at him in disbelief, hoping he might crack up and tell me he was kidding. There was silence ... still I stared as he looked at me for a reaction. What the hell could I do? He was being serious! I sat stunned as he talked. He took out a folder containing what looked like legal documents. It was as outrageous as anything that Ron could throw my way – in fact, more so.

As time moved on, I fell out with Brad and Kim. Brad did not like the fact that I had got close to Reg and started to try and cause trouble between Reg and myself. There was one incident where Reg had given me a few items as gifts, a few of them being books. Brad had written to Reg and said that I had not given him some money that I owed. A total of £85.92, to be precise. Reg had written to me and had put Brad's handwritten note in the letter, and asked why I had not given Brad the money. To me, this was petty, and I was just not going to play along, and in addition to what Reg had now proposed, I wondered if Reg knew what Brad was like. You can't be friends with everyone.

I had no intention of going along with Reg's idea of me being Brad's father, and luckily it was never mentioned again. I suppose that means I'd also have been Kim's husband as well, which is just as surreal. It was certainly one of the most bizarre things I've ever heard in my life. I really don't know how to explain the logic behind it. It was a hare-brained scheme where he had given absolutely no thought to anyone or consideration to anyone's lives.

I could probably look at it from different angles and say it was an honour that he thought so highly of me, then the other angle is the complete opposite. He wanted me to move in and take care of these people who I'd already fallen out with, to be a father to an out-of-control teenager (it wasn't that long ago that I'd been one myself) and be a husband to someone I barely even knew. I couldn't get my head around it.

On that visit we (thankfully) discussed other business. Real business. He wanted my help in republishing a book of his called *Thoughts, Philosophy and Poetry*. My ears pricked up immediately, as there was more potential in this one happening. Originally, the book had been a flop and he wanted me to help repair the damage. I jumped at the chance. Just being connected to the project would have been good, but financially I was offered a better cut than I had expected. Reg was keen to split the profits straight down the middle and I was keen to let him. I was on a high as I travelled home; it certainly was a much more appealing prospect than becoming a father with a ready-made dysfunctional son.

The next few months were spent sorting out copyright clearance and other contractual commitments that had been signed for on the book's first release. Once that was out the way, there was just the task of reading an entire manuscript in Reg's handwriting. I lost count of the hours I spent on it, but after six months, I was happy with the final draft copy. It was back-breaking, eye straining work, but I'd done it. Then came the next bombshell ... "Steve, I've decided not to re-release *Thoughts*, but could you help me with my new book? It's called *Villains We Have Known*. I'll go seventy-thirty with you."

I was outraged, to put it mildly. I mumbled something to the effect that I'd be unable to help him on that one and put the phone down. The thing that hurt the most was that he didn't even apologise for wasting my time. I had learnt a hard lesson. I had wasted near enough nine months on the strength that we were going to re-release the book. It just showed how far removed from reality the man was ... he was so out of touch with the real world that he thought time meant nothing to everyone else. I'm not sure how true that is, or whether he just didn't care that I had my own life on the outside. Whichever one it was, it meant he was inconsiderate.

I'd also begun to publicise the book in the newspapers, and the *Sunday People* had run an article on it. I learnt that Reg was like that – his moods changed like the weather. He could ask you to help with something on one visit, you'd set the wheels in motion and go into the next visit well prepared … then he would have changed his mind and it was over. Just like that. This was usual for Ron, as well; it was all par for the course. To have one friend like that was annoying enough, but two of them was too much at times.

One consolation I got from the book deal, or the ceasing of it, was that there were ten unused poems that he said I could have and use as I saw fit. I knew him well enough by now to let the book deal go. On a few occasions, we got on each other's nerves or let each other down; it meant that we would stay clear of anything similar in the future. We always needed a cooling off period.

So, Reg asking me to help on a different book was out of the question for me, even if it had been a 90 per cent cut in my favour. Once bitten, twice never gonna waste my time for Reg again, as they say. He could see I wasn't taken by the Brad and Kim idea, too, so it was forgotten about as well as the book. Life with the twins was like a rollercoaster … full of ups and downs, so you knew that when you were on either that it wouldn't last forever, and the opposite was on its way. Still, I knew there was always money to be made as far as they were concerned, so wasting time on the book was all it had been. At least I hadn't lost any money.

He still wouldn't give up on the idea of *Villains*, though. On 5 February 1992, Reg asked me to introduce him to Chris Donald, the bloke behind *Viz* magazine, or *Fizz*, as Reg called it. He wanted Donald to buy into *Villains We Have Known* and to buy a share in *A Way of Life*, another book Reg had in mind. The interest in *Fizz* came from the fact that they had run a spoof story on the Krays and Reg assumed they must be supporters.

In consecutive months, I was asked if my mate Paul Hollingshead would print *Villains* for a 10 per cent cut and then to print and promote it with Paul Marcus Henry. He was like a man possessed, changing his mind all the time and phoning me to ask whether I'd ask people to get involved. I'd already given him my answer and I was sticking to it.

Celebrity visits when I knew Reg were a far cry from the Fifties and Sixties. Back then, the twins were celebrities through association; they met everyone who was worth knowing, but now 'celebrities' would only ever visit the twins for one reason – to raise their profile. An aging comedian / now has-been soap star and a washed-up actress are two that spring to mind. Their respective careers were at an all-time low, so what better way to get your name in the papers than to visit dear old Reg?

It really annoyed me, because when their help was needed, they were otherwise engaged. Reg would not have it, though; like me, he believed that any publicity was good publicity, so people used Reg and vice versa in the end. They would argue that there was friendship and say they knew the twins from the old days, but friends are there all the time, not just in the run-up to Christmas when they are in pantomime and want publicity. You could almost start a poster campaign with: 'Reg Kray is in for life ... don't just visit at Christmas.'

Speaking of Christmas, 22 December 1992 became a date that I would remember for a long time. Mrs Dodd, the Governor of Blundeston Prison's secretary, wrote saying that Reg wanted me to visit him on what was known as Family Day. This was a day where lifers could spend some quality time with their loved ones as a sort of Christmas present. Lifers tend to get such privileges and I considered it an honour to be invited. It would be a six-hour visit.

I got the letter two weeks before the visit, so I'd had time to let it sink in and to panic slightly at the same time. All kinds of thoughts were running through my mind ... Would we be able to fill the visit with conversation? That was my biggest worry, as often Reg struggled not to repeat what he'd already said, so how would he cope with a visit three times as long?

I was half an hour late for the visit due to the bad weather causing rail delays. I called the prison but should have known that my message wouldn't have reached him. The various security checks and leaving a few bits and bobs at reception for him just slowed me down even more, but eventually I was escorted to the large visiting room. The room was *alive* ... Children's voices and all the decorations made it just like Christmas Day. Reg was at his usual table in the middle of the room, and sitting with him was the prison's vicar and a nun. I waited until they had finished, and Reg stood up to greet me. He said his goodbyes to them and then he hugged me like a long-lost brother.

"Thanks for coming, Steve, you look fit and well, you're filling out nicely," ... I braced myself for the inevitable.

"You do know you're half an hour late, and I've had to listen to their rubbish for all that time."

I tried to explain that the weather had caused delays, but excuses didn't interest Reg. He had no concerns about the weather ... I was late and that was that, no point in dwelling on it.

We were scheduled for two meals; at midday, it would be a three-course meal of soup, followed by turkey with all the trimmings and ice cream or jam roly-poly for dessert. Then at three o'clock it would be a choice of sandwiches and crisps followed by fruit or cheese and biscuits ... sounded good to me.

The first two hours flew over as we discussed business deals and talked about people on the outside that Reg wanted me to get in touch with. The Christmas atmosphere had engulfed the prison. As we began our first course, I couldn't help feeling that this meal could be taking place anywhere. To take a photo and look back on it, you could have passed it off as a family Christmas dinner at home. It was quite poignant as I looked around and saw all these families tucking into turkey. For that one day in the year, they *were* at home. I also thought about Reg as we ate. For him to invite me that day was like saying I was a member of the family. It wasn't something that we openly discussed, but we both knew what it meant for us to both be there.

After lunch, Reg began to reflect on the past and speculate

about the future. He didn't often talk about his past, so I decided to seize the initiative and ask him if he would have changed his life in any way.

He took a deep breath and stared right at me. "No, I wouldn't, Steve. If I hadn't done what I done, I would never have met people like you. You and others who visit me would never have written to me if I had not been in prison. My one and only regret is not to have made it as a boxer, but it was obviously not meant to be."

On a roll, I asked if he regretted killing Jack McVitie.

His answer was short and sweet, "No, he got what he deserved, and I have no regrets." Reg never showed any remorse for his crimes and I feel that this was the sole reason that the Home Office never showed any compassion in releasing him earlier. If he had said he was sorry for doing it, then he'd have been saying that he shouldn't have done it and that it was a mistake. In his world in past days, decisions were made on the spot and you stuck by those decisions. It was gangland ... there is no remorse in gangland and no going back.

Someone outside of that world – people like you and me, or a grand jury – just cannot comprehend that someone can say the wrong thing or wind someone up and, as a consequence, *deserve* to die. It's as alien to us as it would be for one of them to take a nine to five nice safe office job.

The Krays always portrayed Jack McVitie as a pill-popping-good-for-nothing bloke and tried their best to make him look bad to justify killing him. He took pills so he could stay awake for twenty-four hours at a time. He loved life and hated the night coming to an end; pills and booze were his vice. He had taken liberties with the twins – he was supposed to have fulfilled obligations which he had not, he was forever borrowing money and not paying it back. It was felt that they couldn't let him get away with it anymore. The justification was that he was making a nuisance of himself in gangland – he became a problem they needed to get rid of. The decision was made; they stuck to it, end of story.

Reg introduced me to a few of the other lifers on the same visit, and as usual he would walk from table to table playing the host to other visitors. As I watched this, I could see he was completely in his element ... shaking hands, hugging, laughing and joking and talking business. It was quite sad in a way. I thought of Ron and how his day may be panning out. I always thought of Ron as the one who was stuck in his former life, but now it was just like Reg was reliving the days of glory as well.

As twins, I found them both quite different, but in this mode, there was no difference at all. In this mode, we weren't in prison, we were in the Double R or The Regal. At least we were for those few valuable minutes. It was such a sight to behold – everyone there couldn't wait to meet him. All looking up from their family time to introduce him or to let him pick their child up, to shake his hand and say, "Merry Christmas".

Just after we'd finished our sandwiches, Reg motioned to one of the officers who brought down a large brown box. "I got you a few things for Christmas, Steve, have a look at that little lot." He sat back in his chair, smiling proudly as I opened the box. It was crammed full of socks, shirts, pens and pencils, and books by all sorts of people, including two boxing books featuring the twins by Harry Carpenter and Frank Bruno.

I was gobsmacked ... Looking up, I thanked Reg before diving straight back into it. They say that Christmas is about giving and not receiving, and when I looked up from that box with my amazed expression, I could tell that Reg had got a lot of pleasure from it. So, there was me rummaging through all that incredible stuff and then it began to dawn on me. A lot of people would send stuff into Reg – socks, shirts, pens and pencils, and books by all sorts of people. My 'present' turned out to be the stuff he obviously didn't want. Still, it's the thought that counts, and it's not like he could have nipped over to the local Megastore to buy me Weller's new CD, is it? At least he'd put some thought into putting it all into a box.

The six hours that I had worried about filling came to an end. Reg thanked me for a 'smashing visit', we embraced, and I picked up my box and made my way to the exit. The floor was littered with bits of wrapping paper and streamers as I walked towards the door; the other visits had come to an end and the sound of the children playing became a memory until next year. Reg stood at the table and waved, a visible tear in his eye. It was a sad moment. This had been his Christmas. I always think of Christmas as a time for family – it's what Christmas should be all about.

I thought about this a lot more on my way to the station. It puzzled me why Ron and Reg could not spend this Family Day together, as they had no other family to enjoy it with. I couldn't help but laugh inside as I went through my Christmas box again on the journey home. I opened the first few pages of the Frank Bruno book to see that it was signed ... not by Bruno, but by another boxer, 'God bless. Reg Kray'. It had been a great day, though. One that we'd both never forget. Presents or no presents, it was an honour to spend such time with Reg Kray.

Sometimes, arranging visits was difficult due to work commitments, but it meant when we did catch up, we had a lot more to talk about.

In the New Year, I visited him again in Blundeston Prison and immediately I saw the glint in his eye ... obviously there was news. As another con brought over some refreshments and left the table, out it came, "I've proposed to someone, Steve." Amazing. I couldn't believe it. Rumours of Reg spending 'quality time' with other inmates had been doing the rounds for years – Reg liked to spend his hours with the younger prisoners rather than the older lags ... but to propose to one of them?

I think Reg had read my mind and put me at ease when he announced that he had proposed to a *female* prisoner by the name of Linda Calvey. Linda was known as *The Black Widow* and was serving a long sentence for murder. A match made in heaven, I hear you say. Quite. He had kept up a long-term pen-pal relationship with Calvey and had decided to pop the question. He hadn't received an answer for a time but was quietly confident.

I don't know about you, but if I was proposing to someone

called *The Black Widow*, the last thing I would be was confident. He then talked of his first wedding to Frances Shea. There was no question that Reg doted on Frances and I don't think he ever let go of her or their special day. Having his bride buried in her wedding dress after her tragic suicide was testament to that. The wedding to *The Black Widow* never happened, but I later learnt from Reg that Charlie Bronson had also proposed to Calvey in the same week. She declined on both counts. Women, eh?

With both twins, there were always urgent press duties to take care of. It may have been campaigning on behalf of one of them or setting the record straight for both, but always *something*. I was glad to help if and when I was asked to write to a newspaper. There was one occasion that Ron had asked me to write to John Major, who was the Prime Minister at the time. Ron loved it, but Reg went mad, saying I'd played into the hands of the press and had jeopardised their chances of parole. Ron was keen to keep the ball rolling, though, saying to me all the time that Reg should not be kept in prison any longer and to help get him out.

I mentioned it on my next visit to Reg, suggesting a march to Downing Street to deliver a petition to Major. At first, he wasn't keen on the idea and he killed the conversation dead. Fine – I knew not to pursue it any further. We discussed all the other usual business, and then towards the end of the visit he asked, "How many signatures do you think you could get?" Bingo. That was the sign I needed to start an official campaign.

Reg and Ron had hundreds of friends and thousands of addresses of pen-pals, so once the forms were printed by Steph King, one of Reg's closest friends, we set about sending them to people who would be willing to go out and collect names. The forms were returned in their hundreds over the next few weeks, and by the time the last sheet was returned, there were over 10,000 signatures. Steph organised the walk from Hyde Park to Downing Street, whilst I organised the press and media. The date was set for 9 October 1993.

As expected, there was a low turnout of 'faces', but over 200 supporters turned up to justify the heavy police presence. The petition was handed over to the Prime Minister and all the major television channels and newspapers were there to capture it. It was a job well done. The twins were happy, Steph and I were happy. It was a shame, though, because for all the effort we had put in, I knew it wouldn't make the slightest bit of difference to possible release. It did, however, succeed in keeping Reg Kray in the media spotlight and showed that he could still pull the crowds in.

* * *

I was soon making solo trips to see Ron, and likewise Reg. I visited Ron alone on 20 July 1991; this was the first time that I had seen him look distressed. He was like a different person. He had been shown a newspaper cutting about a tragic young boy named Colin Budd who had idolised the twins. Colin was nineteen years old and his ambition was to emulate his idols … Ron and Reg Kray. He had a collection of cuttings about them and a tattoo etched onto his body.

One day, he walked into a gunsmith's store in Colchester, Essex, in an attempted hold-up. During the hold-up, the owner managed to load a gun and shot him dead. The story upset Ron, and on the visit, he opened up to me, "If I have any regrets, Steve, it's that we are looked upon as heroes by some kids today. There's nothing clever about ending up in here. Kids today have a lot more choices than me and Reg ever had. You make sure you keep on the right side of the law. Don't end up like me. You hear me?"

This was proof for me that he was aware of the things they had done and was aware that they were wrong. I knew all about their younger days and how their mother had conditioned them – the way that they could not differentiate between right and wrong. I can never believe anyone does not know the difference; there are probably extreme cases, but most of the time it sounds like a cop-out to me. Here Ron was telling me he knew they had done wrong in their lives. It's not like he was sorry, though, it was just sounding like he regretted that they had been locked up for those crimes, rather than feeling remorse about the crimes themselves.

For the Krays in their day, there were not many choices – there was petty crime with the ambition to go further, there was boxing and there was show business. Or all three. Ron could accept that their crimes hadn't paid but it was their 'destiny'. He hated reading things like this ... that young people were wasting their lives and their freedom because of some romantic vision that crime was glamorous. Crime had been glamorous for the twins, but not for long. A thirty-year stretch was not glamorous, nor was being shot dead in a hold-up at nineteen years of age.

It was a tiring nine-hour trip to spend an hour and a half with Ron, but it was still worth it. After I took the initiative to produce merchandise that first time around, Ron was so taken by the idea of the Kray mirrors, he mentioned it in his book *My Story*.

Working for the twins in this capacity was not really the money-spinner you'd imagine. Yes, I got my cut, but it was always the twins who benefited from such deals. Right then, for me, the money didn't seem to matter. It was the buzz ... the association of working for them on a business level that kept me going. I didn't treat this as a full-time position – I had my own job and my own life, but I was enjoying the notoriety that came with it. Who wouldn't? It was a good side-line, money on top of what I was earning and becoming known for different reasons other than my day job.

***

There were always con men, crooks and cranks popping up all the time, and I was always given the 'pleasure' of meeting them. Of course, I also met a lot of genuine people who shared a belief that the Krays should be released, many of whom I am still in touch with to this day. Once, I was introduced to a fellow con, "Steve, this is Paul ... he's a good burglar." He just looked like a hanger-on. I said to Reg that he couldn't be that good if he was in prison. Reg had no answer. There was no answer. The 'burglar' then got up and left us.

As we talked, another inmate caught Reg's eye. He beckoned the man over and introduced him to me. His name was Ron Stevens. Ron was a good friend of Reg's and had first met him in a billiard hall on Mile End Road. He later became a regular at the twins' Double R club, and they had kept in touch for years until their paths finally crossed again, this time behind bars.

Reg was always full of business ideas and as I got to know him more, I began to wonder if he was losing his marbles. He asked me to meet up with an assortment of nutters and oddballs the length and breadth of the country to "square a deal", as he put it. These were the scams or 'business ventures' where I became the point of contact.

First up was a trip to Wales to meet the Frayne brothers. These two lads looked the business. Reg had asked me to pick up some merchandise from them and check them out. They took me around the pubs and clubs where they were running the doors and were good company. They handed over the stuff that Reg wanted and that was that. A pleasant time was had by all. A year on and they were arrested and sent down for robbery. The papers said that the brothers revelled in the Kray story and that they had convinced themselves that they were the new twins.

Next on the loony tour was Mike Peters from Birmingham. He had arranged a charity do in aid of a young lad with brittle bones disease and wanted to use Reg's name to publicise the lad's plight. No problem there. Reg sent down some signed artwork. Mike then asked Reg if he would be interested in a fifty-fifty partnership in a used car business. Reg gave me an address and asked me to go and have a look at the place to see if it was kosher.

To enter the partnership, Mike wanted twenty-five grand up front from Reg. I knew a few lads in Birmingham and asked them to take a trip around spaghetti junction a few times to find out what this lad was all about. When I got the call back, I wasn't surprised to hear that our man was known in the area as a con man. Formerly known as Steve Fowler, it was said that his office was a brick wall with a door; the rest of the building lay as rubble behind it. Reg was fuming but grateful that he had asked me to check out the man's credentials in advance.

Scaffolding was next up on the Kray business plan. Jonathan Parlin had set up a company in Essex but felt that because he was such a fan of the twins, that the least he could do was offer Reg half of his business and 25 per cent of any profits. All he wanted in return was Reg to say that yes, he was in business with him. Reg duly obliged and was confident that this man was kind-hearted and genuine.

Another promising sign was that Jonathan even changed the name of his company to incorporate his new business partner's name. Instead of Parlin Scaffolding it was now Par-Kray Scaffolding. He even sent Reg a few sheets of headed paper and business cards to prove he was doing things above board. Reg was proud to be a partner again. I wasn't convinced. I decided to check out Mr Parlin with the help of my mate Christian Simpson. Christian knew Essex like the back of his hand, and it didn't take long to track down Mr Parlin.

Unlike Mike Peters in Birmingham, Jonathan Parlin did own a scaffolding company; unfortunately, he also owed half the population of Essex a lot of money, and we were talking the bad part of Essex, not the good part. So now it was coming together. He owes a lot of bad people a lot of money … so he calls in Reg Kray. What better way to frighten off those people he owes money to than introducing his not so silent partner? After a visit from Christian and me, *Par-Kray Scaffolding* folded. No amount of industrial strength support would be able to rebuild Mr Parlin's reputation after that one.

I lost track of the number of different ventures that fell through for various reasons. A lot of the time, they fell through because they were so off the wall there was no way they would ever get anywhere. Reg had his own ideas – producing champagne, or 'Campaign Cocktail' as it was to be known, red roses in plastic tubes with his name on a card inside – and those are some of the tame ones.

Quite often, these hare-brained schemes would come from an associate of the twins as a money earner, and it wasn't always just Ron who would jump in feet first without looking. I said I would act as an adviser for Reg, for both … kind of like a mediator to suss out the money-makers from the time wasters. If I knew then what I know now, I wouldn't have bothered.

I was getting calls from all over the place with offers, offers and more offers … practically every trade you can think of. Some of them turned out to be lucrative for him and others, of course, turned out to be con men after Kray money.

There was the time I was called by a Scotsman going by the name of John Miller. He wanted Reg to put his name to a business venture called School Dinners. He wanted a five-figure sum that would see Reg earn his money back in no time and promised a lot more on top. Now, those kinds of promises sound good – some bank managers may argue that such a business plan and turnover sounds good enough to warrant a nice start-up loan, in fact, which was the first cause for alarm.

Reg was quite keen to get involved, but somehow, the name John Miller sounded familiar to me. I'm quite good with faces, which comes from doing the door, but names don't mean that much to me unless you are important. For some reason, this name had stuck in my mind, but why? I started flicking through all the indexes of my Kray books, then onto other books till I reached Ronnie Biggs' autobiography, *His Own Story*. And there he was … Miller, John.

I flicked through the pages and began to read about how Mr Miller had attempted to kidnap Ronnie Biggs in return for a reward. When I reported the story to Reg, the deal was dead. Our friend John had also claimed to have found Lord Lucan prior to the Biggs kidnap. Maybe the twins were his next targets, who knows? He was certainly a tryer. The School Dinners scheme did go ahead, though, without Kray involvement. It was so successful that I read about it in the newspapers. It was alleged that he had prostitutes dressed up as schoolgirls to serve more than just food in his eating establishments. What a bloke. It was a close call and would have been an absolute disaster if I hadn't investigated John Miller's background first.

Reg was always interested in what was going on in the outside world. He was fascinated by the fact that you could now get takeaway food delivered to your door and loved to hear about other cultural developments. I mean, the last time he was free, a Big Mac was something he'd hide a shooter in.

One development he was really into was the music scene. He was heavily into rave culture and had even experimented with drugs such as ecstasy. One story about his drug taking even leaked to the press via 'a trusted cellmate', which was titled 'Reg E Kray'. In September 1996, I took dance band QFX to meet him in Maidstone, along with my mate Ray Cann.

Ray was panicking, as Reg had asked for a pair of training shoes and Ray had been unable to deliver. This was Ray's first visit, so as soon as we arrived, he made for the nearest sports shop while Jacquie, Kirk and I went for a drink. Just as we were finishing our drinks, Ray came in out of breath but smiling. He had a bag with a pair of training shoes in – panic over.

The security inside the prison was a lot tighter than it had been in the past. We were searched but luckily had decided not to take in the bottles of scotch as requested. We took our seats in the visiting room and Reg appeared looking fit and well. He took an instant shine to Jacquie and said he'd ask a warden if she could stay the night with him. Reg looked a bit unsure of Ray at first, though making him sit on his 'deaf side' as he did with most new people.

After small talk, it was down to business … Reg brought a portfolio of songs he and cellmate Bradley Allardyce had written, which were surprisingly good – a lot better than his poetry, which was what I would have expected. QFX were interested in taking things further on the strength of his songs.

Reg then asked us all to swap seats so he could talk other business with me. It was the usual mishmash of merchandise, Kray parties, phone cards and sending money to people. He was ebullient on this visit, and business-wise it had been productive, too. He left the visit early saying he wanted to beat the rush back, which is exactly what Ron always said! They were too similar sometimes. It was eerie. Before he left, we swapped training shoes with him so that he had a new pair – Ray got the left, I got the right.

Through my involvement with Reg, I'd been present at some memorable visits over the years. The Christmas Day visit is one I'll always remember, the first time I met him is another … the best one of all was a visit at Maidstone on 12 August 1994, when I was twenty-two. Thinking back about it, I was in such a privileged position, but at the time it was just the sort of thing I took in my stride. It was only after such an event that the relevance of it all hit me. Here I was in the middle of something huge … this visit made gangland history. Present at this one were us younger associates Christian Simpson, Dave Courtney and me along with Frankie Fraser, Charlie Richardson, Charlie Kray and Alec Steene.

So, here I was in amongst one of the most important meetings in British criminal history. As we all checked in with our respective visiting orders, I had a terrific sense of occasion. We all knew that this was a first and definitely a one-off. As we waited, I wondered what was going through the minds of these aging gangsters. They had not all met each other like this in over thirty years. The last time there had been any talk of the Krays and the Richardsons meeting was to go to war … to fight it out to the death … the winners having control of London.

None of these men were strangers to prison, so while it was like a second home to them, I can imagine it was bringing back some bad memories. They had clocked up well over a hundred years of prison time between them, and that's not even including Dave! We made our way through the sequence of security gates and checkpoints and were led into the large canteen that was the visiting room.

Reg wasn't there yet. We made our way to a couple of tables in the middle of the room. People on visits had stopped talking and could do nothing other than stare at us. Dave and I pulled the two tables together, and we all took our seats and chatted amongst ourselves as we waited for Reg to appear. He didn't keep us waiting too long. He was wearing his regulation blue and white pinstripe shirt opened to his chest, revealing a chunky gold cross, a pair of Levi's and a brand-new pair of white Reebok trainers.

He smiled widely as he approached … first he embraced Charlie Richardson and then the rest of us in no particular order. As we took our seats, the conversation from the other cons and visitors started back up. It was an unbelievable sight.

I didn't really get a chance to speak much with Reg, but for once I couldn't care less. It was fascinating to see Reg with Charlie Richardson after all the stories I had heard and read about them. The rivalry and hatred was not just set aside, it was left firmly in the past. Dave made me feel at ease with his jokes and laughter, even when sitting with some of the biggest villains in the country.

I also chatted with Alec Steene. Alec always had a lot of time for me and I appreciated that. He wasn't a villain but a man who loved the whole gangster lifestyle and was proud to be associated with the chaps, particularly the twins.

For once, Reg didn't get up and start talking to other cons – he was full of questions … wanting to know who was alive, where they were and what they were doing. They discussed old times, looking back on those days with fond memories. I decided to get the refreshments in and asked what they all wanted. Charlie Kray wanted a biscuit, as did a few others … "What do you fancy, Charlie? Penguin or a McVitie's?" asked Fraser. We all burst out laughing. It was great to see they could laugh about the past like that.

The visit lasted two hours and it was an emotional Reg who said his goodbyes to his friends. They had tears in their eyes knowing that this would probably be the last time they would see each other alive. In a way, that was the main reason for the visit. None of them were in their prime anymore and it was a way of making up before time ran out. It was good to see them make the peace after many years and while they still could. I also think that it was a good show for the media – there was always talk about the rivalry between the two gangs but now they had put it to rest once and for all.

My last visit to Reg was in December 1999. The visits had been getting less frequent over time and we both knew that they were ending. We didn't fall out or stop doing business fully, it's just that there were other things to be getting on with and we had drifted apart like friends so often do. In not seeing him as often, I noticed the physical changes more. He'd lost a lot of weight over the years and didn't look like the healthy Reg Kray in the prison gym photograph, which he was still sending out to people. He clung onto the image of the powerful gangster for all he was worth.

CHAPTER 5

DOING THE DOOR

The early Nineties saw a big change in the direction my life was to take. I was losing interest in the post office business and couldn't see my involvement lasting much longer. My connection with the Krays and the friends I'd made was proving to be profitable and was taking up much of my spare time. Business with the twins and football seemed to be taking over, both developing from pastimes into occupations. I was also managing a Sunday League football team which over the years has included: Dave, Mark, Steven and Chris Liddle, Mark Collingwood, Andy Wilcox, Rob Wraith, Chris Parker, Anth Vickers, Davey Campbell, Ian Burns, Ian Brown, Joseph Collings, Fred Clarke, Anthony McGowan, David Ball, John Moore, Ade Fasan (RIP), Paul Grey, Dave Butterfield, Steven Spence, Arron Parker, Keith and John Armstrong, John Mole, Lee Gates, David Hills, Mark Lockwell, Andy Green, David Walker, Brendan Mullholland, Willie Dryden, Thomas Pope, Davey Brown, Raymond Oshin, James MacCoy, Dean Askins, Paul Young, Steven Thompson, Mark and Carl Douglas, Lee Lowe, Steven Roberts, Steven Clarke, Chris Heron (RIP), Alan Lamb, Chris Lamb, Shaun Thompson and Paul Donnely.

Professional football was now receiving more media interest, especially with the increase in availability with satellite and digital technologies. Television and radio were always looking for different angles on a story and would often want a supporter to give his view on different issues. Eight times out of ten, they would ask me, as I had become an unofficial voice of the Newcastle United fans through the magazine. It was good to be asked about issues surrounding the club – also good to get recognised by fans, as they would always ask me about what was going on at St James' Park and we'd discuss the latest signings and transfers.

One of the interviews I was asked to do was BBC's *Newsnight* in the wake of the Hall / Shepherd saga at the club. This was when Freddie Shepherd and Douglas Hall (both club chairmen) went on an (alleged) massive drink and prostitute binge and were caught on video tape making derogatory comments about women from Newcastle and criticising United skipper, Alan Shearer.

The media are well known for the ability to manipulate events and report comments out of context, so that the reported version differs from actuality. It is well known that men from Tyneside worship women and football. Whether Hall and Shepherd's comments were taken out of context or not was irrelevant ... they said what they said and were guilty. They were on the television news, in the papers and people could read it all in black and white, pardon the pun. I lost count of the number of press interviews about Hall and Shepherd I ended up doing; I was literally walking from one to the next.

Newsnight ... unfortunately, Jeremy Paxman was on holiday. I was flown down to the studio in London and asked to give my opinion on the state of the club. Asked to dress smartly, I wore my best suit jacket (of the 'track' variety), trainers, jeans and had my head freshly shaved. I sat across from the interviewer with a studio link-up to an intelligent and beautiful woman from Tyneside and ex-Newcastle striker Malcolm Macdonald.

Newcastle United is one of the biggest clubs in the country with a massive following. The scandal caused outrage a lot further afield than just the North East; *Newsnight* was broadcast nationally. The interview went well, with all three of us putting our points across as civilised grown-ups, then out of the blue the presenter asked me, "Yes, Mr Wraith, but isn't it true that you would have the Kray twins playing for Newcastle United if you could?"

For a second, I was gobsmacked, but I quickly retorted with, "Yes, I would, but sadly one of them is dead; you should have some respect." Someone had clearly told him that I was associated with the twins and that it would be a great piece of television to ridicule me in front of millions with this question. All he succeeded in doing was confusing the watching audience, who didn't know me. He just made me look cool, calm and collected. I thanked him after the show, hoping that his producer had shouted all the things at him I'd wanted to.

Like most young lads on Tyneside, I was spending my money as quickly as I was earning it. Most of it was spent in local pubs, The Ship and The Swan. It was not uncommon for me to start drinking on Friday, have a lock-in till Saturday morning, go home, get some kip or go to the match if Newcastle were playing and be back in again for another session that evening. This had been one of the main reasons that Reg had given me a mobile phone – complaining that I was at the pub more than I was at home, which was probably true.

Spending time in my local pubs eventually led me into door work. Looking back now, there were a few factors that led me towards it. One of them was that I could never mind my own business when it came to a fight or an argument. I still can't. I always had to be there amongst it. I liked to stop any bother if I could, one way or another.

Don't get me wrong – I have never been a fighter. I prefer to diffuse situations. Unfortunately, some people enjoy themselves by going out to pick fights. I had the fact that I am physically big enough to step in on my side as well, which was a bonus. It is a case of 'size matters' – a bully will think twice about having a go at someone his size and will back down when faced with someone bigger. If mates were having a drunken fight, my intervention could be a good excuse for them to call a truce.

Most bar fights are a one-way attack on another person who just wants to enjoy a night out. It is unacceptable that some moron who can't handle his booze can ruin someone else's night out – or ruin their life in some cases. If I could do my bit to help, then I was happy. If only people would just think first ... it takes a lot more energy to pick a fight, have one, then live with the consequences than it does to shrug one off.

On nights out in Newcastle, I found it was getting easier to jump the queues outside bars. My face had become known because of television appearances, and I became friends with a lot of doormen around town. My association with Newcastle United and the Krays was the perfect icebreaker. Conversation would start off with talk about football; see if I had any inside knowledge on The Toon (Newcastle United), and so on. Some doormen knew of me from my Kray association and we became friends through that, so I'd say it was an even spread.

When talking to them, I found that punters would mistake me for a doorman, so the progression into the line of work was inevitable. If the shoe fits ... wear it. No one I have ever spoken to has said that becoming a doorman or door*person* was his or her number one career choice. No one. A lot of door staff will have a day job and do door work to earn extra cash; others have turned it into a full-time career. Nearly everyone I know says they just 'fell' into it, but it always related to size, reputation and contacts.

I was on a night out with the lads in Newcastle one weekend when I saw Gary (a.k.a. Lurch) on the door of Masters. We discussed the usual topic – football – then he asked me if I fancied earning a few quid over Christmas. One of the lads had broken his wrist and Gary wanted me to fill in, if I was willing to. I was game enough and couldn't think of a better way of earning a bit of cash than to be standing in a bar listening to music and looking at gorgeous women all night. It literally *did* sound like Christmas to me.

My first shift was a Thursday night, which as anyone will tell you is as busy as a weekend in other cities. I was dressed in a white shirt, black trousers, Dr. Martens and a black bomber jacket. I felt and looked the business. Gary introduced me to the lads who would be watching my back and vice versa.

There was Irish, Buzz, Dave and John Lillico, who remains one of my closest friends. There were two key positions, front door and back door, with buzzers and flashing lights to let you know where a fight had broken out. That night, there were six fights in just over four hours, and this was a relatively tame night according to the lads. I loved every minute of it. It felt right and *definitely* felt like the start of something new and exciting.

The festive season is always a bit on the mental side. Once a year, drinkers and office parties … everyone drinking too much, eating too much, the just-out-of-school-lad getting off with the middle-aged woman in the office and never living it down, being sick in the streets, in shop doorways … and remember, this is people *enjoying* themselves.

Up until that Christmas, I had been doing exactly the same thing (although I'll never admit to the middle-aged woman) and it was only then that I realised that there was more to life than spending my hard-earned cash on booze. It's really only when in this position that you can cringe for the first time, knowing what you must have looked like. You can't beat Christmas time in Newcastle.

Then January comes and it is the quietest time of the year. People realising they spent their entire wages and Christmas bonus in one go. A quiet period in door work means no work; as I had been the last in, I was first out when shifts had to be cut. I lost my Thursday to Sunday shifts and was gutted. I hadn't been there that long, but I missed it. I missed the adrenaline rush that I got when the lights and buzzers came to life and I missed the lads I was teamed up with. I still saw them on nights out, though, so I didn't lose touch altogether. It was like getting bombed out by a girlfriend after a few weeks … just after that 'getting to know you' stage and everything is running smoothly. It was tough to deal with, but there were no hard feelings.

I left it for a while, until an old friend of mine, George Poulter, telephoned in the New Year. He managed The Filament and Firkin, as well as Scruffy Murphy's, and asked if I would be interested in sharing the head doorman's job with Paul Tinnion. I thought about it and decided to give it another go. I had got the taste for it now and wanted to get back in, and a head doorman's job had more credibility than relief work.

By now, Newcastle City Council had decided that all door supervisors should be licensed. This required four days training, covering all aspects of the job, including fire regulations, health and safety, drug awareness, licensing laws and first aid. On the final day, each potential doorperson sat a multi-choice test on what he or she had learned. I passed with flying colours and was given a weekend shift as joint head doorman on George's bars at the Haymarket end of Newcastle.

Paul Tinnion is the kind of doorman you would want in the trenches with you – always on the ball and not someone to mess with. On the doors, you need to know that your partner is going to be watching your back and isn't going to bottle it. With Paul by my side, I never had to worry. He's one of the best to work with and over the weeks and months we handled every situation that came our way.

The bars weren't as hectic as Masters had been at Christmas, but nevertheless, we had our fair share of bother. The Haymarket is not far from St James' Park, so football matches always brought trouble our way. Never anything too serious, though; it was always outweighed by the Newcastle fans, who would talk to me about the beautiful game. Of course, I had to bear a bit of verbal abuse from some of the supporters as well. It was water off a duck's back, though; I am aware that you can't keep everyone happy, and one thing every fan is, is an expert on football. You just can't win – 'sticks and stones', as the saying goes. There were plenty of good blokes as well as bad blokes who would come in ... and we can't forget to mention the ugly ones.

Doormen in general have a bad reputation, but I'd say it's been getting a lot better in recent years. They were considered by the public to be paid thugs who chat up women and give any man who looks at them the wrong way a good hiding. You got a problem with that, eh? Have you? Joking aside, though, that's how things *used to* be and that's how the name 'bouncer' came about ... and it wasn't that long ago.

Bouncers were feared and unfriendly – in a word, bullies. A bouncer would probably intimidate you on the way into a bar so you wouldn't cause any bother inside. If you caused anything, they would clear house, throw people out and hurt as many as they could along the way. That's why they were there and they enjoyed it.

You wouldn't talk to a bouncer – ever. They were unreasonable ... *everything* was settled through violence, because it was the only language they understood. Blokes would see them as a challenge and, again, that's how a lot of fights broke out. The same thing was going on all over the country; bars were getting bad reputations, which meant cities were getting bad reputations. Put a thug on the door to keep the peace and there would be only one outcome.

It was getting out of hand, so the council and the police force called for a change of image. They wanted to rid the bars and clubs of bouncers and bring in 'doormen', who went on to become doorpeople, which is why the licensing initiative was set up. What publicans wanted now was a customer-friendly doorperson – someone who would talk to the customers and eject them with reasonable force if they misbehaved.

There is always a better atmosphere if you greet someone as they approach as opposed to growling at them. Progress ... back then, bars were nothing like they are today. Now it's all about designer labels, designer furniture and designer drinks – a bar is about image and attracting clientele – not about cheap booze and punters. With that, you need the right people on the doors. It's PR now more than anything – conduct instead of conflict.

I learned quickly that doing the door was as much about front as it was physical size. Never back down when you have made a decision, because it shows weakness; always maintain eye contact with a customer who you have a problem with; be aware of who that person is with; and most importantly, make sure someone is watching your back. You need balls, brains and *then* brawn.

In my late teens, I studied drama at college – acting has always been an interest of mine since learning that I was named after

Steve McQueen. Working on the doors, I could see that another element to the job was acting, in the sense that you must become a different person. You need confidence in yourself and what you are doing. You may not be the toughest person in the world, but the way you act will play a big part in whether you will need to prove it or not. Once you put your clothing on, you start to become the role itself.

There was an episode of *Faking It*, a television series on Channel 4, where a doorman and an acting coach trained a young lad. The idea was to place a middle-class Oxford graduate in a fish-out-of-water situation and see if he could convince the public and head doormen that he was for real. He pulled it off and was actually good at it! At one point, there was an arranged confrontation to test him and he didn't back down. He proved he had the front to stand up to a big bloke, although if things had kicked off, they may have had to change the programme's name to *Breaking It*. Skills are required to diffuse situations verbally, but physical skills are needed when the peace talks break down.

I was making regular trips to London to see the chaps, all friends I'd made through my contact with the twins. If I had not become so close to Ron and Reg, then meeting and networking with the likes of Dave Courtney would never have happened. Being connected to them opened a lot of doors sociably and having friends of friends is always useful.

The doors being open sociably soon meant they were open economically, too. Through Dave, I was doing regular shifts on the doors at Diamonds club in Hackney, and at the Ministry of Sound. Working at the Ministry gave me a taste for club life. I loved everything about it, and it was a lifestyle that I got used to quite easily ... with him by your side, resistance is never an option.

I considered moving to London full-time but was advised by Dave that I should stay up North and make my mark. I decided to take his advice. I could see what he meant. Down there, Dave is a big fish in a big pond, but it took him years to get where he is. Newcastle is a major city but is still the right size to be able to make a name for yourself.

Back home, I made further enquiries for club work. A couple of months had passed when Mike, the manager of Legends nightclub in Newcastle, called me to offer some work. I jumped at the chance and, four hours later, I was signing on the dotted line with Geoff Capes' (*the* Geoff Capes) security firm. What Mike had neglected to tell me was that the previous doormen had just been sacked and that the police were keeping a close eye on the club. It's sometimes nice to know these details when you start a potentially dangerous job.

It was common knowledge that the doormen had been running the club by their own set of rules, which basically meant that customers were getting beaten to a pulp on a regular basis with the security tapes going missing each time. Also, the club had gained a reputation as a place for drugs, so the inevitable police raid was on the cards. They had stormed the club with over 150 officers, but to their embarrassment, caught no dealers and only a handful of people for possession.

The ex-doormen were not happy despite receiving a substantial settlement, and they made us work hard for our money. The first couple of days passed by without incident – the calm before the storm. Paul Tinnion soon came on board; it gave me a lift to have a mate there with me.

Because of the trouble from the ex-door staff, Paul and I were now looked upon as outcasts amongst the door fraternity and were subsequently barred from most bars in the city centre, with the threat of a good kicking if we tried to visit. I'll admit now that each night was a nerve-wracking experience. I changed my route to and from work, was careful not to let anyone know my address or telephone number, and I even gave a false name to people I talked to in the club. That's how I had to live.

Paranoid maybe, but you cannot be too careful in this game. Although some of the threats lacked any real danger, you must take each one seriously because one day someone may just call your bluff. You have got to look after number one, and even a half-hearted threat by some numpty on the street must be considered.

I'd thought about calling in some favours from friends down South, but this was my own fight – I couldn't call for backup at the first sign of trouble.

As time went by, the threats died down and we had weathered the storm. There had been a few run-ins, but as the months passed, the lads from other bars started to respect the fact that we had all stood our ground and not bottled it. I suggested to our boss that he lift the ban on doormen entering the club now that the trouble had cooled down. We could let them in so long as they surrendered their licence to us while in the club. He agreed to it and again we'd made our job that little easier.

For many reasons, you can't afford to have doormen as enemies when you work as one. It's bad enough having enemies, but doormen need allies – you can't have any bad blood in your own city. Our bans began to lift one by one, and I was soon able to go for a pint in Newcastle again without having to look over my shoulder. Special mention must go to those who stood their ground and watched my back at Legends. They were Paul Tinnion, Johnny Miller, Vaughn Basset, Maria Gillon, Mark Higgins, Simon McGhee, Biff, Adam, Naz, Andy, Gareth, and Amanda Scott.

The job can be messy at times and it's not uncommon to see a broken bone or some blood spilled at least once a week. Mix testosterone and alcohol together and it often equals bad behaviour. Then there's the stag parties, hen parties, fancy dress parties, the air guitarists, the stage divers, the indie kids, people being sick, drinking sick, covered in sick, falling in sick … you name it, we've seen it.

The 'incidents' are always the best part. A few incidents a night are a lot better than having to fight. Just because we work the doors does not mean we look forward to fighting. The best part about the job for me is some of the surreal sights that you can have a good laugh about even years afterwards.

Monday nights were student nights at the club. Love them or hate them, but it's their debt that pays our wages. Working a student night would have been all right if it wasn't for the students. There was always a Jeremy from the rugger team whose daddy owned most of the world and would have us all sacked for chucking him out. You got used to it, though – each time you were told they would be earning four times as much as you in a few years, you just had to be tolerant ... and be prepared for exactly the same speech next week. I'd always laugh to myself, knowing that in a year or so they may be asking if I wanted large or medium fries. Kicking out time on a Monday night had to be seen to be believed; Whitney Houston would never have sung that song if she'd ever come to Legends.

Then there was Posh Ron. Just add enough alcohol and he'd start stripping! This went on every week, so we were used to it after a few Mondays, but it starts to get boring after two semesters. I remember the last time ... the usual routine after a few pints, the final sock kicked off ... then we gathered his clothes up and hid them. We had no choice but to escort him out ... into the snowy January night. There were still people queuing to get inside, so he kept them entertained until the police came to offer him their hospitality. We handed his clothes over to the police and made sure we kept the videotape in case they needed it for evidence. Clearly, you must be bright to get into university, but common sense and being streetwise are skills that mustn't have been on their curriculum.

There was a restaurant upstairs in Legends that would double up as a VIP room every weekend for celebrities, so on Mondays it was just business as usual up there. I'd stand on the stairs leading to the VIP area and could guarantee that people would want to get upstairs to mingle with the stars. I'd play it cool, saying I shouldn't really let them in ... but we all know that money talks. Five quid usually bought them the privilege of watching people eating a meal.

Life wasn't always fun and games at Legends, though. There were always the odd scuffles, but I wouldn't say it was worse than anywhere else. It was mainly visitors to the city that would cause trouble as opposed to the regulars. Every June in Newcastle, we have The Hoppings; this is where the Gypsies come along and transform the town moor into a huge funfair with rides and stalls for a full week – and they loved causing trouble in the club.

I remember one Thursday in particular as a few of the doormen were late into work, leaving only three of us on duty – Johnny, Paul and me. Inside, there was a group of lads from Edinburgh out on a stag night – doing as Scotsmen do, and doing a good job of it, too. It was a laugh. Thursdays were a bit quiet in there, so it livened the place up … then, of course, the Gypsies arrived to put a dampener on the whole night.

Within five minutes, the Gypsies had introduced themselves to the Scots in a non-too-friendly way, which caused the Scots to do that other thing they do well. We were told over the radio that there was a fight in bar one, so Paul and I went to investigate, with Johnny staying on door duty. We needed more doormen, but rule number one is never leave the door unmanned. We legged it down to bar one and there were twenty blokes beating the piss out of each other. With no time to think, we had to get in amongst it and sort it out as quickly as possible. I was dragging the Gypsies out while Paul had his hands full dragging the Jocks out. It was total mayhem.

As we were rag dolling them up the stairs, Simon and Vaughan arrived and without any questions began hauling them out, too. It was one of the only times at work where I've actually had to hit anyone, a record I'm quite proud of. In that situation, I had no choice. One of the Gypsies had decided to bite my arm, so I caught him with a big uppercut and floored him with a left. I had to move fast, because if he'd drawn blood, I might have turned into one.

The introduction of CCTV cameras was the end of the road for some doormen. Security had to be stepped up for everyone's protection, so they were put into clubs and on the streets. People may protest about privacy, but Big Brother has been watching us for years now – cameras have made places safer. There are pros and cons … you can be caught skiving or doing anything you shouldn't be doing, but you could be getting attacked and need to know who it was or you could be blamed for attacking someone when you were nowhere near. I personally think cameras are a good idea.

In pubs and clubs, every time a punter was thrown out, he'd go to the police and say he was assaulted. Most of the time, it would be only his pride that got hurt, but now doormen could prove their innocence, too. Just after the cameras were installed, I was in Legends on a night out as a civvy. I was standing just off the main dance floor with Richie, Graham, Curly Keith and Iraqi Alan, enjoying a few drinks and having a good time when a fight broke out. It happened too quickly to even call it a fight really, but it was enough to give someone a broken nose.

Doormen are never fully off duty; I caught what happened out of the corner of my eye and rushed over to the lad. He was in a bad way and being surrounded by clubbers; bright lights and dry ice must have added to his confusion. Irish Mark was working the door that night, so I called him over to help.

By that time, the injured lad's mates had crowded round to see what was going on ... and to ask what I'd done. Ever tried convincing a bunch of drunken lads that you didn't hit their mate when you even have his blood on your shirt? Well, I have and it's impossible. My mates wanted to get involved but it wasn't worth it. It was made worse when Irish Mark arrived and got the unofficial story of what had happened from the hostile witnesses. Innocent until proven guilty? *Never.* Not in these situations. It's always the other way round and the only one who could clear my name was falling drunk *before* the punch. His friends were never going to let it lie, so I decided to leave before it became a bad night for everyone.

The following night, I arrived for work and was told the manager wanted to see me. He said there was no work for me that night – I was suspended for assaulting someone the night before. Brilliant. The police had been called after I'd left, and the same story was given to them. It was a nightmare. The manager had to give them my name and now I was a wanted man who'd fled the scene of the crime ... it was getting better by the minute.

I told the manager that I didn't do it and I was trying to help the lad. I remembered the cameras were now in the club and told him to look through the tapes, because he didn't seem to believe me. The police had taken the tapes and I was suspended without pay. I couldn't believe it. I just had to roll with it for a week until the police got back with the tapes and – surprise, surprise – I was innocent and had tried to help the lad out. It was great to get the not guilty verdict, but it had cost me £200.

I'd been working at Legends for almost two years when I made one of the worst moves in my life. I decided to move to Sheffield. I had met a woman from Sheffield on a night out with the chaps in London and fell head over heels in lust. I travelled down to Sheffield for a couple of weekends on the trot to see her. She was ten years older than me, had blonde hair, blue eyes and a cracking figure ... and just happened to be a millionairess.

I was sucked in by the whole thing – who wouldn't be? Within three months, I had proposed for the second time in my life and I had got to the stage where I was handing out invitations. It was obvious to everyone else which head I was thinking with, but I couldn't see what they could. I had walked away from my life on the door and employed another member of staff to cover for my absence at the post office. The magazine was on its last legs and I convinced myself that the retired life was for me.

What was I on? My mates had met her and tried to warn me about her, but lust is blind. She gobbled me up, spat me out and almost cost me everything. I will never forgive her. One of the first incidents was when she was photographed with *the* Nicholas Cage entering a hotel after a night out. Luckily, the *News of the World* covered the story, so everyone I knew could read it and ask me about it. My mates loved it! I mean, it's not that often that your mate's fiancée plays away with an Academy Award winner, is it? She denied everything; I forgave her, thus becoming Steve Naive. I had reporters hounding me for days on that one.

After all that, she started throwing huge tantrums, claimed she was pregnant, then said she'd miscarried ... I really was finding it difficult. The 'honeymoon period' was well and truly over by now. She was taking Prozac, which in theory should have been making things easier. I don't think it was actual depression she had. It was aggression, not depression. When we reached the lowest point, we decided to go on holiday to repair the damage ... her treat, she wouldn't hear of me paying. It suited me fine; I didn't want to throw my money away on a potential holiday from Hell and, anyway, she had some making up to do.

We visited Greece and the first couple of days went well. Amazingly well. We were back on track. Day three was a slight contrast. It could have been planned but it seemed so out of the blue ... She told me that she didn't love me, didn't want to marry me, hated me, and was going to tell all her family that I had been unfaithful so that they would hate me as well. I think she must have had a secret stash of 'don't beat around the bush' pills, too. Her family didn't like me anyway, especially her daughter, so I knew they would believe her.

I'd had all I could take from her. Three days into a holiday, she'd made a story up about me – now, would her family believe it or not? There was no way I was going fifty-fifty, so I decided to phone a friend. I called my mate Paul Donnely in England and asked him to book me on a flight. That was it; I was leaving her and going home.

I packed my things as best I could into two carrier bags and took some money out of the safety deposit box in the room. I was just about ready to go when the apartment door burst open and the bitch came at me with a bottle. I tried to duck out of the way but with two bags in my hand was an easy target as she cracked me across the head.

She started to claw my face as I dropped the bags. I grabbed her arms and pushed her onto the bed. She came at me again, so I shoved her as I made for the door. This time she banged her arm on the rough surface of the wall and it started to bleed. I paused ... she looked down at her arm and smiled ... squeezing the graze and rubbing the blood onto her face and through her hair. I was watching her, panicking, but didn't know what my next move should be. She was starting to look like a *Texas Chainsaw Massacre* victim right before my eyes.

Now she made for the door and I knew I couldn't let her leave the room. To anyone who saw her, it would look like I'd tried to murder her. I blocked her exit, so with no way out, she ran to the bathroom and locked herself in. Now was my chance. I was out of the room, down the stairs and into a taxi before you could say Anthony Perkins.

Instead of taking a direct flight, I took a cross-country flight to Athens and flew to Luton. I had £3 left in my pocket when Paul picked me up later that day. I had never been so happy to see one of the lads. She returned home full of stories about my womanising ways and how I had stolen thousands of pounds from her.

To top that, she tried to turn Reg, Charlie Kray and a few of the other London faces against me. She knew all the same people down there as I did, but if they believed her, I'd be in serious trouble. As soon as I was able to give my account of what had happened, they were happy that I was telling the truth. I do owe Dave Courtney a lot, though. He believed me from the outset and was one of those who tried to tell me that she was bad news. Thanks, Dave.

My family welcomed me back with open arms, glad that I'd had the sense to get away when I did. Now I had to get my life back in order. I thanked the girls at the post office, resumed my shifts and told all my mates – ding, dong ... the psycho's gone. They were glad I'd seen the light and had made the right decision at last.

Another decision I made was to sell the post office. I'd worked there for almost a decade, and always saw it as my safety net. My heart wasn't in it anymore. I needed a clean break, and by selling it, I would be able to get on and do other things.

I called a family meeting to discuss it and they soon realised that I was doing it for the right reasons. My grandparents were upset at first, as it had been in the family for nearly four generations, but they gave me their support.

My jobs on the door were gone after my excursion to Sheffield. Basically, I'd severed my ties thinking I'd never return, so I had to eat a lot of humble pie with Capes (although you'd think he'd eaten it all judging by the size of him). My job at Legends had been taken but I was offered work in other bars. It was good to get back into it and with bars springing up all the time, there is never any real shortage of work. I was taken on at The Union Rooms, working with Gordon, Eric, Mark, Simon, Gary, Amanda and Alex.

I was working again but still had itchy feet – I couldn't seem to settle. I even took a door job while on holiday in Ibiza with a few of the lads. The first couple of days were a laugh as I caught up with friends I'd met on my last visit. I also made some new friends at The Star Club, now called Eden.

It was just as well ... there was a lot of friction between the lads and me by the end of the first week. It was nothing too serious, but I thought it was best not to rock the boat and created a bit of breathing space between us.

I took a doorman job at Eden. This was the sort of breathing space I needed. The lads were bemused at my decision to work but I was sticking to my guns. I teamed up with James, the only other English lad from Nottingham, and a Swedish steroid freak by the name of Magnus. The manager of the club, Mario, explained to me that the hours were from 11.30 p.m. till 6.30 a.m. and that I would receive the equivalent of sixty quid cash in hand. Result!

Working the door abroad is so different to back home in England. It's far more relaxed and not half as much trouble. The only real trouble was when I had to hit someone who went for me as I tried to calm him down one night. It turned out that he was the Governor of Ibiza's son, his dad being the one who granted licences for clubs. It was a close call but ended up fine in the end. It was just like those early days at *Legends* all over again ... so, okay, sometimes they *actually can* get you shut down.

The next night was foam party night with Boy George as special guest DJ. About an hour into the night, a cockney bloke tapped me on the shoulder and asked me to do him a favour. He was in his mid-forties, tanned, with tight, curly hair. He introduced himself as Tony, a partner in the club. He had arranged for a film crew to visit the club and record an advert for the Ministry of Sound. He wanted me to look after them and the girl who they would be filming for a TV commercial.

After the formal introductions, the story unfolded ... I was to carry Lisa, the star of the advert, on my shoulders onto the dance floor, where she would be performing dance moves to the camera. Within five minutes, I was completely caked in foam, in fact choking on the bloody stuff as the director asked me if I could try and look as if I was enjoying it. Take two. I know I said earlier that I'd acted before, but this was a little *too* Stanislavski for my liking.

Like a trooper, I managed to battle on till the end with her safely on my shoulders. The director was happy, I was soaking wet with aching shoulders, and Lisa was looking forward to a blossoming career. The director promised to supply me with a final copy, and a few months later, I got one. Unless you are looking for me, you can't even see me on the advert, but at least I know I was there.

I toyed with the idea of staying in Ibiza and giving up on my life back home for a while. I had enjoyed my time there and decided that if things didn't work out for me in England, then I would return the following year and pick up where I left off. I said my goodbyes and decided I was going to give it another go on the doors again in Newcastle. I wasn't too sure what I wanted out of life.

Working in Ibiza was great because it was a different world. I knew I could never leave Newcastle altogether, though – it's the best place in the world. Ibiza was a good time to gather my thoughts and find myself. There was the saga with her from Sheffield, leaving my door jobs, heading out on holiday, finding work there ... I needed to decide what direction I was going in.

In Newcastle, I left my number with a few people to get some more nightclub hours. I was offered work at *Chase*, a new bar on Newcastle's developing Quayside. A trendy bar, more hours and better money ... going once, going twice ... sold to the man with the bald head. I thanked Capes for giving me work when I needed it and left The Union Rooms on good terms.

The Quayside was a welcome change to some of the places that I had worked and the lads there had years of experience under their belts. Graham, Richard and Keith had worked there since the bar had opened and I was accepted straight away. At first, I was there on weekends only, but as Christmas drew nearer, I gained a lot of weeknights.

There was also the promise of other work with the company that had signed me up. I was soon given a head doorman's position at their other bar, Jonny Ringos, more hours and more money ... and soon after I was given six nights a week at *Sea*, a new nightclub on the Quayside. I've worked there on and off over the last few years, working with a good bunch of friends: Alan Scott, Wayne Keepin, Steve Leng, Terry Grey, Mark, Julie, Peter, Clyde, Heta, Nigel White, Billy, Barry Dorner and David.

It took me twelve months to get my life back together, but I'd done it and I promised myself that I would never walk away from any job like that again, because I might not be as fortunate next time.

The trips to London carried on. I'd meet up with Dave Courtney and his mates Mad Pete, Bulldog, Brendan, Seymour, Wish, Marcus Tucker, Andy, Lou and a New Zealander by the name of Christian Simpson. Christian is a real character. Like me, he read about the twins at a young and impressionable age and sympathised with their plight.

Living day to day in New Zealand, he wanted to speak to one of the twins to pass on his respects and offer his help in whatever way he could. He'd read an article about the Kray family, which said that they still had the same solicitor. He left a message at the solicitor's office for both Ron and Reg, saying that one of their great aunties had died and left the twins a huge sum of money by way of inheritance.

Christian waited for a reply, which came a lot sooner than expected. Within an hour, Reg wanted to know more about the money. The news had also influenced Ron, who had reacted badly to a change in medication because of the stressful news. Christian panicked and when quizzed further by the family's solicitor, he buckled under the pressure and had to tell the truth.

The solicitor was far from amused, even when Christian explained that all he wanted to do was speak to the twins and wish them well. No sooner had he put the phone down than it rang again. It was Reg. He said that it was an irresponsible thing to do and he should have known better. He then asked him how old he was; when Christian replied that he was sixteen, Reg told him to learn from the experience and that if he was ever in England, that he should come and see him. The call ended with the usual 'God bless' and now Christian was even more determined to make further contact. He came to Britain as soon as he could and is now highly respected amongst the chaps. Apart from Dave Courtney, I have to say that Christian is one of the closest friends that I have met through the twins.

I'd stay at Dave's flat in Woolwich, South London. The life down there was amazing. Now if you think your life is hectic, you really want to try living Dave's for a few minutes. His wife Jenny has her hands full with the kids – Jensen, Beau and Courtney – but she still finds time to answer the phones, make countless cuppas and cook meals for the never-ending guests that pass through … and that's *before* looking after Dave! She really is one in a million.

Dave has been called the Yellow Pages of Crime and it was easy to see why. Dave has a friend in every major city, and by picking up the phone can help you out without having to get out of the Jacuzzi. I felt that I had to earn my keep when I was down there, although Dave said it wasn't necessary. I took my door supervisor course in Wembley and gained my certificate and badge, which now enabled me to work legitimately, instead of what I'd been doing on earlier trips.

I worked at a few pubs and clubs for Dave, mainly filling in when his places were short of cover. Places such as the Ministry of Sound and The Aquarium were becoming third and fourth homes to me now. If I wasn't working at them, you could guarantee I'd be drinking in them. I was really neglecting my jobs, friends and family back home, but at the time I didn't really care.

I was having too much of a good time to even think about home, which looking back sounds bad. I was messing around with drink and women; doing the whole 'live fast, die young and leave a bald corpse' lifestyle. I also picked up work doing personal security for a lot of famous people, such as Elton John, Robbie Williams, The Spice Girls, Michael Flatley and soap stars Steve McFadden and Martine McCutcheon. They always ranged from good fun yet hard work to being a complete nightmare and incredibly hard work. Stars would never fail to amaze. They can be down to earth and friendly, or the complete opposite. I always got on well with Steve McFadden – he's a top bloke.

During the day in London, I made my money debt collecting, and being teamed up with Christian Simpson, we always had a good laugh along the way. Often, you can tell when you are introduced to someone whether they are for real or not, and in the Kray circle, there were a lot of fakers. Chris is the genuine article.

At the time, he had just got fixed up with a new flat after a rather hair-raising first experience on his way onto the property ladder. Reg had always told him that he would set him up with a place to stay if he ever came to England, so Chris took him at his word. Reg asked Gary (one of his many gofers) to sort it, and surprisingly he had sorted it within a week. "£500 for the first month's rent and it's all yours, geezer!"

Christian was a little wary, but after reassurance from the gofer that Reg and Charlie had sorted it, Chris paid the money. Although Gary did look like a used car salesman, you still wouldn't buy one from him ... so handing over £500 to him would never feel right.

That night, Chris got a taxi to his new home – imagine his

surprise as he found it existed and the key actually fitted and turned in the lock. Now imagine his surprise as an axe-wielding Turk greeted him as he entered what was also *his* house. The Turk was far from being delighted. He swung at Chris a few times, narrowly missing his head as he dived back into the taxi and tossed the key out of the window. The driver needed no encouragement to step on it at that point.

The gofer was a hardman to find for the next couple of weeks, but when he finally surfaced, he refused to pay the money back, saying that Charlie had it. As we got to know more about Gary, we realised what a scheming little toe-rag he really was. I've always been a great believer in 'what goes around, comes around' – I just don't believe that you can go around walking some kind of walk, pretending, and hope to get away with it forever. What Gary did with Chris – ripping him off or 'doing a Rickaby' as it's known in the North East, is the lowest of the low.

Debt collecting is to me a job like any other. It has its ups and downs and you can sometimes wonder to yourself, *Why on earth am I doing this?* – just like any other. Although we had some laughs along the way, I never did see it as a positive career move.

In recovering any debt, there are always some people who will take a little more persuading than others. There was one guy who had ripped a friend of mine off to the tune of £10,000. The lads and I were asked to get what we could and we would be given 10 per cent each for our troubles. The bloke in question owned a taxi office in the Edmonton area of North London, but decided to do a disappearing act ... along with the ten grand. We had to find him and retrieve the cash or property to that amount.

Now, if you do a Rickaby on such a large scale, you would make sure you moved away, or at least laid low for a while (or would wear disguises in public, not go out 'jogging' or organise boxing events. Or reinvent yourself as a cosmic ordering guru). Not this bloke. He set up a new taxi firm just three miles from his old place! Amazing.

Outside his new empire stood a gleaming silver BMW. I'm no

expert, but I knew that this was worth our wages, so the lads and me entered the office for a chat. I have always been a good talker, or a gobshite as some would argue, so it was up to me to explain the situation to our friend. The rest of the lads, all six-foot tall and wide, with an array of sporting bats and clubs, stared menacingly to prompt him into a friendly solution.

The jobs always paid well, but there was considerable hassle. I'd have to work with learners a lot of the time, who turned out to be walking liabilities.

I remember one job with a learner where we got no answer at a house. I went around the back to investigate while he stuck a shopping trolley through the front window. Great intimidation technique … if Dale Winton is putting the frighteners on someone.

The job could sometimes be quite dangerous, too. I have only ever been *slightly* hurt on a job. It was a simple cash-in-hand job where the bloke in question attacked me with his mother's walking stick before she joined in with him. He paid the money in the end and we all had a nice cup of tea afterwards, but it was another wake-up call to think about calling it a day. I could laugh about fighting the bloke, then having to restrain his mother, but the job was losing its appeal.

Hanging around with Dave always made me forget about my day jobs. His life is one big adventure and it's great to be a part of it. One night, there was a 'tip-off' call to say that someone he had a score to settle with was in a club and would be there till the early hours. So, together with Dave's best mate Tucker, we set off to this club to look into settling the score.

Along the way, Dave had been making a few calls – which is nothing new – but the calls were all about an old record called 'Strollin''. We reached the club, where a rave was in full effect, with glow sticks, whistles, white hats and gloves … the lot. Dave had a word with the security on the door, and then … well, and then nothing. The lights came on, the music stopped and the doormen started parting the clubbers like the Red Sea.

Suddenly, the speakers crackled into action once again, and all the clubbers looked on in confusion as 'Strollin'' began to play. I followed Tucker and Dave towards this big bald bloke loitering next to the DJ stand. In Dave's words, it was 'the bollocks' – like a scene straight out of a Scorsese film, as we walked through the club, honing in on our prey. As we neared the fat bald bloke, Dave pulled on his knuckleduster, and within a second, fatty was out for the count. We strolled back out, shaking hands with all the door staff on the way.

Dave Courtney had become public enemy number one in the eyes of the Metropolitan Police; they were determined to have him, one way or another. They tailed him and photographed us all at every opportunity. It was like a game of cat and mouse, and I found it quite amusing that the Met were wasting taxpayers' money at first, but as it continued, I thought it was a disgraceful waste. The police spending thousands of pounds on surveillance equipment just to take pictures of a bunch of blokes was a waste of money and police resources to me.

They kept watch across the road from a pub Dave owned, The Albion. They were on the second floor of an old youth hostel and had been there for weeks, watching all the unspeakable atrocities such as pool playing, drinking and the odd game of darts. We were all there one night when Dave told us to 'watch this'. Armed with a tray of lagers and bar snacks, he crossed the road and asked the receptionist to send the tray up to the police officers on the second floor and said that if they fancied a game of darts, they were more than welcome. Within minutes, the police had packed and fled the building ... another victory for Dodgy Dave! I know I was photographed throughout this period, but it didn't bother me. I was not a major player; I was just a friend.

Back in Newcastle, work began to take off. Because of the personal security I'd done in London, I was always top of the list when pop stars or sports stars were in town and wanted a hassle-free night out. One club had been pre-warned that Robbie Williams may or may not be showing his face after his gig at the

Newcastle Arena – then he turned up with thirty of his entourage in tow. The management had asked us to look after him and his own security firm, so first up I had to ask a lot of clubbers to clear some room, which didn't go down too well. Of course, I was just doing my job as usual, but this was something I have never agreed with.

One thing I've noticed is that the stars who love meeting and mingling with people are always more down to earth and there are no problems, whilst those that make a fuss about not wishing to talk to fans generally cause animosity. Which it did. Each to their own, though. Robbie and his guests made themselves comfortable and started drinking like there was no tomorrow ... the champagne stocks were the first casualty.

Robbie was being a pain, jumping around all over the place like a little kid. If he'd been anyone else, he'd have been out on his backside, but these superstar-international-pop-idols are good for business, no matter how irritating they are. It was a tough job to keep people (mostly women) back from trying to get close to him, and it was made that bit tougher when they even began to offer me sexual favours in return for turning a blind eye ... mostly women as well.

Just as things started to calm down, the cheeky chap jumped up and sang "Angels", sending the entire club into a frenzy. I was glad I wasn't part of his personal security team, as they would have quite a job on their hands. I couldn't imagine babysitting like that on a full-time basis. The next day, there were reports in the local newspaper that Robbie had bought everyone in the club a drink. It amazes me where they find these stories.

Steps caused trouble in their own unique way when they visited the club. There weren't as many followers as what Robbie had, but it was still quite hectic all the same. We were asked by their security team not to let anyone take any pictures of the band. This really was mission impossible – especially with Faye from Steps (as she's now known) in the room.

The usual suspects tried to gain entry to the VIP area and were given the usual answer. The manager had now started switching his phone off when VIPs were in because these people would phone him up in another desperate attempt to get past us. As expected, people took photographs, the security team started to cause trouble with our punters, and we were expected to pick up the pieces ... just another example of the sort of behaviour that gets stars bad reputations. I dare say that a lot of the punters had bought their records, maybe been to the gig and now were pleased to see the band in their local nightclub; surely the odd photograph wouldn't hurt.

Whilst still doing club security, I received an offer to work on the door of The Groat House in Newcastle's Bigg Market. I couldn't let this one pass. I loved the Bigg Market, and The Groat House was just a kick up the arse from where I took that first job at Masters. I had three great years there before I was headhunted by a classy wine bar on the flourishing Quayside called Chase.

I went in as part of a six-man team there and it was a *lot* different to the Bigg Market. All the movers and shakers were ploughing their cash into the tills at Chase and were averaging 8,000 punters each Friday or Saturday night. As head doorman, I was freezing my balls off on the front door during the winter, which was the only downside. The other occasional one was that I witnessed a few tragic souls jumping off the Tyne Bridge as well. I upped my hours by taking on some nightclub work at Sea Nightclub just across the road.

In the four years at Chase, I had the best times of my life. My team of Shaun Charlton, Peter Lucy, Freddie Suadwa, Mick Bradwell and Les Jackson was as good as it gets. The atmosphere was good and they all did the job the way it should be done.

All good things come to an end, though, and our boss moved on and wanted us to go with him. I moved to Bar 55 as head doorman and from there to Sam Jacks. I found it difficult to adjust to life at my new bars and decided to take up the offer of a job at Yates, which would fit around the Performing Arts degree (I'd been looking for a way out of door work and acting had been my first love, after all).

My final job was at Tiger Tiger, which is part of the new Gate Complex on Newgate Street. I was appointed head doorman a year after taking the job there after my old mate Buzz from Masters had decided to call it a day. I found the job harder than most. I was dealing with fourteen doormen's egos every night, as well as the changing face of laws in the licensing trade. Later drinking hours meant longer nights for all and the smoking ban meant that we had the added hassle on the front door of a smoking area. You had to stamp people's hands and make sure that those ejected from the club didn't get back in: it was a pain in the backside.

Newcastle city centre had also become a haven for stags and hens from all corners of Europe, and I was becoming more impatient with drunken punters, which, as a doorman, is never a good thing. Even though I was on a good wage, £15 per hour, it was nothing to the £25 per hour I had started on eighteen years before this. Had the job gotten any easier in that time? *No.* If anything, it had gotten bloody harder.

It was time for a change; I just had to summon the courage to walk away from a job that was paying my bills. A few situations on the door in quick succession helped me make my decision. I ended up in situations which, as a single man, I may have faced head-on but now, as a married parent as I had since become, I had my family to consider.

I had a chat with my manager Chris Kyle on 1 December 2008 and he agreed to give me a month off at the busiest time of the year until I got my head sorted. I met up with him and my line manager Rob Fisher on 2 January and I told them that I was hanging up my gloves and black coat for the final time. They wished me well and I trudged off through the snowy streets of Newcastle wondering what adventures lay ahead for me in 2009.

People often ask me what I got out of doing the door. Well it's simple … it was a means to an end. It paid my bills, kept a roof over my head and gave me good spending money. I'd say that one of the best things about door work is meeting people. I had some laughs and met some characters that I wouldn't otherwise have met – punters as well as colleagues.

I also met my wife, Dawn, while working on the doors (although she wasn't my wife at the time. That would have been too strange). It was through knowing the twins that I got into the whole security game, so I suppose in a way they indirectly had a hand in me meeting Dawn.

As I have already said, I'm no hardman. I'm a good talker and can handle most situations. I had to hit two people in eighteen years. Not a bad record. I removed a lot of people from venues and most came back the following week to shake my hand and apologise. I treated people with respect and they appreciated it. I fronted a lot of people who wanted to cause trouble at all venues I worked at, but if it had come to a fight, I can't guarantee I would have come out on top; I suppose it's the best bit of acting I've ever done.

CHAPTER 6

PARTY TIME

During the Sixties, the good old days, there were parties every night. There was not the excuse of having to be up for work in the morning. It could be said that in Kray work circles, it was pretty much flexi-time all year. The twins were photographed with celebrities, well-known faces, stars from stage and screen, sports stars ... they loved having pictures taken at their clubs, and would always ensure that they were seen mingling with the people of the moment. This was the lifestyle they loved. It was what they had worked for.

Many events or social gatherings were held to raise money for charity, or to rephrase that, they were *advertised* as charity events. The charity did benefit at each event, but not as much as the twins did. It was their way of doing something for two good causes at the same time. In that respect, everyone was happy. What better way to raise their profile? They impressed and made money. It was the perfect set-up.

In the early Nineties, the Krays had their 'Second Coming' ... the film was released, and Reg brought out his book, *Born Fighter*. Almost monthly, a new book came out by a 'firm member' or an old friend, and Reg was quick to spot the business potential in this renewed interest. They already had a tried and tested formula. It was obvious to Reg that what the world needed was 'Kray Nights'.

Ron and Reg received countless letters week in, week out from families with sick children (as well as from dozens of con artists), and now the time seemed right to do something to help. They knew charity nights worked and there was no shortage of charities to help. After all ... charity begins at home, doesn't it? Even if you happen to share it with a few thousand others.

The time was also right to heal the rift between the twins and Charlie, mainly because they needed something from him. They fell out with him over the film deal – the twins were not happy with the way Violet had been portrayed in the film by actress Billie Whitelaw. Ron had told me on a visit that she never swore like she did in the film.

Because Charlie was an adviser to the film's director, Ron and Reg held him responsible for the script, dialogue, direction and the final cut. They needed someone to blame, so their one-man-production-company brother took the brunt of it.

As part of their research, the Kemp brothers visited Ron and Reg, and they said they were pleased with how they were portrayed. For the rights to make the film, the twins were paid £110,000 and a further £145,000 was paid in royalties. When the film went on to gross £3.5 million, they held Charlie responsible for not getting them a better slice of the action.

Roger Daltrey, frontman of The Who, originally owned the rights to *The Profession of Violence* on which it was based and sold the rights on for it to become the film. It's not as though they were given a bad deal, but when you feel you have missed out – you look for someone to blame.

They had also fallen out over another matter. Reg was told there had been T-shirts sold in London and other major cities in the country, including Newcastle. These T-shirts were unofficial Kray merchandise with a picture of the twins on the front. Reg asked me to get to the bottom of it, which took three weeks of phone calls and a trip down to London ... and it turned out that the T-shirts were being manufactured in Croydon by none other than Charlie. I had no choice but to tell the twins and so the biggest pile of shit in the world hit the biggest fan in the world. Charles James Kray was now affectionately known as Mr X. Every call, letter and visit, they never mentioned him by name.

So, he had some making up to do and now he was given the

perfect opportunity to do so. He would act as host and compère for Kray Nights, and in doing so, Mr X would once again become known as Mr Kray. Reg was the king of manipulation and soon enlisted more fans to do his gofering. He just needed to click his fingers and people would come running.

It was now that I could look at my relationship with the twins and see how it had changed. I didn't see myself as a fan anymore and this was something I hadn't really stopped to consider before. I knew I was a fan before I'd met them and certainly was a fan in the early days, but now, I was part of their inner circle. I was a friend, an associate. If I didn't agree with something or didn't want to get involved, I told them so. I didn't just go along with anything. I could take from the friendship what I wanted, and this helped me gain their respect. The relationship wasn't just one of 'Steve do this, Steve do that'. It was like any other friendship.

This led to a new set of gofers being brought in. I was only gofer to one person ... me. Reg was smart enough to judge what people were like and what chain of manipulation he could utilise to his best advantage. A lot of people fell into the 'I'll do anything for the twins' category and that's all they were, people who would live off a slight notoriety because they earned them a few quid. Getting something out of it for yourself, favours in return, backhanders, you name it – was what it was all about. It was also the networking I was interested in, and contacts were one thing the twins were not short of.

As the party idea progressed, one of Reg's young gofers – A cockney kid called Gary – turned up on the scene and we did not get on. There was just something about him I couldn't put my finger on. Reg had this annoying habit of giving your phone number to anyone he took a fancy to. God only knows the amount of ex-cellmates, and so-called old firm members, who have called me up at stupid o'clock for a chat.

So, sure enough, I received a call from Gary. He'd been enlisted by Reg to organise the venue, food and entertainment for the latest Kray Night. Reg had given him a list of numbers to sell tickets to, my number being one of them.

It went something like this:

"Hello, my name's Gary. I've been asked by Reg Kray to let you know about a party that I'm organising for him. Do you want any tickets? They're twenty-five quid each."

News to me, I told him. Again, he asked if I wanted any. You know when you can dislike someone just by their *voice*? I told him I'd call Reg myself and hung up. He was just so cocky and irritating. The lack of respect showed that nothing had been thought through. I phoned Reg at Nottingham and left a message on his landing for him to phone me, and two minutes later, he did.

I told him I was pissed off at this cockney wide boy's attitude and pissed off that Reg had given him my number. I didn't expect an apology and wasn't disappointed. The nearest to an apology was, "He's just a gofer, doing some running around for me. I'll have a word with him and make sure you get your tickets for the do. How many do you want?" I told him I only wanted one and left it at that. I felt better for getting it off my chest, but I didn't expect him to phone Gary at all. The next day, a rather sheepish and respectful Gary phoned to get my address to send a ticket ... I take it back, Reg, you kept your word.

The ticket stated that it was a 'gala night'. I travelled down to London's East End not knowing what to expect. The ticket also said there would be television stars from *EastEnders*, *The Bill* and *London's Burning* ... and that all proceeds would go to "a little boy with muscular dystrophy" ... sounded good.

I arrived early at the Tudor Lodge. It sounded just like a grand English banqueting hall, and when I walked into the place, it looked absolutely nothing like one. It was basically a social club without any pool tables in. I was one of the first there, but within an hour, the Lodge was almost full with 200 people dancing to hits from the Sixties.

I cringed as Carl Douglas was wheeled out to 'sing' his only hit "Kung Fu Fighting", unsure if it was for real, then grimacing as I found out it was. At least Carl had turned up, though. The celebrity turnout consisted of Carl, Mike Reid from *EastEnders* and Kate Kray. There were a lot of disgruntled punters, to say the least.

I made a few useful contacts, though; one was a bloke called Mike, who looked just like John Gotti. He told me he owned a cab firm in Hackney and that he used to work for the twins. I nodded and smiled … I'd heard it all before. He said I could stay at his place whenever I was in London and I thought nothing more of it. I also met Frank and Noelle Kurylo, who were friends of the family and were in the process of helping Reg with a few projects; I exchanged numbers with them, too. I said my farewell to Kate Kray at the end of the night and told Mike Reid that he was much better in *Runaround*. I returned to my hotel happy that I'd been an invited guest and not a paying customer.

I was still quite intrigued about Gary. He'd organised this event and hadn't turned up for it, and come to think of it, Charlie wasn't there, either. When I was invited along to the next gathering, I questioned if it was worth the effort. Weighing up the pros and cons (no pun intended), I decided it couldn't be any worse than the last one. I booked my train ticket and called Mafia Mick to see if his offer still stood. It did. No hotel bill for me!

The party was at a club called the Guvner's in the heart of the East End. Bare-knuckle streetfighter, boxer and all-round hardman Lenny McLean had a share in this bar. The night for me was a great success … the circle was complete as I shook hands with Charlie Kray for the first time. Having spoken to him dozens of times on the phone, I knew we'd get along fine.

He introduced me to many of the faces as well as Dave Courtney, who was climbing up the criminal ladder with a knuckleduster and a smile. As I was talking to Dave, someone tapped me on the shoulder. I turned to confront … a young lad with cropped hair, a dodgy suit and a gold tooth. I later found out that the phrase 'all over him like a cheap suit' had its origins in his wardrobe. He introduced himself as Gary and I shook his hand half-heartedly before turning back to Dave. I wasn't impressed with him on the phone and in person I was glad my gut reaction hadn't let me down.

There were well over 200 people crammed into the pub at twenty-five quid a head. This time, though, they got value for money. In attendance were: West Ham footballer Julian Dicks, *EastEnders* star Steve McFadden, Shane Richie, boxer Jimmy McDonnell, actor Ray Winstone (amazing in *Sexy Beast*), Lenny McLean, Tony Lambrianou, Alec Steene, Patsy Manning, George and Andrew Wadman, Charlie Kray, his biographer Robin McGibbon and also Charlie's son, Gary. There were also many friends of the twins there: Scott Mytton, Dave Clarke, Colin and Andy Fanning, Christian Simpson, Ray Cann, Janet and Alan Alsop, Frank and Noelle Kurylo, Andy Gravonor, Eileen Sheridan-Price, Irene Hart, Ron Proffit, Kiwi Andy and Les and Ellie Martin.

For members of the general public, this is what it was all about. The parties were a chance to mingle with stars and rub shoulders with the gangland faces they had read or heard about courtesy of our mutual friends, the Krays. For any stars that turned up, they knew what to expect; they knew that they could relax and talk to people in a hassle-free atmosphere. The party was great, and it seemed like there would be a lot of money raised. There had also been an auction of all kinds of Kray memorabilia, including paintings, that raised a further thousand plus.

As the night wore on, I'd noticed Gary was in and out of the kitchen like a yo-yo. I just didn't trust him, so I thought I'd investigate. As I opened the door slightly, I saw Gary standing with his back to me counting a large wad of cash and handing it out to two other lads. One of the lads was Paul, who I'd met on a visit to Reg ... the 'great burglar'. I could not believe what I was observing. People had paid good money towards what they thought was a good cause and here was this little tosser handing it out to two other tossers. At a rough guess, I'd say £5,000 would have been raised, at least, and here it was being divided up. I pushed the door wide open and Gary turned around like a startled rabbit ... no, make that a startled thieving bastard.

"All right, geezer?" he asked.

"I will be when they give you that cash back," was my reply.

Paul stared at me … "Reg said I could have it, so mind your own fucking business." That was it. I punched him straight in the face and turned to face the other two. I wanted them to try something … they stood there panicking. They knew I'd caught them out. Gary was squirming. Then he took out the rest of the wad and asked me how much I wanted … he counted a hundred out and offered me it. I just stared at them, long enough for any guilt to take hold if they had a conscience. I walked out and back to the bar to order a triple Jack Daniels and Coke. A few minutes later and the three rats emerged from the kitchen.

Paul was defiant. "Wait till Reg hears about this, just wait."

I was fuming, and said, "I can't hear you, cos your mouth is full of shit."

I was still fuming as I stared over at them. Gary brought a drink over to try and calm the situation down, or to talk himself out of it more like. I listened to what he had to say and still wasn't impressed. He told me that Reg had told him to sort a few people out for coming; okay, some celeb's taxi maybe, but not some ex-con who was just gonna shoot it up his arm. This had ruined what had started out as an excellent night.

I made sure I told Charlie Kray all about what had happened. I didn't want to see this sort of behaviour again; they were scum as far as I was concerned. Charlie said he always thought Gary was bad news and thanked me for telling him. He was going to tell Reg the next day. I was still thinking about the incident as the party ended. A lot of people had paid money under false pretences. I'm sure those who paid would like to have known who had ripped them off and tricked them. I could see that calling these events a 'charity' event was just a big con. Gary had no intention of giving any away unless it was to his friends. He was conning people, but he was also conning people by using the Kray name.

I got the train back to Newcastle the following day with Ray Cann. I became good mates with him. We were buzzing with talk of the night before and I asked him if he fancied organising a party with me in Newcastle. We could invite Charlie Kray up, a few of the others from London, get some local celebs involved and do it for a Northern charity. We agreed there and then to work together.

Ray had some contacts that could help us out and we both knew we could do it. Importantly, we knew we could do a decent job. The first thing needed was a venue; Ray gave me the number of a lad called Davey Falcus, who ran a social club in Bensham, Gateshead called The Elysium Lane, and I arranged a meeting the next day. Davey was 100 per cent behind us and willing to help in any way he could.

The room was spot on ... seating around 170 people, with enough room for a further hundred standing. What's more, it had a long bar and a big stage with lighting. Perfect. It had everything we needed, and Davey was letting us have it for free. We scanned the bookings erm ... book, and made a provisional booking for 8 July 1995. Here was the carrot I needed to dangle in front of the former Mr X. All I needed to ask him was if he wanted to spend his birthday in the North East. He was hooked as I went through our plans, "As good as there, Steve," came the reply.

Just two more hurdles left – the tickets and the buffet. A quick call to Steve in South London (a good friend of Reg's) solved the ticket problem, and a bit of grovelling and a few promises to our respective families got the buffet sorted out; we were now on the home straight. Everything was falling into place.

Next up, I contacted the family I wanted the money we would raise to go to. The Morans were a close-knit family from Felling, Gateshead, and I was friends with father and son – both called Terry. I'd met them through football. Young Terry was a natural with the skill, confidence and commitment that he dreamed would one day earn him a place playing for Newcastle United.

On Guy Fawkes Night, 1994, Terry was involved in a horrific accident. He was wearing a shell-suit that night and was standing too close to a bonfire. His clothes caught fire and he suffered 80 per cent burns. He was rushed to hospital and was not expected to survive the night. Terry was strong and pulled through … he was still in hospital when I contacted the family about the charity night. I told them it had the full backing from Reg Kray and that Charlie Kray would be in attendance. I warned them of the publicity – some good, some bad – which the event would attract in the coming weeks. They seemed okay with it but asked for a few days to think it over properly.

During that time, I contacted some local celebrities for their help: Boxers Glenn McCrory and Billy Hardy, and footballers Paul Gascoigne, Lee Clark and Steve Watson all said they could make it. Soon after, I got the green light from the Morans … it was all systems go for 8 July!

Key to holding events was primarily doing so for a cause. It was apparent that the Kray name could attract a lot of attention, and holding events was a way of using that name for something positive instead of all the negativity that had surrounded it. That is what pissed me off about the Gary incident. He was using the name and the event to line his own and his friends' pockets. To do something like that is the lowest of the low … to claim that someone's money is going towards a charity and then keep it for yourself, it's hard to put into words.

From my point of view, I saw it as a chance to put right any damage that this had caused. What he'd done wasn't made public because he is still around, but from my involvement in the incident I was keen to see a real charity event take place. Hearing the Morans say they were happy to accept the offer made all the work worthwhile. From that moment on, I was bombarded by phone calls from Reg about it.

There were still a few weeks to go and I thought the calls were slightly on the neurotic side but hadn't considered the fact that Reg was locked up and always thinking about life over the walls, and wanted to be constantly updated. Then, out of the blue, Reg got one of his gofers to send me the money up to buy myself a mobile phone, along with the message: "Steve, buy a mobile phone. I'm sick of missing you at home. God bless, Reg. P.S. Ring me with your number."

It was a nice gesture ... until you put '1995' and 'mobile phone' together and come up with 'house brick'. Within a week, I was the proud owner of a top-of-the-range phone and boy did I milk it with the lads. Remember that vision of someone walking along the street with a ghetto blaster to their ear? That was not unlike using this phone. I tried carrying it in my trouser pocket once but could only walk round in circles. I got some cards printed up to give everyone my new number and Reg would always call me on it, knowing he could reach me. That was until he saw how much it cost him to call and he never bothered again.

It was ideal for organising the event and gave me a number to stick alongside all the publicity. It seems weird to think back now ... it wasn't that long ago that I was one of the first in the area to get a mobile phone; now, it's unusual not to have one.

The publicity side of organisation was what really gave me the buzz. Still does. Whether I'm in the limelight or promoting something, it's something I thrive on. There's a certain knack to getting coverage in all the local papers for the same event, and this time I cracked it. Give the same story to the morning papers and the evening papers on the same day and nine times out of ten they will both print it. Give one or both of them the story a day earlier and it's yesterday's news. So, *The Chronicle*, *Journal*, *Sunday Sun* and good old *Gateshead Post* all ran with 'Krays to attend Charity Night'.

Soon after the locals, I had the national press calling the house brick for a story. The publicity worked well and within a week, 150 tickets were sold at ten quid each ... a week later and still the brick was ringing until the event was a sell-out. Due to fire regulations, we were only allowed 210 people in the venue, so that meant that straight away we had already raised over £2,000.

A week before the event, I was nervous. I received another call from Reg asking how things were going and if the little boy was okay. I told him that everything was fine and that Terry was looking forward to the night. I think Reg telephoning contributed towards my nerves. This call sounded familiar, though; I knew he was leading up to something with the usual tone and small talk … ready to spring something onto me when I was off guard.

Then it came, "Steve, I don't want Charlie or Tony Lambrianou at the party, okay?"

I couldn't control myself; was this bloke for real? "You're fucking joking, Reg, the party is a sell-out because of them."

There was a long pause and then I knew he was serious. He said that I should do as he said or cancel the party and hung up on me. This sort of 'twist' was not uncommon, but his demand was outrageous. I called Charlie up immediately and asked what the problem was – he was as stunned as I was. He said he wouldn't let me down and would come up regardless of what Reg had said. He didn't want to let Terry down, either.

I phoned Tony next and got a better insight into the problem. Reg had loaned Tony two copies of a portfolio to show someone who was interested in buying them. The portfolio was a limited-edition photograph album released by the twins, which were retailing at £250. The bloke wasn't that interested and sent them both back to Tony, who only sent one back to Reg, holding on to the other. Apparently, he hadn't got round to sending it back and suggested this may be the reason. It made sense and it was the sort of thing Reg would spit his dummy out over.

I put it to Tony that he should send the album to Reg immediately to smooth things over. As a compromise, he said he'd bring it to the event, and I could send it to Reg … Result. I spoke to Reg again and explained what was going to happen, again saying it was a sell-out because of Tony and Charlie, and that he'd be bringing the album up with him.

"I don't fucking want Tony there. Tell the papers up there that Tony and me are no longer friends."

Non-result. Typical stubbornness.

I asked about Charlie and was told he was okay, but to make sure Tony was *not there*. I had no intention of calling the papers, but to keep Reg happy, my brother Rob helped. He designed an authentic-looking newspaper layout with all the right typography, and I acted as reporter on this 'gangland rift' exclusive. It looked spot on. I sent a copy straight to Reg, who was over the moon with the article and the fact that I'd acted so quickly. I knew he would find out that Tony had attended but people had paid money for tickets, and we could not disappoint. Reg would get over it anyway.

This left me in an awkward situation, to say the least. I knew what Reg was like and I knew his ideas and plans could change at the drop of a hat. There was no way I was going to call the whole party off just because he suddenly changed his mind about it at the last minute. Everything was organised, the local and national press ran stories on it, and it had completely sold out. Now he wanted it scrapped because Tony hadn't given him a few photos back?

We'd raised £2,100 so far and there was no way we could hand it back after we'd promised the Morans. All that time spent planning and arranging to give the money to someone ... then Reg wakes up in a bad mood, so we must cancel ... it was not on. Again, this was another case of not being on the outside and realising the full extent of what he was doing. You cannot just mess people around like that – famous gangster or not, it's not right.

Monday, 4 July and everything is running along smoothly again. I was working as usual in the post office when three masked raiders burst in and attacked myself and a member of staff. Quite a lot of money and stock was stolen, but luckily, I'd spotted them just before they came in and hit the alarm. It was all over in an instant but something like that stays with you forever. Fortunately, neither staff nor customers were hurt, just badly shaken.

It's true that everything slows down in that situation ... it's like you are on autopilot, watching from a third-person point of view. Until you have been in that position, you can never fully appreciate how you will react. My advice to anyone is don't try to be a hero for a few quid; life is too precious. You mean nothing to an armed robber, especially if you get in his way. The reason

I say don't try to be a hero for the sake of a few quid is that when the post office representative came to investigate, his first question was, "How much was taken?" He didn't even bother to ask if anyone was hurt.

In the last few days before the party, the Gascoigne family confirmed they would be attending, though were unsure whether Paul would be there or not. And then the day before the party, Charlie left a message on my answer machine to say he would be up later than expected due to family illness. I was still happy he was coming, but when it's out of your hands, you just have to sit back and see what happens.

Ray and me got some people together to help with looking after the partygoers – meet 'n' greeters. Basically, we wanted every angle covered and wanted it to be a talking point for a long while to come. The biggest disappointment for me was that my mam, dad and Rob had already arranged holidays and wouldn't be able to make it. I knew they were thinking of me, though, and that was what mattered.

Then it was time … the big day. In the morning, a package from Reg arrived. It was a recorded message from him to be played at the event. I played it through a couple of times and was happy with it; listening to him made me feel sad that he couldn't attend. I knew he was proud to be associated with this fundraiser, and I made sure I'd have a drink for absent friends on the night. The message was his way of being there and I thought it was a nice touch.

I kept checking my watch all day and was convinced it was going backwards; it was taking forever for the hands to reach seven o'clock, then they just seemed to speed up as the time neared. I put on my tuxedo and bow tie and headed for The Elysium Lane, arriving with time to spare.

Inside, there were already queues at the bar; all the usual suspects had arrived: Alan and Gordon Fanning, Scott Mytton, Andy Gravenor, Christian Simpson, Kiwi Andy, Dave Clarke, Steve Marshall, Gary the Gofer, Carl Carty and Sharon, Mad

Marilyn, Les and Ellie Martin. Also a few of my closest mates ... Dave and Mickey Butterfield, Halpin, Mickey D, Chris, David, Mark and Steven Liddle, Carl and Mark Douglas, Parker, Paul Donnely, Croany, Babbsy, Maccoy, Colly, Ballsy, the Clarkes, Browny, Weasel Wilcox, Moley, Wheatley, Steppy, Tappers and a couple of 'cool cats' called Toby and Britney ... apologies for anyone missed out, I'm sure you'll point it out to me sometime.

Ray had Geordie, Simon, Alfie and Sean driving people to the club who'd spent all day travelling up. Then we got news that Paul Gascoigne couldn't make it as he was in the process of signing for *Glasgow Rangers* ... some people will make *anything* up to get out of a party. His family brought some extra signed football tops up, which more than made up for it. Nice one!

The Morans arrived with all their friends. It was an emotional time for Terry, as he'd just been released from hospital that week. His parents, Terry and Gillian were concerned that he'd be overwhelmed by such an event, with everyone there for him, but we had reserved a large room for them to relax in. It was great to see them there; we were amazed at the recovery Terry was making.

Inside, the buffet looked amazing (thanks to Ray's wife Bev and other contributors, including the Morans) and the place was really starting to fill up. All that we needed now was Tony Lambrianou and Charlie Kray. Tony was first to arrive, looking dapper in ... well, in a safari suit. He said he'd just got back from Kenya and had literally just rushed straight to Newcastle. I was wondering ... had someone misinterpreted 'dress fancy'? We had another room for him and partner Wendy to get changed into their evening wear. Phew, one down – one to go.

The press had gathered at the door to get photos of the first Kray in the North East since the Sixties and you could hear the buzz of anticipation from them as well as the punters. We had Kenny Dick DJing and the place was jumping ... then he mixed straight into a Sting record and our 'special guest' arrived. Neil Grant, a Sting lookalike, stunned the crowd as he walked in as though it was his local. Within seconds, he was being mobbed and could easily have pulled it off until he gave out his business cards with 'Sting Lookalike' printed on them. Still, it was a good laugh and kept everyone in high spirits.

I received a message informing me that Charlie had arrived and was waiting in a car outside. I made my way to see him and as I approached, he got out to greet me. I can still remember it like it was yesterday. "Hello, Steve, mate. How are you?" We shook hands as we greeted each other. Charlie was looking fit and well with his customary suntan. The photographers moved in and we were mobbed on our way to the club.

Ray got the drinks in for Charlie and Tony, and introduced them to a few of the North East faces while I told the press there would be a photo call in thirty minutes. There were a few groans from them, as they had to get the story out that night, but that was how we wanted it. Next up were the formal introductions; I took the microphone as Kenny lowered the music. "Ladies and gentlemen, if I can have your attention please. First, I would like to thank you all for coming on behalf of Terry. I would like to take this opportunity to thank all those people who have made this night possible. Now I would like you to put your hands together for our main guests of the evening ... Mr Tony Lambrianou, and Mr Charlie Kray.

Ray was flanked by two lads to keep people back as he led our main guests into the lounge. They received a standing ovation that lasted a few minutes. It was a strange feeling to be standing there introducing these two people to a North East crowd. I'd known them both for a while now and for me the whole 'Sixties firm' days never really registered anymore. To be in this position, I could see in the eyes of a lot of people something like what must have once been in mine. It was an honour for me to introduce them, and it being the first time I did something like that, it was something I'd remember for a long time to come.

Ray led them to their seats, where everyone wanting a photo, a signature or a handshake besieged them. It was complete madness.

To say they were well received would be an understatement.

The music restarted, and then the buffet was opened and gone in an instant. The auction of signed Kray memorabilia and celebrity signed odds and sods raised a bit more cash, and I must admit I enjoyed shouting, 'Going, going, *gone!*'

The most moving part of the night and the most silent was when it came to the playing of the tape that Reg had sent me. Once I had everyone's attention and the tape was in place, you could have heard the proverbial pin drop. The silence just added to the moment; it gave the impression that something historic was taking place. I pressed play and Reggie Kray's voice crackled into life over the PA system.

"Hello friends there in the North East. I would like to thank you this evening on behalf of my friends Steve Wraith and Ray Cann and myself for the fact that you are present in support of our young friend Terry Moran. I would like to thank all of you and the celebrities present and my brother Charlie for being host.

I wish I could be with you there physically, but I am with you in spirit and I hope that you all enjoy the evening as much as possible and I hope that the night is a success. I also wish to give a personal message to young Terry. Terry, I would like you to know we are all here for you. We all love you as a person, and if there is anything I can do for you personally to make you happy, I am willing to do so. Try to have happy thoughts and think happy thoughts and this will make you happy. I pray and hope that you will get better in the future and lead a happy life. That's all for now, Terry. And once again, I would like to thank you all. Goodnight. God bless, Reg Kray."

The tape fell silent. Looking around the room, I could see that everyone was captivated. They were listening to *the* Reg Kray. Seamus Watson, a well-known face in Dunston, began to clap, and as he did, the rest of the room joined in as if awoken from a trance. It evolved into deafening applause. I was grinning. I would swear that Reg could have heard the reception he got that night; it was a proud moment for us all … the looks on the faces of the Morans, the message from Reg, Tony and Charlie showing up, the other celebs *and* all the punters.

As the cameras flashed again at the photo call, Charlie turned to me, put his arm around me and said, "Thanks, Steve, this is the best birthday I can remember. It's taken me back. I've never had a night like this since the Sixties." Comments like that also made the effort worthwhile.

As the night ended, I lost count of the number of people who came up to me and shook my hand. The night just shot past me. It was amazing but exhausting … thank God for last orders. As people made their way out, I counted the money. The grand total was £2,400. The Morans were overwhelmed and asked me to donate the money to the Newcastle Burns Unit that had looked after and nursed Terry through the early days. How good did it feel to be able to do that? It's hard to explain. Okay, so we hadn't exactly raised millions, but it could still go towards helping people.

Charlie was keen to go clubbing, so we arranged a night out in Julie's nightclub for him on Newcastle's Quayside. He said his goodbyes, and as he was going thanked me again for "the best night I've had in years". With that, he was gone. Ray, Tony and I chose to wind down with a few select friends after hours in the club to reflect on what had been a successful night. The night had gone well, and without any problems.

Then, of course, something had to happen … A young lad had apparently been making a nuisance of himself all night, and on more than one occasion had asked Tony absurd and insulting questions.

To his credit, Tony had ignored him. But the lad persisted and somehow found himself left behind in the club with us. It's hard to imagine what this lad was thinking; was he drunk, slightly eccentric or did he have a death wish? I'd put money on the latter, but I dare say it was a good combination of all three, with a large dose of stupidity for good measure.

When he asked Tony whether he had ever slept with Ronnie Kray, it was the straw that broke the camel's back, which led to the punch that broke the tosser's face. Tony cracked him on the jaw with such force that it sent him flying into the wall on the other side of the room. It really was some punch. Tony had kept his cool for long enough and this idiot had tested his patience one time too many. I dragged the lad outside and made sure he was okay, then shut the fire doors on him. Now would be a good time to leave; the last thing I needed was the headline, 'Kray Firm on Rampage at Charity Bash'. We retired to Ray's to chill out and boy did I need it.

In the run-up to the party, Tony had mentioned it in passing that his mother was originally from Consett, and so, theoretically that made him half-Geordie. He also mentioned the fact that he had never seen his mother's grave and did not know its whereabouts. So, having the time and the inclination, Ray set out on a mission to locate Elizabeth Lambrianou's resting place.

After a lot of phone calls and good detective work, Ray traced her grave to a plot in Shotley Bridge Cemetery. We took time out to visit the site, tidy it up and place some fresh flowers there. The day after the party, we made the sentimental journey once again to the quiet leafy village, but this time with Tony and Wendy. Once we had pointed it out, we left them alone.

As we stood back, it was quite a touching sight to see this former gangster and hardman pay his respects to his mother. He placed his own flowers around the grave and then said his goodbyes. He came over to Ray and me and, after drying his eyes, thanked us. It was an emotional moment for us all. We said our farewells to Tony and Wendy and thanked them for coming. It was the end of an amazing couple of days, and Ray and I had achieved everything we had set out to do and more. Like a jigsaw, everything had fallen into place and we both knew that we couldn't have done it all without the support of our families and friends.

Charlie phoned the next day to thank me again. "One of the best nights of my life, Steve." I felt content and a sense of righting the wrongs that I had witnessed in London.

After the success of arranging two charity nights at The Elysium Lane for my young friend Terry Moran, I always said that I would never do another charity night again for the Krays. The second party for Terry was on 16 December 1995. We did this for him as he gave all the money in the summer to the Hospital Burns Unit to show appreciation for the care that they had given him.

Charlie was to play host and Tony Lambrianou came as a special guest. Running like clockwork, Reg phoned me two weeks before the party and asked me for the bar takings on the night. Again, it was an outrageous request. I could not believe that he was doing all this again, but looking back, it's quite easy to believe. Asking for the bar takings was something that would be done in the Sixties and people would think nothing of it. Asking for the bar takings in the Nineties was something Reg Kray would do and think nothing of it.

I really thought it was a selfish act. Why was he doing it? I can only assume it was because he saw there was some money being raised for a charity and wanted a part of it. We already had the room free for the night and he expected the money that the bar made to go into his pocket. Things didn't work like that anymore; it was only the Krays who did. Time had moved on, but they stayed firmly rooted in the Sixties. If I had gone with Reg's suggestion, I know I would have a lot less friends than I have today.

We argued over the bar takings on the phone and I hung up on him, seething with rage. He rang back immediately, swearing and warning that he was pulling out and that I better not have Charlie there ... then he hung up. Jesus, at least he didn't say, 'My dad is bigger than your dad' first. I rang Charlie, and told him not to bother turning up. I didn't want to drag him into it, as he took enough crap from Reg over the slightest things. I told him I would go ahead with Tony.

Reg phoned the following day to see if I had agreed to his terms, and I told him he could stick it. He was asking the impossible. I was doing this for Terry, not him. I informed the local papers that I would give refunds to those who had paid to see Charlie. I couldn't be any fairer than that. No one wanted a refund and the party went ahead successfully. Reg didn't speak to me for around a month after that. Neither of us would back down.

At the party, we raised £1,000, but they were beginning to feel like too much hard work. It wasn't just because of all the hassle that went with it or the constant arguments with Reg over money, but because the organisation of these nights was so time-consuming.

In 1998, I had a rethink when my attention was drawn to another young lad, whose family I knew well through the post office. Alan Hedley from Wardley had impaired hearing and a serious bowel disorder but remained upbeat and cheerful. I admired his parents for the love and determination that they gave to Alan, and I wanted to help them in whatever way I could.

Three years had passed since the last party. I was still in touch with Ray Cann and phoned him to ask if he was interested in coordinating another party at the same venue. He jumped at the chance to do it again, as did Davey Falcus ... he let us invade his social club again, so we began to put our heads together. This would definitely maybe be the last one.

I already had an idea of what I wanted to do with the night and what I wanted to call it but would need Reg's blessing. I rang C-wing and waited only a couple of minutes for the return call. After the usual chit-chat about how each of us were doing, I told Reg of young Alan's health problems and that I wanted to put on a night in the North East with his help. I then explained that I wanted to call the night *The Firm Friends Reunion*, as it was thirty years since their arrest in 1968. I wanted to hold it on 8 May, which would be thirty years to the actual day. Reg was impressed with the idea. I asked him to compile a list of people who I could invite from his past. The wheels were officially in motion.

Local friend and DJ Kenny Dick agreed to do his usual turn with Premier Discos, and my mate Paul Martin agreed to bring his band, Cryin' Out Loud, free of charge to perform. We decided against a buffet and priced the tickets at a reasonable ten spot. Next up, a few calls to local former footballers John Anderson,

Malcolm MacDonald and Mick Martin, who all pledged their support and agreed to make an appearance for Alan. I couldn't believe how well everything was coming together. The venue, entertainment and now some football heroes ... couldn't be happier.

A few days later, Reg phoned me again to say that he wasn't too keen on the idea now. *How 'out of the blue'*, I thought. He also wanted to know how much he could expect to make from the night. I told him that the money was all going to Alan and that none of the guests or acts were being paid, i.e., a *charity* event. I must have caught him on a good day, because from that moment on he never mentioned it again. Instead, Reg asked me to contact his wife Roberta to ask her to send up some merchandise to sell for him on the evening.

I liked Roberta. They had got married in July 1997. She had been arranging parties for a while herself since the marriage. I had no real interest in attending them anymore and when asked to help by Reg I said I could organise security for them and that was all my input could be. Roberta made the events credible again. She wasn't everyone's cup of tea but that's because she was doing things for Reg and not for herself. Reg had surrounded himself with so many idiots and 'yes men' over the years, but many of them crawled back under their stones when she came onto the scene. She had a good head on her shoulders both personality-wise and business-wise and had a good nose for sniffing out certain smells that tended to come out of people's mouths instead of words.

As for *Firm Friends* guests, Reg told me to use my discretion, so I played safe and asked Roberta. I was given a list that included Frankie Fraser, Freddie Foreman and Tony Lambrianou. That was more than enough, so I set about publicising the forthcoming event in the local and national press. I provided them with a photo of myself with the three principal guests, and it went down well.

After speaking to Fred and Tony and receiving confirmation that they would travel up with my old mate Christian, I called Frankie Fraser. I had met Frankie quite a few times and had always got on well with him. From the tone of his voice, I knew he wasn't too interested, so decided to leave it at that and wished him well. I rang Freddie and asked him if he knew of any of the old firm that would be willing to travel up. He said he would make a few enquiries but, if all else failed, that he would bring up a celebrity friend. I was intrigued.

Once the publicity had gone out, I was swamped by calls for tickets. I contacted people who had attended previous nights and we were almost guaranteed a sell-out. Good news for us and even better news for Alan. I had asked John Lillico to help arrange the security and he brought down a few of his mates from Ashington to help. John also came with me to meet Freddie, Tony, Christian and the mystery guest when they arrived in Newcastle. The guest was none other than Gary Webster of television show *Minder*. Freddie had done us proud.

They arrived in the afternoon, so I arranged for a quick tour of St James' Park, which was much appreciated. As we were waiting to go into the ground, an armoured security van was pulling in and Freddie had us in stitches with his comments, "Well, that is good timing!"

From the football ground, we took our guests to the Cross Keys in Dunston, where they received the warmest of welcomes from landlady Val. After a quick bite to eat and a chance to freshen up, we were on our way to the venue. I was more relaxed this time than I had been previous occasions.

We arrived just after seven o'clock and there were already a group of thirty people mingling. By eight o'clock, the room was a mass of men suited and booted and women wearing their best evening dresses. This was going to be a night to remember.

We had reserved tables for Alan and his family next to Freddie and the chaps, as well as the ex-footballers. Alan loved it and it was great to see him enjoying himself so much. Again, there was a long silence as I played Reg's taped message for the evening, and then an explosion of applause and cheering as the tape whirred to an end. There were endless photographs taken … flash after flash, and the night seemed to end all too quickly.

The night was a great success and raised a lot of money for Alan and for Reg with his merchandise stall. Instead of staying back at the club for a late drink, we had been invited to a nightclub in Sunderland called The Palace by a friend of mine, Tony Currie. Somehow, the words 'Sunderland' and 'Palace' just didn't seem right to me, but I was willing to give it a go.

Tony was a doorman by night and a private detective by day, and said that we would all be more than welcome in Sunderland. His friend had laid the taxis on, as getting there and back was my major concern. The club itself was huge and, as we approached, I recognised a few of the lads on the door, Andy Walker and Mickey Armstrong, who I introduced, and they led us through the ravers to the VIP area upstairs.

It was a great atmosphere ... people wall to wall, with most of them wanting autographs and pictures of Fred and Tony. I took time out with Christian, John and Tony Currie to toast a successful night. As usual, there was an absentee – this time it was Dave Courtney. He was attending a wedding as the best man but promised he would pop up to see me the next day.

After clubbing it, we made our way back to the Cross Keys at about three in the morning and I sat up with Tony and Fred, talking about the old days. They talked about how they felt about Reg and his continuing imprisonment. We stayed up for a couple of hours, talking and unwinding, before we turned in. They were good to listen to. I could see in their eyes how they looked back on those days with some fond memories. They didn't really dwell on the bad times; it would have spoilt the night ... just a couple of retired men talking about work.

We got the chaps up and out to the station for the eleven o'clock morning train to London. I had no sooner said my goodbyes to one set of friends than I was back at the Central Station a few hours later to welcome in Dave, his wife Jenny and close friend Brendan to town.

I brought John along and compared hangovers along the way ... it's safe to say that I had possibly the worst hangover in the country that day. We filled Dave in on the previous night's events and he was gutted that he had missed out. I assured him that we would make up for it that night with a trip down Newcastle's legendary Bigg Market. We dropped them off at the Cross Keys into the capable hands of Val and made our way home to grab forty winks in preparation for the night ahead.

With Dave in town and up for a night out, there was no way you could be at anything less than 110 per cent fit. Saturday is always a good night out in Newcastle and this night was no exception. I had told all the lads that Dave was coming up, so with me there was Chris and David Liddle, Chris Parker, Ian Brown, Steven Spence, Arron Parker and Anthony Halpin. Together with Ray, John and Graham Borthwick, there was a nice little squad of us assembled.

As a doorman, a good perk is not to have to queue at bars in the town you work, but if you are out with a big group, it is unfair to take the piss. So, at each bar we went to, before attempting to queue-jump, I asked the lads on the door if it was okay. We had no problems. Most of the lads were just pleased to meet Dave and Jenny, and Dave loved the fact that people wanted to talk to him. He is usually a shy and unassuming person, but he must have come out of his shell for a few hours on this visit.

I had let Tony Currie know that Dave was in town and asked him if the offer was open to take him down to The Palace. Tony checked it out and said there would be no problem. He sorted the transport out and, as last orders were called, we found ourselves on the way to Makemland once more (Makems being natives of Sunderland).

The club was jumping again as we made our way upstairs to the VIP lounge. It was only *foam party* night! Try to imagine a big bubble bath with a few hundred strangers and loud music. The club closed at two in the morning and we were amongst the last to leave.

We watched as one of the lads (alcoholically and chemically enhanced) decided to mimic Germany's predatory football striker

Jurgen Klinsmann's goal celebrations by diving headfirst into the foam from the balcony. The impersonation was perfect, but his landing wasn't … he staggered from the foam with a gaping head wound. The rest of us were howling with laughter at the state of him but eventually managed to compose ourselves and help get the wound covered.

Whilst Klinsmann headed off to the Accident and Emergency Unit, we made our way to the Cross Keys and chilled out with Dave. Dave was in the process of writing his second book, *Raving Lunacy*, after the huge success of *Stop the Ride, I want to Get Off*, and assured me that he would give me and the lads a mention. I'm pleased to say that he kept his word as he always does, so am not ashamed of giving his books a free plug.

Both twins always made sure that my expenses were looked after. Our friendship took off at a tremendous pace, with Ron writing or calling a few times a week. I seemed to get on better with Ron, as our visits were all about conversation. Unlike Reg, he had no reason to get up and start socialising with other patients while I was there. He'd phone me to ask if I could investigate different ventures he'd been approached about, could I send some money to this person or that charity, or did I get that money he'd sent up.

On 29 April, I received a letter from Kate Kray with a cheque for £200 in it and on the same day, another letter from Ron saying a further £200 would be coming my way shortly. It was good to see that it wasn't just a one-way friendship of me visiting all the time and using my own money. Receiving expenses meant he was thinking about me.

As money was now a major part of our relationship, I contacted Ron to ask what I should do with the money being made (I was careful to make sure that every penny was accounted for and listed in detail any expenses I had). He told me to open a bank account up and keep any money they were owed there until further notice. No way. I had visions of putting a thousand quid in one week and being asked "Where's my ten grand?" the next. I didn't need that sort of hassle at any stage in our friendship. We could be good mates, but enemy status is only a mood swing away.

He was still the same person who had been locked away in 1968, and I had to keep it in the back of my mind no matter how well the present situation was panning out. I hung back from the idea of a bank account for a while, then as more money started to come in, Ron was always telling me to send it to this boy and that boy, the bank account forgotten about. It began to feel like a race to get rid of the money as soon as it was earned ... it was going out all over the country to any Tom, Dick, Harry, Larry or Barry.

Ron would never cease to amaze me. Quite a few times, he asked me to make statements to the press highlighting their plight or just commenting on a current affair on their behalf. A lot of the time, the stories didn't make it to print, but when they did, I was always rewarded for my effort. One day, I received a call from Broadmoor and Ron was seething at a news report he'd just heard on the radio.

"That bloody rat Major [John Major] is trying to jeopardise our chances of parole! He said he doesn't want today's kids being the Krays of tomorrow! It's slander. The slag. I want you to make a statement on our behalf, use your discretion, Steve. I'll be in touch. God bless."

With that, he was gone. I barely had a chance to speak. This was how many of our 'conversations' would take shape when he was in this mood. Once the 'God bless' was spoken, I always knew the conversation was over. I tried to get in touch with Reg to talk it through first but was unable to do so. So, it looked like I had to put my Kray Media Liaison hat on again and take on the most powerful man in the country on their behalf.

The press release I put together was as follows:

In response to Mr Major's speech, we would like to say that in our day, no one would dream of mugging and battering old ladies, stealing from their next-door neighbours or molesting and killing innocent women and children. The people of our day would not tolerate any such behaviour. To be compared to people like that by our own Prime Minister saddens and hurts us deeply.

Ron was so happy with it that he told me to "tell all the papers". It got good coverage the next day in the broadsheets, giving the twins their right to reply and hopefully making John Major take note for any future remarks. I got a letter back from Ron saying I'd done well with the write-up and that it worked out for the best.

He was always urging me to campaign on Reg's behalf as well. He'd say that Reg didn't deserve to be locked up like an animal and to help get him out. Reg, on the other hand, wanted them both to be released, though I think he knew deep down that it was highly unlikely.

It felt good to be trusted to such a degree by them, I just had to remember to be cautious. Ron was obviously unstable at times, and Reg could also be unpredictable. Anything I went into with them would have to be carefully considered. Whilst many of the visits were filled with talking about nothing in particular, I felt quite honoured that they had brought me in as an unofficial business adviser. They wanted me to cast my eyes over deals and give them an honest opinion as to the money-making potential of them.

I knew that I wouldn't be the only person who would have a say, but to be asked whether I thought they should part with their cash for various deals was quite a responsibility. In their position, they needed to rely on people. I saw straight away that they were surrounded by 'advisers' who couldn't care less about them. Many of these people were just out for themselves and could not be trusted. I'd always need to be on my guard; there was a lot of talking behind backs and playing people off against others for personal gain. There were some decent blokes, though, and I made some good friends, but some of the others made me wonder what the twins were thinking of to even talk to them.

I took my old mate Matty to visit Ron in Broadmoor one time. On our way down, we were involved in a serious car crash.

A drink driver had skidded in front of an articulated lorry that had to brake suddenly, forcing Matty to brake hard and swerve to avoid it. We clipped the back of the lorry and spun three times before crashing through the central reservation and landing on the other side of the motorway. The car was a total write-off.

I don't know how, but we were okay apart from a few cuts and bruises, and a rip in my new suit. We counted our blessings that it was only seven in the morning and not midday, because in rush-hour traffic it could have been a lot different. I had my camera that day and took some shots of the car, because I couldn't quite believe that we had escaped with so few injuries between us.

I called Broadmoor to let Ron know that we wouldn't be able to make it, and got my mother and grandmother to do the same. I sent some pictures of the car and an apologetic letter to Ron, asking him when the next available visit was. Over the next couple of days, I received four letters from Ron calling me a rat and a slag and telling me that he was 'right disappointed in me'.

I didn't think it was right that we were in a crash and here he was mouthing off to me like this. I hadn't known him for that long, so this was our first 'falling out'. It made me think about what I was into and how deep I was in.

I know there are friends who can fall out and once things are off their chest and all is said, it's back to normal and the friendship is still there. I know others where they can argue and the friendship is over. It was a learning curve for me. I could have taken it to heart and ended it all then, or I could let it go, knowing it had come from an emotionally unstable criminal who had been away from society for some time.

It seemed he couldn't take disappointment well at all. In his eyes, I'd let him down and upset him. That's when I found out that Ron had been sitting in the visiting room at a table by himself for the full two-hour visit. Whether it was a breakdown in communication or some form of mental torture, I wasn't sure, but I hoped at least the photographs would reach Ron. Luckily, they did, and he was quick to apologise and arrange another visit.

He also wanted to know if he could do anything to help us with any costs we had incurred. After refusing money, a cheque still arrived for £200. It was a nice gesture and said a lot about the real Ron Kray. Sure, he was disappointed, and I dare say humiliated at having to sit there for two hours … I'm glad to say that when he knew I was on the level, he showed a different side to his personality.

If this was a guilty conscience or real concern, I was unsure at first, but now realise it was a bit of both. There was never a conventional apology, but I knew he knew. Just like Reg, though, once something like that had come and gone, that was it. It would never be mentioned again … it was in the past. It seemed slightly ironic to me that the 'immediate' was gone in an instant, yet they were both firmly stuck in their own past and they were still hanging on to it every day.

The rearranged visit took place two weeks later and this time we decided that the train was the safest option. The journey went without a hitch and we reached Broadmoor with an hour to spare. We left Ron some John Players at reception and were escorted to the visiting hall. We made our way to the table in the middle of the room and pulled up three chairs and waited for Ron to join us. Within five minutes, the familiar dapper figure of Don Ron appeared in the doorway and he looked over his gold rimmed glasses to see where we were sitting. Waving him over, we stood up to greet him.

I shook hands first, and he said, "Hello, Steve. Good to see you, good to see you," in his customary whisper, and I introduced him to Matty as we sat down. Ron clicked his fingers to attract the attention of one of the nurses. He ordered six cans of non-alcoholic lager and Matty and I had tea. He had his first cigarette lit and we were off … then a silence seemed to fall over him and I was beginning to wonder whether we had picked a bad day to visit. He was hunched up and tense; I could see something within him starting to rise, his eyes fixed behind me.

It was then I felt someone nudge my chair from behind, trying to squeeze past, which distracted me from Ron for a second. Turning sharply to see what was going on, I could see it was a patient. No problem, but no 'excuse me', either. He stared through me and pulled up a chair at his table, where an elderly woman was sitting.

I turned back to Ron, who was livid. "Slag ... the fuckin' slag." He was staring right at the patient who'd knocked my chair, seriously wound up – his anger was like a volcano about to erupt. I tried to calm him down by telling him it didn't really matter, but I sensed it was nothing to do with that. Ron continued, "He's a fuckin' rat. He's a slag and a rat."

I'd heard this kind of talk from Ron before and recently had been on the receiving end of it but had never seen such hatred in Ron's eyes since I'd known him. Matty was as intrigued as I was. I asked who this bloke was. "Sutcliffe, Peter Sutcliffe, the Yorkshire Ripper. He's a no-good slag."

I already knew that Ron had a dislike for Sutcliffe. In 1983, Ron organised an attack on him and Sutcliffe was left with one side of his face slashed open. The pair had never fallen out over anything, and had never exchanged words, for that matter. Ron despised him for his crimes against women; he needed no excuse to feel how he did.

Hearing Ron in what sounded like him preparing for a fight was an unreal experience. Matty and I turned to each other in disbelief. There was total silence between us as it began to sink in. Suddenly, Ron jumped up ... we flinched as the chair legs scraped back ... looking up at him, I realised what a powerful force he would still be against any opponent.

Then, the anger just seemed to leave his whole being within a millisecond; he turned to Matty and said, "Well, thanks for coming, Matthew, I'd like to have the rest of the time with Steve now; we have business to discuss." We never did talk about it but we both thought he was going to do Sutcliffe right there in front of us; it was something where you just had to read the other's expression to know there were no words to describe it. You could feel the relief in the atmosphere as Matty shook Ron's hand and we arranged to meet back in reception. His visit had lasted a mere fifteen minutes.

Ron had something on his mind and he wanted to tell me. He was a talker anyway, but the past was his favourite topic. Get him on a good day about the old days and you could forget about getting a word in edgeways.

Once we had discussed a few more merchandise ideas, Ron revealed that he had just finished reading a book by a former member of the so-called Kray firm and he wasn't happy with the inaccuracies that had appeared in it.

"I'm sick of people writing lies about us, Steve," he said. I listened intently as he started to talk about his life at the top of the criminal ladder. "People think I killed George Cornell because he called me a queer. That's rubbish. I didn't like him, Steve, he was arrogant, but Cornell got his because of what he told me. You see, he told me he killed Freddie Mills."

I was taken aback by Ron's frankness, but he continued, "Cornell and I were not always enemies, and we had confided in each other. He and Mills fell out and George killed him, simple as that. He told me this in good faith and I have kept it until now." Ron was being deadly serious as he told me, and that is word for word how I remember it.

No one was ever found guilty or convicted of Freddie Mills' murder. Ron was certainly sincere when he told me, though I still wouldn't like to guess one way or the other. It was something else I was unsure of – a mind game? I don't think so.

It was said that Ron shot Cornell because he'd killed someone close to Ron – maybe that someone was Freddie Mills and not Dickie Hart. At the time of Cornell's murder, it would have been easy for Ron to just go along with the 'fat poof' theory as his motivation. All his spies would tell him Cornell had been heard saying something about him *just* to put themselves in favour, but at the same time, anyone heard badmouthing Ron Kray was reason enough for him to put a bullet in their head. I can only share what he told me and can't prove it one way or the other, but Cornell – if it was true – had confessed to an unsolved murder.

Ron went on to describe how he had walked into The Blind Beggar public house and shot Cornell through the head at point-blank range. "It was great, Steve, I can play that moment repeatedly in my mind, I can smell the fear. Good, good." With that, Ron had another Player lit up and patted my hand with his.

He was revealing different sides to his personality like this all the time. I knew he'd murdered in the past – everyone knew – but I'd never heard him describing it so graphically before. It's unusual to hear someone reminisce so fondly about murder; I'd read about this murder many times but hearing of the pleasure that committing it had brought Ron really disturbed me.

He went on to describe it other times after that. He said he went through it over and over in depraved sexual fantasies, using the scenario to reach orgasm. I found it sickening.

I think today, people can be desensitised to murder and crime through being constantly bombarded with it through film and TV. When faced with it in such cases like the Rodney King incident or 11 September, you can see the media effect on whole nations and society, as opposed to just a community. Many people can feel distanced from it because it can become an everyday occurrence that does not affect their lives, and then an event like the twin towers unites everyone in shock, grief and repulsion.

I'd say this was the effect Ron describing a murder had on me. I could read a murder ... a murder ... a murder all day and not be moved by it. I had no personal connection with the bloke, and it happened before I was born. Now I'd got to know Ron Kray and he was telling me how good it felt to murder – to physically end someone's life in such a violent and ruthless way.

To see his face light up as he told me was a real eye-opener to some of the repressed thoughts that could resurface from the mind of a paranoid schizophrenic. It was one side to Ron I didn't like. It's almost impossible to hide a reaction to something like that, but obviously I would try to keep my true feelings to myself.

The eyes and the hands of a person are always a giveaway. You can tell when people are lying or telling the truth, if they are guilty, embarrassed, angry ... you name it, just by things they do subconsciously.

He loved to tell stories, though; he could sit for hours losing himself in recalling memories about events or scrapes they'd been in – the good old days – or tell me of his dreams for the future, of people they had known, taken on in battle or were just good friends with. I remember these stories because it was Ron's sixtieth birthday when he told me. (His best present was to follow two days later, with a visit from Reg. They were allowed only four visits a year under supervision, a grand total of eight hours ... how the authorities spoilt them.)

As usual, he was immaculately dressed, sporting a jazzy pair of crocodile shoes and a grey pinstriped suit, from Savile Row, of course. He was on top form and was keen to introduce me to his fellow patients on this visit. I met everyone from Hannibal Lecter to Freddy Kreuger; they were all good to their mums and were just misunderstood, according to Ron. Maybe some of them were. We sat down and Ron poured me a cuppa and started to recall other inmates he'd had the pleasure of doing his bird with. One of those people was none other than Michael Peterson, a.k.a. Mr Charles Bronson.

* * *

The twins had first met Charlie in Parkhurst in 1978. They were on C-wing together. Ron said that he could see the potential in the young Bronson and that he took him under his wing. He would give the young Charlie twenty quid a time to exchange for baccy (tobacco) so that he could have a more comfortable life inside. They built up a good relationship and I think that the twins could see a hint of themselves somewhere within Bronson.

Ron wrote him a letter when he was locked up in solitary confinement after one of many misunderstandings with a screw.

In it, he told him to, "Slow down, don't end up like me, life is too precious to throw away your young and full life. Think of your mum when you feel bad. I don't want to see you like this. God bless, Ron."

He told me he remembered writing the letter in his cell at the time but described his cell as The Lagoon. It threw me a bit at first; I didn't know if I'd heard right or whether he'd lapsed into the past, but I didn't recall The Lagoon as one of their clubs. He continued ... remembering writing the letter so vividly as his cell had been decorated like a small nightclub. All the other cons called it The Blue Lagoon.

He smiled as he told me how cons would pop in and share a drink and a smoke with him. I could picture it ... the smoky atmosphere, the drink flowing, the conversation, the business ... not unlike one of the clubs on the outside ... always with The Colonel holding court. This was what he'd loved on the outside, sitting in his clubs in amongst all the smoke and soaking up the atmosphere. He loved being the host.

To hear such a story made me smile, too – to me, it signalled more escapism for Ron. Being in The Blue Lagoon was like being a million miles away from Parkhurst. It was good to see that there were things he'd enjoyed as a free man that he'd always hung on to. He could lose himself, whether it be for five minutes or five hours.

Ron explained to me that prison life wasn't for him and that it was slowly driving him mad, eating away at him all the time. Violence could erupt at any time on C-wing and in Bronson the twins had a valuable ally. He recalled with such joy the days when he would bash a screw or a con, and then Reg would follow up the attack.

Again, I found this interesting, as it seemed that when they were in prison together, it was still Ron who was the dominant of the twins – still leading the way in battle.

Once, Reg even had to restrain Bronson from bashing up a con called Dave Simmonds, who had slighted him. The twins were not bothered about the con, but the more damage Charlie inflicted, the greater his punishment would be when he finally stopped.

Ron inevitably bashed one screw too many and was sent to isolation, losing his sanity all over again in the concrete coffin. Bronson remembered Ron's letter of support and returned the gesture. "Keep it together, be strong and don't let the authorities grind you down," something that Ron would never forget.

In solitary, the screws tormented Ron. For them, it was like having some wild animal in captivity that they could have their fun with. The hardest thing for him was that he felt for Reg. He knew that the same screws torturing him would be dealing with Reg in the normal manner; he knew that Reg would be suffering mentally, not knowing how his twin was. No doubt they would have had their fun with Reg, too, getting their revenge by taunting him about Ron.

After the incident, Ron was admitted to the hospital wing for assessment and was finally categorised as a mentally ill patient who could not be treated by the prison authorities. There was no other option but to transfer him to Broadmoor.

Ron was happy in Broadmoor. A lot of people couldn't understand why, as Broadmoor is not well known for releasing patients. He was allowed more visits than he could have dreamed of in Parkhust. He also had a locker full of tinned salmon, fruit, chocolate – you name it, Ron had it. When you have everything you want, why would you want to change it? It was a regime that would suit him a lot better than prison ever could.

It wasn't long before Bronson joined Ron in the nuthouse and their friendship started back up. Charlie became an unofficial minder to Ron, fending off a lot of the lunatics that would harass him, and in return Ron would arrange for a lot of good-looking females to visit Charlie.

Ron was always bemused by the attention and fan mail that he received from women all over the world and was never short of love interests in Broadmoor. Not a bad arrangement if you ask me.

With Ron in Broadmoor and Reg in Parkhurst, visits for Violet were exhausting and time-consuming, but as Ron used to say, "She never let her boys down."

It must have been one hell of a strain on her; first to have both twins locked up, then one in a mental hospital, and then have to visit them separately. It proved their love was strong and the family ethics that bonded them during the war years shined through. Violet would even send in items for other cons that the twins wanted 'looking after', so Charlie never went short of tracksuits and training shoes thanks to Mrs Kray.

Ron, when talking about Charlie, said, "I told him he still had a fighting chance in the outside world. If he had the chance on the outside, then it was a fighting career he should go for." He could see the potential in him, and Charlie obviously listened to the advice. Bronson was eventually transferred back into the prison system to serve the rest of his sentence. When released, Reg put him in touch with a bloke by the name of Paul Edmunds, who was a boxing promoter from Canning Town. Edmunds arranged a fight in East London but needed to give him an alias, as the fight was not what you would call a legal show. That day Michael Peterson became Charlie Bronson, and Charlie Bronson became a legend.

Ron and Reg called him before the fight to wish him luck and made sure Charlie Kray was at ringside to cheer their mate on. Ron laughed loudly during the story ... he had run a book on the fight with the other patients on Somerset Ward, and Bronson won with convincing ease.

Bronson's brief taste of success (and freedom) did not last long, however, and shortly after another resounding win in the ring, he found himself back behind bars.

Bronson went on to Rob a jeweller's to get a ring for his girlfriend Alison as a surprise for New Year. He selected and kept a ring and gave it to her as a present and sold the rest of the jewels lifted from the robbery. He was then arrested on 7 January 1988, when he was out for his morning jog. He has never been out of jail since.

Ron, just like his brothers, loved to name-drop into conversations and stories. The countless names of toy boys and lovers Ron had in prison would be reeled off, all just names to me, but I would listen all the same. I don't think that listing their names was ever meant to shock me, because I know that he was comfortable with his sexuality and had been for many years. He'd already tried it on my first visit anyway, so he knew I wasn't bothered by it.

There was one story he told me about an artist he used to know. I guessed the time of this to be around 1964, when the Lord Boothby scandal had broken. I know Ron paid weekend visits to Brighton and was quite taken by the place. The circles he'd begun to mix with at that time, 'The Chelsea Set', would invite him down to parties, as a lot of them had country retreats and what have you down that way.

He'd get that glint in his eye as he'd start to tell it: "You know, Steve, when I used to go down the South Coast, I used to know this artist. Lots of talent. A bit of a drinker, but always full of ideas." He looked back on it with fondness as I tried to picture the scene. Here's how it went.

One day, while the two of them were sat on the pier, his artist friend was almost in tears.

"What's wrong?" asked Ron.

"Oh, nothing," came the reply.

"It's such a grand sight. The high tides, the rocks, the gulls, they bring back such sad memories."

Ron told me how they couldn't pursue a meaningful conversation out in the open, so they found shelter in a nearby pub and the artist elaborated on his tale of woe. They sat down with a couple of Brown Ales and Ron listened to the story just as I was now, as the artist went into more detail.

He'd met this beautiful girl at a dance, they courted, and he found out that it was soon to be her birthday. He wanted to give her a special present and as she had come to mean so much to him in such a short space of time, he wanted to show her in the best way possible.

She was fond of a part of the bay where they had first met, and being an artist, he decided to capture it in a watercolour. He waited until the next beautiful sunny day before he made his way down to the bay. The thing was, he realised he'd forgotten to take water along with him once he sat down in front of his easel to paint.

Instead of going all the way back home to get some water, he decided to just use some seawater.

He did so and the painting turned out brilliantly. Ron went into detail of how he'd caught the sea crashing against a ridge of rocks with the water spraying up into the air, each drop catching the light of the sun on its way down ... the untouched and golden sandy beach, the deep blues of the sea on the horizon, vibrant yellows and the pale blue cloudless sky.

In due course, the painting was presented to the fair maiden on her birthday. She loved it – absolutely adored it – and hung it up in her bedroom in pride of place.

I was intrigued. Ron lowered his voice to his barely audible mode. I leaned in so I could hear him.

"The thing is, Steve, that the part of the painting that depicted the sea, yeah? Well, because it was created with seawater, it was subject to the attraction of the moon, which meant it was tidal. This meant you could see the sea in the painting coming up over the rocks by the shore's edge, and then down again at low tide."

I'd had my head slightly cocked to one side to hear properly, but now I turned to face him. What on earth was he talking about? I looked at him in disbelief as he went on.

"One night, it was the highest recorded tide in the country's history. The entire South Coast was hit with thunderstorms, rain, hurricanes ... everything. The next day, my friend went to visit his girlfriend. The whole household was in a state of complete despair. It was the watercolour, see. The watercolour had overflowed during the night and it fucking drowned her in her sleep. And since that day, after what had happened, he could never paint anything again."

He timed that story perfectly. Just as he finished it, he stood up to leave and we said our goodbyes. He was smiling to himself, knowing he'd had me believing the whole thing all along. I stood and watched his exit, the other visits now ending with Ron 'beating the rush' back to his room. I smiled as he turned back to wave.

He really was a man of many dimensions. That story proved he had a wicked sense of humour, but to anyone else listening, it probably confirmed his insanity. There were so many times he'd have me in stitches with his sense of humour. He'd be so dry in his delivery, sometimes I'd have to think first before knowing I could laugh. There would always be a slight pause and he'd look at me as if to say, "Have you not got it yet?"

Every time I visited, he would always ask what I wanted to eat and drink – usually tea and most often I'd join him in a snack. I remember once I declined the offer of food, as I'd had something on the way down. Ron didn't eat, either. I thought he was just being polite, but he said the reason why he wasn't eating was because working in the kitchen that day was none other than Graham Young, The Bovingdon Poisoner.

Young was convicted in 1972 of murdering two workmates by Thallium poisoning and administering poison to four others. He'd already poisoned his stepmother to death and attempted to poison his father, sister and a friend for good measure. And now he was working in the kitchen at Broadmoor! I couldn't believe it; I know people in there have mental problems, but if this was true, then the Governor must have been as mad as a box of frogs. It was insane.

In 1995, the same year as Ron's death, a film called *The Young Poisoner's Handbook* was released, which was all about Graham Young. I watched it with interest to discover he'd died of a heart attack while serving a life sentence in Parkhurst on 1 August 1990, a year before my first ever visit to Ron. I couldn't help but laugh at the fact I'd believed him all that time. Broadmoor was surreal enough at times, so I was glad to wipe that vision from my mind.

Speaking of extremes, Ron's mood swings were exactly that. He could go from one to the other as quickly as he went through his cigarettes. In his environment, I don't suppose there was room for any beating around the bush; there was no time to waste in building up to something with Ron. I was summoned to a visit with him one time and he was absolutely seething.

On this visit, I got to see a chilling side to him that I hadn't seen since he'd described the Cornell murder. This visit was similar; he had the same frankness, the same cold and serious expression ... he moved closer and asked me to arrange the deaths of Kim Lane and Pete Gillett.

This was not just an off-the-cuff remark. He wanted them murdered for upsetting Reg and he wanted me to do it. This was the Ron I'd read about from the Sixties ... in this mood, he was relentless. I could picture him now giving the same orders to The Firm. He insisted I organised it.

I had to keep a calm exterior, but inside my conscience was screaming for me to get the hell out of there. We discussed other business, but I couldn't take any of it in; I don't think I even heard anything else he said.

The visit came to an end and, as far as Ron was concerned, their death warrants had been signed and he could go back to his room a happy man. I left the place disgruntled. At that time, the only hit man I knew was Pete Waterman, and although his music was bad, I'd never heard of it killing anyone.

I'm joking about it now, but at the time this was serious. I knew what Ron's moods were like and I was banking on him changing his mind. I left it a few days. Nothing. I spoke to him on the phone. Nothing. I knew he wouldn't discuss it over the phone, so I could be a bit more relaxed in talking to him ... but he was phoning to arrange another visit to see if I had 'sorted that thing out'. In a week's time, he'd be expecting to hear results.

What could I do? It was a no-win situation. I'm not sure if he realised exactly what he'd asked me to do, but there was no way on this earth that I could even contemplate doing it. It was constantly on my mind leading up to the visit, then on the journey … and eventually during the visit itself.

We sat facing each other at the usual table. He got his cigarette lit, keeping his eyes firmly fixed on me all the time. After the usual small talk, he asked if I'd sorted the pair of them out. I told him I hadn't, and I didn't elaborate any further by saying I needed more time. "Good, good" came the reply. It was as casual as that. He'd called it off as casually as asking me the time.

Imagine now if I had been mad enough to get in touch with someone to carry out his order. I wanted to tell him he could not just go around ordering two murders and not even think to tell me he'd changed his mind … but I realised how ridiculous it would sound. It would sound as ridiculous as the murder request.

I was just glad it was over. He had no right to even ask me in the first place. The more I thought about it, the more I wanted to tell him – but it was in the past now, forgotten about. Thinking about it now, though, he couldn't have been serious about killing them at all. He knew I was not even a petty thief, never mind a killer; and he knew I was not the type who could live with myself if I arranged for such a thing to happen.

If he was that serious about it, he had his pick of anyone throughout the underworld to carry it out. In which case, it would have been over within days. It was all about mood swings. He had already managed to get to Pete Gillett in another way, though, through the film *The Krays*.

As Charlie was an adviser on the film, Ron had made sure he got a favour out of him before renaming him Mr X. In the film, there were a lot of 'real' extras used – friends and associates connected to the family. As Gillett had shared a cell with Reg, it was a perfect guise. Charlie, under instruction, secured a part for Gillett. The part was one of two blokes who get beaten up by Reg, played by Martin Kemp.

On screen, Reg catches him and the other bloke as they admire Frances sitting in his Mercedes as he emerges from a shop. Reg gives them both a severe kicking and leaves them both semi-conscious on the road as he and Frances drive off. Charlie had suggested to Martin Kemp that during fight choreography, sometimes people *can* get hit for real, and if it happened that Gillett *did* take one or two enthusiastic shots, then he would merely be suffering for his art as an 'actor'. Apparently, Mr Kemp was only too happy to help, though I'm not sure how many takes were needed to get it right.

Ron acted in the same manner with Dominic Anciano, producer of the film. As you know, the twins were less than happy at the deal they received, so as well as blaming their elder brother, they blamed Anciano. The fact was that it was all down to Charlie that they got such a bad deal. They already held him responsible but couldn't really do anything in way of revenge to their brother. They looked elsewhere and found the producer.

Ron told me that they had been mugged off and that he should be 'done over properly'. The anger would build but he would never raise his voice or lose his cool. You could see a rage burning within him, ready to explode, but somehow, he kept it under control, if you can call ordering a hit on someone a form of control that is.

I learnt to spot the signs. He'd be agitated ... fidgeting ... anxious, looking at me like it was an inconvenience for him to be there after I'd spent nearly ten hours travelling to see him. Again, the chain-smoking would give the impression of anxiety, whether he was anxious or not. I don't think Ron ever actually *wanted* anyone killed. Not really. It was just his reaction, and once he'd said he wanted them killed, it was his way of eliminating the person and the upset they had caused from his mind. Once he'd 'killed' them, the anger left, and he could go relax.

Next on his hit list was his own wife. I, along with most others, knew Ron was gay. I never asked any questions about his reasons for marriage, as it was obviously a business arrangement no matter which way it was disguised.

This visit was on 25 September 1993. It seemed that during most of my visits, he was at odds with somebody, and I found myself playing the part of agony uncle. This was one of the few times I'd seen Ron not wearing a suit. He appeared in a black jumper, white shirt, dark slacks and polished shoes, and looked distinctly dishevelled.

Saying he was in a bad mood comes nowhere close. This was the worst I had ever seen him; he was like an animal. His first and only topic of conversation was Kate Kray and her book. She had upset Ron by including revelations of an agreement they had over sex in her book, *Murder, Madness and Marriage*. The book had been serialised in a tabloid newspaper and she had revealed personal details about an alleged 'sex pact' between them.

Again, he changed his mind eventually, but this was the most wound up I'd ever seen him. I knew that he would drop it once he'd vented his anger, but this time he took a lot longer to vent it. His fists were clenched tight, the white knuckles bulging as he kept calling her a slag throughout.

He said that a lot of things revealed in her book, like having in her possession the gun that killed Cornell, were all lies and that she had just used him for his name. I don't know if she said she had the gun, but I do know that it resides in the Black Museum at Scotland Yard.

On a visit on 3 June 1992, Ron again was not in the best of moods. The trial of Lindsay and Leighton Frayne was receiving a lot of media coverage at the time. The Fraynes were charged with robbery and conspiracy to rob the Halifax Building Society in Gwent.

The thing was, they had also become involved with the twins and taken it upon themselves to become some sort of updated version of them. They dressed in sharp suits and visited all the old haunts in the East End but didn't really rate as bad imitations. All the ambition was there, but they just came across as an outdated pastiche.

Their naivety in getting caught meant that not only were they looking at a long sentence each, but they were also attracting a lot of bad publicity for the twins. Bad publicity was the last thing they needed with the parole board looking for the slightest excuse to refuse them each time; now the Frayne brothers were handing the authorities an excuse on a plate.

As more and more was revealed during their trial, Ron was getting angrier. "I can't believe these boys, Steve. They've done Reg and me a lot of harm. Do you know they tried to kidnap your pal Gazza?" He was referring to the footballer Paul Gascoigne; this I had to hear ... "Yeah, they tried to get his bodyguard, Paul Edwards, who used to be in the SAS, to help them kidnap him and hold him ransom. How stupid can you get, Steve?"

I had to agree. Reg had told me about them, too, although I don't know if there was any truth to the kidnap part. I'd heard that the Frayne brothers were connected to the Krays a lot further than the Krays would ever let on.

The Krays are said to have made an arrangement with them to help maintain their stronghold on the underworld. They would give them all the contacts they needed, with the intended plan that the Fraynes would take over London and hand control over to Ron and Reg when they were released. Knowing of the deals the Krays got involved with, this does not surprise me.

It was reinforced when I heard that the Krays funded the Fraynes, too. They would travel to London each day in a bashed-up car and eat pitiful meals in order to save every penny they could for themselves. The plan failed, though, and it was easy for the Krays to deny all knowledge.

In 1993, just over a year to the day of that visit, Ron's behaviour was still up and down. It was a sad sight to see, as he could be calm and in control on one visit, then agitated and irrational on the next.

He was in a good mood but made it quite clear that he was becoming increasingly irritated with a fellow patient by the name of Lee Kiernender. As I drank my tea and he his non-alcoholic lager, he pointed Kiernender out to me, and I thought nothing more of it. He told me that he had an annoying habit, which I must admit is one of the most annoying things in the world ... he whistled whenever Ron was within earshot, and always out of tune.

Ron told me he was on a reduced drug treatment and, as a result, he felt unstable and irritable. The rest of the visit passed without incident and I left him feeling happy and upbeat. Two days later, I picked up a newspaper to read that Ron had taken exception to the out-of-tune whistler and had tried to strangle him. Five nurses were needed to drag Ron from him.

I could not believe it ... I rang the hospital for an update; as I was quite friendly with one of the nurses, she told me that Ron had been moved to Abingdon Ward and stripped of all privileges. He was allowed to call those on his phone list, so I passed on a message to him. He phoned me a couple of hours later ... still sounding as upbeat as when I'd left him.

"I just flipped, Steve. I told you they were messing with my drugs, didn't I? Still, that's that. I'm better off here anyway. I'm off gardening and kitchen duties. No privileges, see. But it means I've got time to think here. I get forty quid here from the NHS, so that's a result! Anyway, I must go. Will you do me a favour? Phone the papers and tell them that this attack is the last act of violence Ron Kray will ever carry out."

It was as good as done. Bizarre.

In the same year, Diana, Princess of Wales visited Broadmoor. The visit was publicised in all the newspapers, with the tabloids making out that she was having tea with the Ripper and Ron. Not so. I visited Ron a week later and the first question I asked Ron was, "How was the princess?" Ron glared at me over his spectacles and then said, "She didn't want to see me."

Further questioning revealed that she had the option of visiting Ron but had declined. He wasn't impressed. "I'm just as mad as everyone else in here!" Maybe it was for the best. It was unlikely that any member of the royal family would have been permitted to visit one of the Krays, or Sutcliffe for that matter. The press would have had a field day and the public would have seen it as an unforgivable act of condoning their crimes. They were too high profile.

On the same visit, he asked me to pick up an envelope on the way out that he'd left at reception. It contained an old newspaper that he wanted me to send to Reg. In it was a photo of the Queen Mother visiting the East End in the 1940s. There in the background was a young Ron Kray. His non-visit with the princess had jogged his memory about this paper and he wanted to send it to Reg to remind him of his brush with royalty.

I enjoyed my visits more with Ron than I'd had with Reg. Ron was a likeable man most of the time. Making my way home after the visits would always be my time to reflect – the Ripper incident, the murders he wanted arranged, when he spoke about killing Cornell, they were all added to the times when he would tell me all kinds of funny stories, listen to my life outside, learn all about my family and even ask me to help produce greetings cards with a polar bear on the front and one of his poems inside. He was a hard man to work out. I found him to be different to Reg, but they would always be 'similar'. They had a tight bond that could never be broken by distance.

Ron was the youngest of the twins and had emerged as the dominant one. Within the Firm, he was the more dominant of his other older brother, too. His life was a troubled one that seemed doomed by his illness. He changed physically, too – the medication, giving up on exercise, chain-smoking – but he always appeared to know what he was doing. Even when agitated, he knew it was down to a change in medication.

Many people have asked me whether I think he would ever have been released – I don't think he would have. Patients in Broadmoor are at a disadvantage to begin with. For example, if locked up in prison, a convict can abide by the rules and stay out of trouble to increase their chances of parole. In a mental institution, the criteria are not that well defined. They don't know how to behave to increase their chances, and different behaviours may evoke different responses in the observers. Mental illness is not something that should be taken lightly – it should be treated and not just swept under the carpet.

We hear all the time of mentally ill people committing murder, and all the time the signals were there for the authorities.

Ron Kray had been accurately diagnosed in prison in the Fifties yet did not receive any treatment for his schizophrenia. Locked up for murder, it took the authorities around eight years to take him out of a conventional prison and transfer him to Broadmoor, where he could receive help. He was a lot happier there, even with his ups and downs. He had his own clothes and could dress like the London gangster he'd always be remembered as.

CHAPTER 7
MR X

I became good friends with Charlie Kray. He was a good bloke who would do anything for a mate. I got to know him well through first getting to know his brothers, meeting him at parties and later when hosting our own parties. He would always be the life and soul and would make anyone welcome. He was image-conscious as well ... always wore a suit, always had his hair dyed and groomed, and always had a year-round suntan.

There are plenty of misconceptions about Charlie. He was always going to be in the background compared to his notorious brothers, but he was still very much 'a Kray'. Like many East Enders, he'd been a boxer and was streetwise. Taking more of a silent partner role in The Firm meant that he could be the business brain behind operations and leave Ron and Reg to run the public relations angle. It was a perfect partnership, and all three were happy with the arrangement. Ron and Reg could mingle with the rich and famous in their clubs, while behind all the glitz and glamour, Charlie would be doing all the real work – the work that nobody saw going on. He would make sure everything ran smoothly and he was good at doing so.

The happy partnership was unsteadied one night in *Esmeralda's*, though, when the silent partner was anything but silent. *Esmeralda's* was a good earner for The Firm; it had a discotheque on the first floor and a gambling joint on the second. It was in Belgravia in London, a particularly affluent area. The usual arrangement was that the sons and daughters of the rich gamblers would go to the disco while their parents would enjoy themselves upstairs.

Charlie was the right face to be running this place. Gamblers wanted a relaxed atmosphere; they didn't wish to know about the gangland side of things and didn't want to feel threatened. Charlie fronting the operation was enough to put anyone at ease. He would be the perfect host as usual, ensuring everyone was happy. Charlie mixed with everyone, suited up with his overcoat hanging on his shoulders, shaking hands and welcoming his guests.

One night, all three brothers were there, and the customers began complaining about the behaviour of one of the patrons – it was obvious there was going to be trouble. The person they were complaining about was Ron Kray. He had been going to the disco, and made unwanted advances to young men, so the relaxed atmosphere became tense. Ron's behaviour was upsetting people. Charlie was not amused. Business was good but Ron was going to mess things up by acting so stupidly. Charlie took him to one side and told him the score, but Ron was stubborn; he could not see the problem.

Charlie picked a chair up and hurled it at the bar, saying, "We may as well smash the place up now then!"

He began smashing the bar up and hurling abuse at Ron. Reg stepped in to try and calm Charlie down, but this time neither of them could stop him. He clearly made his point. Charlie was always known as the easy-going Kray brother. He *was* easy-going ... until he was wound up to the point of eruption. After that night, everyone knew he could be as dangerous as the twins if pushed. He silenced a lot of people that night by standing up to both twins at once and proving that he certainly was not a man to be messed with.

When I consider my memories of Charlie ... I recall the many times I met him in London and Newcastle. In all the time I knew him, I never saw a side to Charlie that wasn't likeable. He was always a gentleman – an East End character with a lust for life, who always seemed to have a smile on his face.

On 1 August 1996, I heard news concerning Charlie that was so unlike Charlie that anyone who knew him could not believe it. He was arrested for his involvement in a £39-million cocaine deal. It was shocking enough to hear that he was caught up in the crime, but to hear that he was the mastermind was difficult to comprehend.

To the general public, it was as sensational as ever, but to people who knew him, it was a different story altogether. The 'quiet' Kray brother, an OAP no less, caught in a huge drugs bust, was something that the news teams and tabloid reporters around the country could not wait to jump on.

Video footage of Charlie at a party with undercover policemen was shown on the national news … it was as though there was a huge sigh of relief that the third Kray would be safely locked away.

When I heard, it just didn't sink in. As far as I could see the situation, a man who couldn't cover his tracks on a poxy T-shirt scam was hardly a criminal mastermind. It was as though what I was reading and hearing about involved a different person altogether.

Charlie and two others, Robert Gould and Ronnie Fields, had been arrested in an elaborate sting set up by two Geordie police officers. He was allegedly caught on tape offering to supply cocaine to two businessmen (in reality policemen) who he had met and become friendly with.

On two occasions, Charlie had asked me to meet up with him to check his new friends out, but I couldn't make it due to other commitments. On hearing that it was those friends who turned out to be undercover policemen made me feel sick, and the fact that they were from up here didn't help. I could just picture him telling them how much he loved Newcastle and these two policemen just reeling him in.

One part of me was saying that if I'd met up with them, then just maybe, I could have sussed the pair of them out. *Maybe*. And then *maybe* Charlie would be a free man. The other part of me was saying that if I had been present at *any* of those meetings, then the chances were that I would be in a cell next to Charlie. In that sense, it was a huge relief.

He was remanded at Belmarsh High Security Prison in Woolwich. I kept in touch with him by letter and spoke to him on the phone. He was being held as a triple A category prisoner on twenty-three hours lock-up, high risk and likely to abscond … at seventy years of age.

I tried to keep his morale up and to let him know that we were all thinking of him. He wrote back saying how much he appreciated my effort. He remained as positive as he could in his situation, but he knew that if things went the wrong way for him, the consequences were not worth thinking about. On 6 August, he wrote to me asking if I could sort security out for him if he got bail. *That's* how positive he was about his chances. Inside, he had the likes of Charles Bronson and Dave Courtney as company. I was in touch with Dave, as he was waiting for a court date, too.

Charlie was coping well, and in telephone conversations he always sounded upbeat. I could always read between the lines, though – he would never say it outright, but he was worried beneath his 'typical Charlie' exterior.

He talked a lot about his girlfriend Judy Stanley; he asked me to send her cash and to make sure she was all right. He was never selfish in that respect. In one letter dated 2 December 1996, he said he wondered when it would all end … that he sat on his own, thinking, contemplating the future, and said he didn't know what he'd do without Judy. It was obvious that his thoughts of her kept him going.

When Dave walked free from his appearance almost a year later, we both agreed to meet up in June to stand as character witnesses for our mate Charlie. Charlie had written to me just after Dave went free saying "what a result" it was and that he was pleased for him. He said it must be the best feeling in the world. Now he had to prepare himself for his own trial.

I travelled down to London by train and arrived in King's Cross on 5 June 1997 to attend Charlie's trial the following day at Woolwich Crown Court, next door to Belmarsh Prison. It was nearing a year since his arrest now. Christian met me off the train just after midnight and we went for a drink. We made our way to a quiet, shady-looking snooker club just outside the station and as we reached the bar, I couldn't help but feel we were slightly out of place.

We were the only white people in there; the rest of the punters were oriental ... then it dawned on me that we were in Triad territory. The snooker club was one of their many after-hours dens but after initial apprehension and a few drinks, I began to feel quite at ease. We played snooker for a while and had a quick bite to eat, leaving at 3.30 a.m.

We talked a lot about what we'd each been up to recently, what other friends had been up to and just generally caught up with things. Chris is one of those people that no matter how long it has been since you last met, you can catch up immediately like you only saw each other last week.

Always one for surprises, he then told me that we would be sleeping at the Hammersmith Apollo. He was working there for a security firm, so he was able to get us into one of the dressing rooms to doss down for a few hours before the trial. The dressing room had just been used by Sir Cliff Richard during his *Heathcliff* show, but we tried not to let that bother us.

After a restless sleep, we made our way to Woolwich. We arrived on time and were greeted outside the court by Frankie Fraser and Charlie's QC, Mr Goldberg. Frankie said that another solicitor, Michelle Haeems, was looking for me to clarify a few points relating to the evidence I was due to give. Not knowing which way to go, I followed Frank and Goldberg into the court buildings. As we entered, we went through the security checks and emptied our pockets for inspection.

I found Michelle Haeems waiting for me on the next floor up. She asked if in May 1996 I had ever met Charlie or arranged to meet him. I told her I had spoken to Charlie but couldn't meet him due to a prior engagement. Michelle was happy with that and told me to wait in the canteen and that my name would be called on the speaker system when I was needed.

The trial was to be held in court number one. The canteen was full of familiar faces – Frankie Fraser, Charlie's close friend John Corbett, Eileen Sheridan, the former Miss UK, Billy Murray from ITV's *The Bill*, Ray Burdis, and Les Martin, one of Charlie's biggest supporters.

Whilst seated in court with a tense atmosphere, this was the first point that I let the enormity of the situation hit me. I could see the anxiety in people's faces and that made me stop to think. When I first heard about the charges, like many others, I just dismissed the whole episode as a mistake or another attempt to get the Krays that was so absurd that it would be laughed out of court.

When encountering the scale of security, the police, the hype, the press turnout – it began to hit home. The conversation centred on Charlie's chances. We all made positive noises, but there was an underlying feeling of a long, long sentence. We seemed to be spending too much time in the canteen, and as I downed my fourth cup of coffee at 11.10 a.m., an announcement informed us that council had been removed from court.

The clock ticked slowly ... at 12.20 p.m., an early lunch was called ... at 1.30 p.m., another announcement ... there would be no evidence heard that day due to legal arguments. We were told that a member of the jury had either recognised or had had an encounter with a defence witness the previous day, so as a result, the juror was removed, and the jury reduced to eleven. I felt deflated. There had been bad vibes throughout the day, and this was the icing on the cake.

On leaving the canteen, I met up with Christian, sank a few pints and then caught the train back to Newcastle. There didn't seem like that much to talk about as we sat in the pub. We made small talk and arranged to meet up on the following Tuesday, when we would be going through it all again.

Tuesday, 11 June arrived; I had travelled down on a late-night train again. I went to the court the following morning. Already there was Fethi, a Turkish restaurant owner from Birmingham, and Jon Ivey, the director of a recently released play based on Tony Lambrianou's life and book called *Inside the Firm*.

That day, there was a prompt start. As we reached court one, we were all flanked by armed officers and were once again searched thoroughly as we passed through the security cordon leading to the court and the public gallery. I was led through to the defence witness waiting room, where I made polite conversation with Fethi and Jon, and we discussed Charlie's chances. The atmosphere once again felt gloomy. No one sounded positive about the outcome; sometimes, people put on a brave face and say that everything will be all right when they know it is unlikely. Well, no one even bothered going through the motions in this case.

I was the last person called in the morning session. The usher called out my name and I got up and walked to the packed courtroom. The air was stifling, making me immediately uncomfortable as the court usher led me to the witness box. It was a tense situation to be in. I caught a glimpse of Charlie behind a glass partition, standing between two burly prison officers. If I felt this uneasy after a few minutes, I could only imagine how he was feeling.

I swore an oath and was questioned by Goldberg for the defence. Goldberg, like Charlie, was suntanned and expensively dressed. I thought he seemed a bit smug, almost arrogant, as though the case would win itself. I just hoped his overconfident manner was justified.

After confirming my name, address and occupation, Goldberg went straight into asking about the magazine, *Number Nine*. I wasn't too sure where the line of questioning was leading. I was asked about how many copies I'd sold and was asked about Newcastle United – had I met them, did I know them ... then was handed an autographed football and was asked to comment on it. I said that it looked like an autographed football, but after looking closely, realised they were all fakes and told the court that none of the signatures were genuine. He then asked if I'd heard of autographed footballs being auctioned, and how much one would fetch if it were genuine.

"Anything up to £100. I have also seen footballs like this autographed by Sunderland's team, but they don't make very much, sir."

I don't think they understood my attempt to be court jester.

He then asked how I had got to know Charlie.

"Basically, through my magazine. Others involved sent copies to sporting heroes such as Kevin Keegan and Peter Beardsley, I sent mine to Ron and Reg Kray, as I had heard a lot about them and was curious as to their response. They replied to my letters, and to cut a long story short, I visited the twins in prison and was then introduced to Charlie; it was a natural progression. I spoke to Charlie on the phone at first."

"When did you first meet the defendant?"

"The 24th of February 1994 at Guvner's pub in the East End of London."

"What was Mr Kray doing there?"

"He was playing the host, meeting people and generally socialising. It was a charity event in aid of a young child suffering from cerebral palsy."

"Was it true that you held a party at which Charles James Kray again played host?"

"Yes, it was. I organised a party for a young boy called Terry Moran at The Elysium Lane social club in Bensham, Gateshead. Terry had suffered 80 per cent burns in a bonfire night accident, and both Charlie and Tony Lambrianou agreed to travel to Newcastle to help support this event."

I also told the court that Charlie did not receive any payment or travelling expenses and that a member of his family was quite ill at the time, and while others may have cancelled, Charlie honoured his agreement and attended. I went on to say he socialised and was a great host. He posed for every photograph, signed every autograph, and said it was one of the best nights he had ever had.

"Was footballer Paul Gascoigne at this event?"

"Paul was invited, and indeed his mother, two sisters and aunties were there, but Paul could not make it as he was signing for his new club, Glasgow Rangers, at the time. In summing up, I was asked to describe him. I said he was affable, friendly and a good host. "I am proud to call Charlie Kray my friend," I concluded.

"No further questions."

I looked over to Charlie. He winked and smiled; he was obviously pleased with my performance. I reluctantly call it a performance, because it hints that I was putting on a show or lying. I'd told the truth throughout. I glanced around the courtroom; it was such a strange feeling standing in the box defending one of the Krays; I couldn't help but imagine what the people in the courtroom were thinking, especially the jury.

I just hoped that I'd helped in a small way to reduce whatever sentence Charlie was going to receive. Judge Carroll interrupted my thoughts by asking QC for the prosecution, Mr Kelsey-Fry, if he had any questions for me. He did.

Kelsey-Fry was concise. He certainly knew what he was doing throughout. He had a Kray in court and knew he would be the one to put Charlie in prison. He asked me if I had ever let Charlie Kray down, arranged to meet him and not turned up, or ever arranged to meet Charlie Kray for a drink in Croydon. I replied no to all three questions. He and the judge thanked me, and I was free to go.

With that, I looked towards the jury, then Charlie, who once again gave me a reassuring smile, and I was led down from the witness box and escorted up to the public gallery. All the chaps who were present congratulated me on my 'performance', as that's how court is always perceived in gangland; compared to a stage. Act innocent ... make him sound like a good person ... do this, do that. I was just glad it was over for me. I had done my bit, and now it was up to the jury to see that justice was done.

I was curious as to Kelsey-Fry's line of questioning. I now know that Charlie was recorded on tape arranging to meet a Steve (not me) in Croydon, and the prosecution just wanted this point clarified. Goldberg, with his questions, wanted me to portray Charlie as a kind-hearted man who would do anything for anybody, and make out that the police were liars intent on setting Charlie up. He was trying to build a case for entrapment, and I personally didn't think that was the greatest of ideas, but I was only a post office manager, not *Columbo*. As far as I was concerned, I'd told the truth and had hopefully helped a friend out.

I had followed Frankie Fraser into the witness box. Charlie's chances had not been helped after Fraser managed to turn the whole thing into a farce. On leaving the witness box, he told everyone that it was the first time he'd ever left court a free man. Okay, it *is* funny … until you put it into context. He was supposed to be a character witness for someone in a serious situation. Did he think that saying what he did would help Charlie? These were the kind of favours he could do without.

I left Woolwich that day with a lot of thoughts running through my head. I wasn't sure what the outcome would be of the trial. It wasn't looking good, but I still believed in a man being innocent until proven guilty. Charlie was on my mind. I felt I'd done all I could and now it was out of my hands. His whole future was at stake in that courtroom, though for a lot of people it was just treated as a day out.

On my way home, I thought a lot about the Krays and my relationship with the family. It had been a long time since my first meetings with them, a long time since I had contacted them as a fan … and that day I'd just stood up for one of the brothers as a character witness in court. That's how much our friendship had developed, and I'm proud to say I was able to support them in court. I wasn't a mobster from the old days, but I was respected enough to be asked and it meant a lot to me. I know it meant a lot to Charlie that I had been there, too.

I was unable to attend the rest of the trial but, as fate would have it, I could make it for the verdict. My football team always had an annual trip away and for the second year running, we visited London. We set off mid-afternoon on Friday, 20 June, and by 7 p.m. my mobile phone battery was close to exhaustion with the news breaking that Charlie had been found guilty on both counts, and that sentencing would be delivered on the Monday. I was devastated but, if honest, I'd expected it. All Charlie could hope for now would be a lenient sentence.

On the day of sentencing, the usual security was in operation, but this time we were made to queue up outside to make our way to the public gallery of court number one. I can only imagine this was for the benefit of the media, who had gathered to capture us all on film. There were all the usual Kray fans trying to get their faces on TV and in the papers, but my respect goes to the loyal friends who attended – Dave Courtney, Christian Simpson, Les Martin and Kiwi Andy – and kept a dignified silence.

That day was also the first time that I had seen Charlie's co-defendants. In stark contrast to Charlie, who was immaculately dressed as usual, Robert Gould and Ronnie Fields were dressed in drab, everyday civvies. Whether this was just pessimism on their behalf, I don't know. I'm sure they could have tried to look respectable if they wanted to, and it may have worked a bit in their favour. It is possible to pick a suit up for a few quid these days or a tie for even less. Maybe they were trying to avoid appearing like ruthless drug barons.

Charlie gave it one last throw of the dice, with an emotional plea to the judge and jury. He was desperate – desperate to somehow convince them and desperate for a way out. He knew his fate was sealed and had to say his piece.

"All my life I would advise people, particularly young people, never to be involved in drugs. Juries have got it wrong before about me, and this jury has got it wrong. I swear on my son's grave I have never handled drugs in my life."

He was given twelve years on count one (offering to supply five kilograms of cocaine every fortnight for two years), and eight years on count two to run concurrently (helping to supply a two-kilogram consignment). I looked at him as the sentence was read out. He was stunned, essentially given a death sentence. I think he knew it as well … it is certainly what everyone in that room was thinking.

Judge Carroll's retort was short and to the point, "Throughout this case you have professed your abhorrence against drugs. The jury's verdict has shown your oft-repeated protestations to be hypocrisy. Those who deal in drugs can still expect justice from the courts but little mercy." He appeared like the headmaster you always disliked at school. As far as he was concerned, Charlie was a Kray and he was guilty – end of story.

Gould received five years for his involvement and Fields got nine. Once sentencing was passed, Charlie turned and blew a kiss to Judy Stanley, then waved to all of us in the gallery. He was led down to the cells beneath the courtrooms to begin his sentence. That was it ... over. We filed out of the gallery, outside to the waiting media, and whilst the usual 'friends' waffled on about how they had known the Krays for years, I quietly slipped away with Dave Courtney and the chaps for a few drinks in The Albion, something Charles James Kray would never be doing again.

On subsequent visits to Charlie, and through letters and phone calls, he told me in detail about the events surrounding his arrest and eventual imprisonment. On my first visit to him, he told me about the operation that had him recorded, set up, entrapped – call it what you want – that was called operation ACID.

The first meeting between them all took place at the Medallion Vert Hotel in Moseley, Birmingham, on Thursday, 9 May 1996. Present at this meeting were Patsy Manning (Patsy is from Birmingham and it was his sixty-sixth birthday party), Deano and George, who had travelled together from London, Jack who had travelled from Newcastle, and Charlie. This was one of the times Charlie had asked me to come along and for reasons that I am now glad of, I couldn't make it.

Deano and Jack already knew each other in this scenario. They were the two undercover policemen from the North East. Patsy was a long-time friend of Charlie's and the twins. As the meeting progressed, they had a few drinks and began to acquaint themselves, talking about times they had visited one another's hometowns and friends they had in common.

Patsy and Jack discussed how depressing the atmosphere in Newcastle was until the mid-Eighties, when money was injected into the pubs and clubs of the Quayside. Jack claimed to have invested money in the area around ten years earlier and mentioned that Deano should bring Patsy up to Newcastle some time. Patsy said he'd use Jack's name when he was there in the usual manner of 'I'm a mate of Jack's ... nudge, nudge' to get looked after.

Jack also claimed to have "done some work" in London, but all this boasting was an obvious front to make himself more credible in his present company. He was talking the talk and bluffing about a fabricated criminal past. Charlie also mentioned Newcastle, telling of the charity event I'd organised that he and Tony hosted. He told them that he met Gazza's family there and had his photo took with them, and went on to tell them about me. I know this to be a fact. My name brought into the conversation – no matter how innocent – associated me with Charlie.

I didn't know it at the time, but the police would most likely have been watching my movements. They would have been aware of me anyway, but would now be aware of my name for another reason, because of Charlie's name-dropping.

As he told me this, I thought back to the night of the charity event. I remembered that we'd shared jokes about police being present ... singling out a few people we said looked like coppers, but it was all in good humour. Now the irony was that we were most likely right.

It would stand to reason that there would be a police presence, as Charlie and Tony in the same room were quite an attraction. I was frantically trying to think if I'd noticed anything out of the ordinary at the party, but it was impossible. The whole night was out of the ordinary. All eyes had been on Charlie.

Their meeting in Birmingham was full of 'any friend of mine is a friend of yours' conversations. They had even discussed the twins themselves ... Patsy reminiscing about the first time he met them in the Sixties, around a week after arriving in London. I could imagine them both in their element discussing 'the days'.

Jack and Deano must have been convincing. They told of connections in Brussels and discussed a piece of work they had recently handled. It was a general bonding meeting of 'friends.'

The criminal language was apparent – doing 'jobs' and 'work' is not the sort where you send in a résumé and sit an interview. Such claims from an undercover policeman are to earn respect and trust within the group. Charlie told me that he had no reason to doubt their credibility.

Charlie loved to tell his stories about meeting this person and that person … he told them about Jackie and Joan Collins, Barbara Windsor, times he met Sonny Liston and what they talked about. He and Patsy took turns in retelling one story about Charlie, the twins, George Raft and Rocky Marciano. They had got together in Bethnal Green and Patsy had been told by Reg to get over and meet them. He got there as quick as he could in a taxi but missed out on a photo opportunity with them by one minute. Billy Daniels was brought into the conversation as well. Famous names … boxing … it was all déjà vu.

More déjà vu was about to come. As I was learning about these conversations after the trial, there were things that started to come together. There had been conversations from these meetings on tapes, which were used as evidence and played to the jury at the trial.

In one of these tapes, Jack was heard asking Charlie if he wanted a signed football for a charity event to help raise money. If I were a gambler, I'd put money on it being the football I was asked to comment on in court, where the signatures were all fakes.

For such a large-scale operation, I would have thought that the signatures would be genuine. As I was hearing all this, I was kicking myself. If I'd been there, maybe I could have sussed them out at this point – ask how they knew the team and other details which would have put them on the spot.

Charlie's memory for detail was impeccable. He could tell me every date they met, where they met, what they discussed – everything. It was like the museum curator confessing to a crime at the end of an episode of *Scooby Doo*.

As he told me about the meetings, I couldn't help but wonder about the whole 'deal'. To begin with, I had been under the impression that he'd been innocent all along. Now I wasn't so sure. It was difficult to know what to think.

He told me that they stayed over at the hotel and the next day arranged further meetings. Jack and Deano discussed business in Amsterdam and 'a problem' over there, where someone died suddenly.

This was the first time where drug activities were hinted at. Someone dying suddenly, a problem and Amsterdam equals drugs and gangs to me. He didn't elaborate the story any further but said that Jack wanted to do business with Charlie's firm because he had been 'let down' on a deal.

He was interested in Charlie (cocaine) and Nordle (cannabis), and the supply of it all. Charlie (Kray), whether we like to admit it or not, had offered to supply a large amount of drugs to someone.

The gist of the discussion was that Charlie said he could not discuss a price just then, but they would have to wait until further arrangements were made. It would be possible to arrange a regular supply of drugs soon. Charlie was enthusiastic about the whole thing. They exchanged phone numbers, Jack not wanting a lot of people involved ... only he and Deano would be involved from their side, well, those two and the rest of the police force.

Charlie arranged their stay at the Selsdon Park Hotel in Croydon under different names. Apparently, he'd seen O.J. Simpson there before, "He was guilty as the day is long. I don't mind people getting a result, but not him." I wondered if this was because he thought that O.J. was guilty all along, but good lawyers had made sure he walked free. Maybe he was bitter that his own lawyer had not done the same for him, I don't know.

Jack brought someone else to the hotel instead of Deano – another officer going by the name of Kenny from Manchester, but any friend of Jack's was a friend of Charlie's. Okay, so he had just met Jack to discuss drug trafficking and now Jack had brought someone else in on it who Charlie had never laid eyes on in his life ... and this was all right with Charlie. It sounded odd ... naive that a drug trafficker would have such disregard for caution. They were talking tens of millions of pounds, not just a ten-quid wrap of speed.

I found it hard to work Charlie's logic out. He'd tell me all this so matter-of-factly ... sipping his tea at intervals, leaving me hanging on his every word. I couldn't believe some of the details he was recalling. To me, this was one of the most important Kray stories. I think more so because it happened in my time and I knew him when it happened – I was almost part of it, too. It also has importance to me because, like all other Kray stories, it was controversial. The more Charlie spoke, the more amazed I was that we were not having the conversation in Broadmoor.

Charlie told of his outlandish boastings about himself in Manchester, where he lost £100,000 on a deal. On hearing this, you may be hoping that drug trafficking is not Charlie's day job, but he told them that he had sorted the problem out by putting 'five grand' up to eradicate the issue, which in gangland terms suggests only one thing.

I'd rarely seen Charlie with more than 100 pence in his pocket, let alone £100,000, or £5,000 for that matter ... it was just part of his personality, his trademark.

Of course, they didn't believe him. They may have pretended to believe him at the time, but in reality, they would have known all his moves for some time and known it was a lie. It was all talk. I know from sources that they said a lot of his comments were, "Bullshit ... all big talk ... not a word of truth in it."

If Charlie was a big-time drug dealer and they knew it, I don't know why they would laugh off his stories as false. It seemed to suggest that they knew Charlie was just talking the talk without walking it. The whole situation seemed to be one contradiction after another from both sides. He'd told me in the past that he knew the police had turned a blind eye to some of the minor crimes he'd been involved in and he knew he had been watched on several occasions, but this time it seemed he was oblivious to the fact that he was meeting up with police and saying he could supply them with a load of dust.

They discussed quantities, which Charlie said would be tonnes … a serious deal from the size of it. This interested Jack; he told Charlie that he could move a regular supply in large quantities, but the price of the cocaine would have to be right. I'm not sure what the norm is for cocaine deals, but if I were buying from someone who kept meeting up with me and repeating how big it was going to be, I'd lose my patience and go elsewhere for it.

At no point could Charlie have sounded like he knew what he was doing … he just kept making the same promise to them over and over. I don't know whether it was a bluff or complete nonsense, or both. The police were quite prepared to wait for him to set the deal up, discussing it so many times on tape that he would incarcerate himself.

As the visit ended, we embraced as we said our goodbyes. I felt sad for him and for what he had done. My visits from then on consisted mostly of conversations about the deal and the trial.

The next time we met, Charlie looked much different. His suntan had faded, his grey hair had grown through the dye and he had begun to look like the old man that he was. He always looked healthy with a tan, adding to his flamboyant 'playboy' appearance. Now he just looked like any other man in his seventies.

Straight into the visit and he picked up where he'd left off on the story. There were things he'd told Jack that really made him feel like a 'mug'. There was the part in the last visit where he mentioned knowing the police had watched him in the past, which he'd even told Jack; there was some other information he told him, too.

Charlie had a friend, an ex-policeman, who had told him this originally. Scotland Yard have a list of criminals whose phones they periodically tap for two weeks at a time. He told him one time, "You're hooked up," which is why Charlie wouldn't discuss any business over the phone.

Now Charlie could think back to their meetings and realise

he'd been offering this kind of information to an undercover policeman. He'd start by saying he told Jack about being out with Denny Laine, formerly of Wings and The Moody Blues, then go on to tell me about a group called Phoenix, who he had done a "publicity thing" for around that time, with David Bailey taking pictures for them. The group was going to play at the Royal Albert Hall, and he was going to get tickets for Jack and Deano. If Dave Courtney was known as the Yellow Pages of Crime, then Charlie should simply have been known as the Yellow Pages.

We didn't talk much about the charity event where the football was auctioned, other than it was to raise money for St Christopher's Hospice, where Charlie's son Gary had died. It was at The Mermaid, and he told me it was a good do. They met up again around a week after the charity event … Jack phoning round as he'd been 'away' doing some business in Brussels. He called Charlie from Newcastle Airport, telling him he'd met up with the 'Brussels Firm' soon after the party, which was why he'd disappeared for so long. Maybe he just had the week off to spend with his family, who knows?

Charlie told me something that made me laugh. When he'd arranged the hotel rooms for Jack and Kenny, he told Jack to see a friend of his there who would "sort him out" – meaning he'd get a good deal. Jack didn't ask the bloke, though, and so ended up paying the full price for the rooms, which was ninety-five quid each.

Patsy heard about this and said it was Charlie's fault and that he should have phoned up to arrange the rooms for Jack and not left it down to him. Jack just shrugged it off … well, it had all come out of the taxpayer's pocket anyway. Charlie was told that Patsy had said this and, whether true or not, knew it was just to try to break their friendship up. It really meant nothing to him in the scheme of things.

Things got moving. Charlie and Ronnie Fields were invited up to Newcastle. Jack sorted some plane tickets so they could fly up, with the idea that they would get together somewhere quiet to discuss business. Charlie contacted Ronnie and they flew from Gatwick to stay overnight in Newcastle. Jack made it clear he wanted it to be low profile, with just Charlie and Ronnie, and none of Ronnie's firm.

Then Charlie let rip with another bombshell – they asked for the airline tickets to be booked in their own names, Charlie Kray and Ronnie Fields. I later heard that the police were in their element over details like this. Here were two known criminals, each with a long history, travelling together to discuss drug trafficking and using their names.

Knowing the conversations that took place, actions were inconsistent with the use of common sense. Using their own names was hardly the actions of two major drug dealers. I assumed that even small-time criminals would have used different names; again, it looks like the work of rank amateurs. Both men had criminal pasts and were still active, so I'd have thought just trying to cover their tracks at least *slightly* would have been second nature to them.

They spoke on the phone for the next few days, until 26 June, when Jack met Charlie and Ronnie at Newcastle Airport and they got into his four-wheel drive jeep. Along the way, Charlie mentioned that Fields had noticed a cream Vauxhall following them for quite some time, but they just laughed it off as paranoia. Still, they didn't seem too paranoid when arranging bookings in hotels and for plane tickets, as they were booked into the hotel under the same names as well.

They made their way over to The Linden Hall Hotel in Longhorsley, near Morpeth, making small talk along the way. Charlie remembered that they discussed things such as Fields getting married in September, and that his ex-missus had been a staff nurse who was always handy for "patching people up".

Also, they talked of a mate of theirs from the North East called Dingus McGhee, who was serving time for killing two policemen. They even joked on, with Jack saying that if he pulled into a quarry, neither Fields nor Charlie would get out of the jeep … they said they wanted it to be the start of their business relationship, not the end of it. They talked about bodies turning up in similar vehicles in London. I suppose at least in their present company, they were safe in that respect.

They reached the hotel, a big stately home out in the country; Charlie was well impressed with it. Kenny was there to meet them, and another bloke called Brian, who was part of their 'firm', i.e., he was an undercover officer, too. Charlie and Field's room was obviously bugged. They'd had plenty of time to set microphones. On the night, they had drinks and watched England playing Germany in the Euro 96 semi-finals, and then on the Thursday morning they met up in one of the rooms to discuss the drugs deal.

Jack apparently started by saying they wanted cocaine and they wanted it regularly. Charlie told me that Jack and Fields discussed the purity of the cocaine at a 'wash-up' of something like 90 to 92 per cent, Fields assuring him it was of high quality. Part payment was to be made up front, with only those present at the meetings to be involved in it.

Brian had suggested a driver might be used, though he would have no idea that it was a drug deal. Also, using their own driver would cut costs down. Fields said they could have five kilos to start with and Jack said they would want that every fortnight. They agreed a one-week timescale for Jack and Brian to raise the cash and would contact Charlie if they got hold of it any earlier.

Jack and Fields discussed a price for five kilos – it was set at £31,500. There was talk of other drugs, too, as they discussed buying and selling cannabis.

As Charlie started to tell me the sort of prices and quantities they were discussing, I couldn't help but think how foolish they had been. I have no doubt that the policemen excelled at their job … it must have been difficult, stressful, dangerous work for them. Charlie and Fields *were* setting up a major drug deal with them – there is no ambiguity there.

There was no false evidence, tapes were played, and it proved that they had discussed all this. There wasn't any way out as far as I could see. Charlie even recalled a veiled threat from Fields, where he'd said the money had better be real – the last person who tried to pay in fakes ended up in a Range Rover (hinting towards an *Essex Boys*-style murder over counterfeit money). Okay, he was joking, but when we know he was saying it to policemen, it could be something else for them to investigate.

The deal was set at The Selsdon in Croydon, where the five kilos would be handed over and driven up to Newcastle. Brian and Jack were to bring money to pay for three kilos and settle the rest once they had sold some of the cocaine. This was in July of 1996, when there was a lot more calls and sorting out to be done for the imminent deal. Charlie, in true Charlie form, had told them he was skint and wanted to borrow an advance of £500 for a trip to Birmingham. It was sent to him by registered post.

Each time Charlie told me of their meetings, whether face to face or in letters, he'd say what 'nice blokes' they were. Again, it just emphasises that they were good enough to fool these drug traffickers. I always wonder if undercover police ever do genuinely like the people they deal with or if it is all an act where they really can't stand being in their company.

Charlie always did have a love for storytelling and name-dropping; he told stories to the police in confidence that others would never hear, as did Ronnie Fields. Things like well-known underworld figures having mental breakdowns while "doing bird", unable to handle prison life and various other scams they were running … all of which they were kicking themselves over once they sat back and remembered all the conversations they'd had.

Tony Lambrianou phoned me a few months after Charlie started his twelve-year sentence, offering me the chance to supply the security for a gala night in an Essex golf club to raise money for his appeal. I'd already had a letter from Charlie on 6 August 1997, after his sentencing, saying he thought the appeal would be his last chance.

I told Tony I would be proud to if I wasn't stepping on anyone's toes, namely Dave's. He told me I wasn't and that it was on Dave's recommendation that he had called me. I recruited the best of the best ... John Lillico, Christian, Andy, Kiwi Andy, Darren Newmass and a couple of Christian's mates.

The clubhouse was brand-spanking new, and the guest list read like a who's who of gangland. There was Joe Pyle, Frankie Fraser, Freddie Foreman, Tommy Wisbey, Tony Chris and Nicky Lambrianou, Roy Shaw, Dave Courtney and Les Martin.

There were the usual celebrities, such as Billy Murray, Ray Winstone (brilliant in *Lenny Blue*), Karl Howman and Shane Richie. The Rockin' Berries provided the entertainment, and Frankie Fraser's wife Marilyn performed a couple of numbers, too.

The night was a great success and Tony raised a healthy five-figure sum for Charlie and his appeal. Les Martin was often looked upon as a bit of an oddball amongst the 'Kray Circle', and a lot of his so-called friends slagged him off behind his back. Les is a bit of a Super Fan and would get carried away with events, hiring limos and the like, and just enjoyed his time. He was well into the Kray story and was a good friend to Charlie.

Les was the only one who would ask the questions and campaign on behalf of the Kray brothers; others may have had the intention, but he was the one out there doing it. His name is well known at the Home Office and for me, he is one of the unsung heroes of the Kray story.

After Charlie's trial and subsequent conviction, he worked tirelessly on his behalf to clear his name, even to this day, years after his death. Les had asked Christian and me to help him with the security at the court of appeal, as sometimes these events can get out of hand, especially if the appeal is successful and the conviction overturned. We accepted the invitation and were both present throughout the hearing.

Unfortunately, all his work was in vain. In February 1999, three judges at London's Law Courts – The Lord Chief Justice, Lord Bingham, Mr Justice Ian Kennedy and Mr Justice Jackson – rejected Charlie's appeal. He was told he'd be able to appeal against the length of his sentence once he'd served half of it. He had made a plea for mercy on the grounds of old age, but it was apparently up to the Secretary of State to release someone on compassionate grounds. There were plans to write to the Home Secretary, Jack Straw.

He was moved from Belmarsh to Long Lartin Prison and then to Frankland in Durham.

With him in Durham, it meant that I was closer to Charlie than any of his friends or family, and I helped by taking visitors to the prison from the station at Durham. When I had visited him earlier on in the year at Long Lartin, he had started to look his age as he settled into prison life. At Frankland Prison, he looked unwell.

As we talked, he would clutch his chest, sometimes pausing to catch his breath. I was concerned for him; he was in obvious pain but would try not to show it. He would love to reminisce about "that night" in Gateshead. It really had been one of the nights of his life and he had never forgotten the welcome that he had received from the Geordies.

He had accepted his sentence now and knew in his heart that he would never see the outside world again. My only disappointment was when Charlie's ex-wife Diane came to visit him. I had arranged for her to be picked up and driven to the prison. Unfortunately, I was let down, and so let Charlie and Diane down at the same time. It meant she missed half an hour of her visit, and it's something I've always felt bad about.

I had not visited Reg for almost six months when, out of the blue, he called me to thank me for what I was doing for Charlie. He never ceased to amaze me. Sometimes, he could be completely insensitive and ungrateful, and then just when you didn't expect it, he would surprise you. It was good to hear from him again, though.

We discussed our concerns for Charlie, as he was not looking well at all when I had last seen him; I told Reg I'd do all I could to help Charlie out. It was hard to imagine right then, but the reality was that the Krays were dying out. Both surviving brothers were in poor health and in prison for what would surely be the rest of their lives. They remained eternally optimistic about their predicament. They had to … in prison, you can never give up.

On my first visit to Charlie in Durham, he asked me all kinds of questions about the policemen who had nicked him. He wanted to know who they were, but I could not provide answers. He even employed private detectives to try to find out who they were. It wasn't that he wanted 'revenge' in the sense you may be thinking – nothing like that was ever discussed at all.

What he wanted was to find out who they were and find out as much about their past as possible. In short, he wanted to know if they had any skeletons in their closets … anything he could find to tarnish the reputations of these men, in doing so questioning the validity of the evidence against him. His appeal had been rejected and this was how Charlie wanted to try to beat the police.

The way he had been caught was for Charlie a bitter pill to swallow. He wanted to play as dirty as he thought they did … he wanted to find as much dirt on them as he could before launching his next appeal.

My next visit, we chatted more about the events that put him where he was. He was still thinking about the future, though; he wanted out of prison desperately. The wheels were still in motion for his next appeal, and he told me of his birthday bash in 1996 … the second time he'd asked me to make it to "meet his new friends".

I felt worse now. I know he knew he'd asked me to Birmingham that night, but we both never mentioned it. We knew it would have been difficult. He spoke to Jack the day before, which was 10 June 1996. It was held at the Wake Green Lodge Hotel, Fethi's place. Ronnie Fields couldn't make it as he was 'waiting for a delivery'.

Jack was bringing Brian down to it from Newcastle. Not much was mentioned of the party itself. He just went on to tell me that the drugs they were to supply Jack with were delayed; there were a lot of calls between them over the next two weeks and a lot of waiting around. Charlie remembered that Jack was asking for specific times, which was annoying him, so he said he'd get Fields to tell him.

Fields called Jack to arrange further details. Apparently on 'business' calls, Fields would be called 'Mr Floyd' and would give out the number of a safe phone box for Jack to call him back on. *Good thinking, Ronnie.* They agreed to meet and make the deal in a few days' time, and Jack phoned Charlie back to confirm. He also asked if Charlie could sort some rooms at The Selsdon again for them.

There was some sort of problem when the two officers, Jack and Brian, met up with Ronnie Fields to do the deal. Charlie was not amused by whatever it was, but as he had to keep his voice low, it was hard to make out what he'd said. Basically, the deal didn't go according to plan and Fields had asked them to come back down in the next day or so. It was always difficult to make out the entire story, as there were always officers around during visits and we couldn't let anything be overheard.

The deal was back on and they were to meet at Waltham Abbey. Charlie made sure he was never present at the drug deal. That part of it was not his scene; his involvement was just to introduce people and help set things up. Ronnie Fields and Robert Gould turned up at The Swallow Hotel at Waltham Abbey in Essex as arranged. Gould was part of Fields' firm. The 'deal' took place ... they handed over two kilos of cocaine worth £63,000 to Jack and Brian. Both Fields and Gould were arrested on the spot. Charlie was arrested at Judy Stanley's flat in Sanderstead.

I've heard so many different stories about the whole drug case since it happened. Some parts are true and others are plain ridiculous ... others, I suppose, we will never know if they are true or not. All I can do is provide the information that I know and leave it up to people to draw their own conclusions.

Personally, I think the accusations against Charlie were true. I also think he had grounds to protest that he was 'stitched up'.

I can see both sides and that's how I want it to remain. I find it impossible to say that he was completely innocent. I could have believed it until I heard what went on at those meetings. Charlie only acted as a go-between to set the deal up ... at no point did he handle drugs.

I know that there were many things that Charlie said at these meetings that the police did not believe – that they knew he was making it up to make himself more credible in their company. This was no different to what they were doing. They were out to get him, there is no denying that. Charlie was a talker. He was looking for any deal. He was old and a deal like that would have been his retirement package.

I have no doubt that he would have sold Big Ben to them if they wanted it. They basically allowed him to talk himself into it. The way it dragged on and on only proved that he was no big-time drug trafficker ... but let's face it, Fields and Gould were arrested with the drugs on them. The deal *was* going ahead, and it was all down to these meetings ... all down to the big talk, the lies and seemingly inept means of bluffing his way through the whole affair.

Entrapment basically means to charm, delude or trick someone into doing something. They went for him, they charmed him ... they deluded him into thinking they were Geordie wide boys who wanted to buy cocaine. He had not approached anyone to try and push drugs. Operation ACID must have been planned for some time.

Undercover police could not have just infiltrated a gangland party one night wired up on the off chance that a coke deal would happen. It meant befriending people over a period (charm) and coming across as people of the same ilk (delude) in order to set up an elaborate deal (trick). I think they wanted Charlie Kray and he made it all too easy for them to get him.

But what could they possibly want him for? Why would they go after an old gangster who was still clinging onto the past and the legend that surrounded his name? This is where some of the rumours come in. It is alleged that the twins met Princess Margaret at society parties in the Sixties. It had been alleged that 'substances' were present and pictures were taken – typical Sixties parties, but the photos would be damaging to the monarchy or anyone else present.

It is also alleged that the Krays kept hundreds of files containing information about royalty, politicians and famous people – basically a huge collection of secrets about household names that could bring in millions of pounds in blackmail demands alone. These files are claimed to contain enough damning information to bring the country to its knees.

Therefore, it was imperative that all three brothers remained locked up until their deaths. It's no secret that the Krays knew a lot of influential people, and in the Sixties, their rise to power had a lot to do with knowing the right people ... more importantly, knowing the right things about the right people. The files are said to still exist. True or not, it is a theory that regularly does the rounds.

Another rumour was that Peter Beaumont-Gowling had offered Charlie Kray to the police as part of a deal. Beaumont-Gowling was a restaurateur from Newcastle, and had big connections in the drug world. He served four years of an eleven-year stretch for trying to launder £540,000. It was drug money from cocaine deals.

It is believed that he made a deal with the police to set Charlie up in exchange for his early parole. I don't know if this is true or not – it was certainly never discussed between Charlie and me.

Beaumont-Gowling was shot dead in his Jesmond flat in Newcastle, an area known for its wealth. It was said that Charlie ordered the hit on him from his deathbed and that Reg had suggested it, wanting revenge on the one who'd grassed him up. I just think it's another sensational story to link to the Kray legend. Of course, it *could* have happened, but it probably didn't happen ... who knows. It is something that all three took to their graves.

It could just be that Charlie and Fields had been involved in this type of activity for some time and the police went after them. The way the deal went, the build-up and the meetings, it is hard to imagine that they were experts in the profession, though.

Maybe they would have been better off going for real drug barons, the ones who own properties all over the world and turn over millions upon millions of pounds, the types who kill at the drop of a hat ... who are feared and consider the use of violence an everyday necessity. But instead, they chose to go for a couple of blokes who never had much money at all, relying on favours from people all the time who never even thought to cover their tracks by using different names.

Charlie had been naive and careless in getting involved. All the signs were there that this was a honeypot waiting for a bee ... the ultimate sting. His partners in crime should have known better, too. Charlie thought that if he did get caught, it would be okay, because he only introduced the two parties.

In the eyes of the law, that is known as setting up a drug deal and not simply known as 'Ronnie, this is Jack, Jack this is Ronnie'. He never physically handled drugs and made sure he had no part in the actual deal itself. Charlie was indeed always looking for a fast buck, but I'm convinced he wasn't trying to set himself up as the next Mr Big. Les Martin is carrying on the fight to clear Charlie's name to this day.

The Kray parties were still ongoing, but I had no real interest in attending any of the shams. Reg had asked me to help him out on more than one occasion with these events, but I told him I would do the security and nothing else. Reg had married a graduate named Roberta in July 1997 and although she had made such events more creditable, it was the people that they attracted that put me off.

Following on from the success of numerous books and of course the film *The Krays*, actor-turned-director Jon Ivey adapted Tony's book *Inside the Firm* into a stage play. Tony once again gave me a call regarding the security. I told him it would be a pleasure. We would only be required for the opening night, when the VIPs would be attending. I recruited the same chaps as I'd had at the party. The night ran like clockwork, and the play itself was excellent. The only pity was that the play never toured nationally.

Funerals

The day started just like any other. It was 17 March 1995. I had opened the post office as usual and went through my daily routine of serving the first few customers and then, when it was quiet again, retiring to the back of the shop for a cuppa and a read of the paper.

I always had the radio turned up high on Radio 1 or Virgin … as I sat down to glance at the headlines, the top news story was announced across the airwaves, "Former East End gangster Ronnie Kray has died." He had previously suffered from chest pains and had died of a suspected heart attack. He was sixty-two years old.

The news knocked me out of my routine. I was numb. I turned the dial on the radio from station to station to confirm what I had just heard. I couldn't believe it, but it slowly began to sink in. Only a couple of days earlier, I had sent him a get-well card. Everyone knew of his illness. Death may be inevitable, but it is often unexpected.

It did not take long for the phone to start ringing, but for a change, I was lost for words. I asked the journalists to give me a couple of hours to absorb the news before I answered their questions and made comments. I needed to make some phone calls of my own first. I phoned Reggie, then Charlie, Frank, Noelle Kurylo, Janet Alsop, Gary the gofer, Brad and Kim.

It was still sinking in the next day, when predictably the papers were full of stories about the twins. I had declined to comment to any of the major tabloids in case I was misquoted. I did talk to the locals … *The Journal*, *The Chronicle* and *The Gateshead Post*, whose journalists I knew I could trust.

During all this, my mate Ray Cann the tattoo artist asked if I intended to go to the funeral, and said that he would be willing to give me a lift there and back. I had not even thought about the funeral at this point, but I agreed and thanked Ray for the offer.

I had already got to know Ray well from our early involvement putting the charity events together, and now we were good friends. Over the next few days, the newspapers carried a different headline or different slant on the Kray story. It was a feeding frenzy. They ranged from Ron's alleged last words, to a statement he had made before his death that he was the evil twin and that Reg should be exonerated of all blame. For many, it will have made for an exciting read, but for me it simply hyped up the Kray legend and could only be detrimental to any plans of imminent release that Reg may have had.

Four days later, Reg called me with the details for the funeral.

The conversation was as follows:

"Hello, Steve, Reg here, have you got a pen? [I had.] Good. The funeral is Wednesday, 29 March. Make your way to English's Funeral Parlour for nine-thirty; your name will be with the security staff. I want you to make sure you get there. If you can't for whatever reason, be at St Matthew's Church for eleven; I will make sure you are on the list there as well. I'm organising the service, so you will get in."

I told him that Ron would be proud of him for all he was doing and for being strong. He agreed, saying he was now at peace. He had others to call, so after his usual 'God bless' he was gone.

I noticed he was a lot calmer than he had been on the day that Ron died. Reg seemed to have come to terms with his brother's death and was at peace with himself for a change. He seemed to be coping well with it. I phoned Ray and let him know that Reg had asked me to attend the service. He would start making the relevant arrangements ... time off work and use of a car for us to travel down.

I then phoned Michael Russen, the taxi company owner who I knew in East London, and asked him if it would be okay for us to stay at his flat overnight. No problem. He too seemed excited. Okay, I see the attraction of a Kray funeral and all that goes with it ... but to be *excited* about a funeral? Never mind.

My next call was to the local florists. My mate Fitzy's wife, Colleen, worked at Sarah Gaskin's in Newcastle and said they would make me a custom wreath, whatever I wanted, for a discounted price. I appreciated the gesture. I had given the wreath a lot of thought and decided that a cruise liner was appropriate, as Ron had told me on my first visit that that was his dream, to go on a round-the-world trip. I only wish that his dream had become a reality. But he was free now – free from the torment that had imprisoned him.

The day before the funeral, Gary phoned me to organise meeting on the day. Nine-thirty at the funeral parlour were Reg's instructions so I arranged to meet Gary fifteen minutes earlier. He did not seem too clear on the arrangements – if he was so close to Reg, why did it seem that I was telling him things for the first time? I had suspicions about Gary and his relationship with the Kray family; I decided not to dwell on it for the time being.

Mid-afternoon, Ray picked me up in a borrowed car, and after a quick photo-shoot with the wreath for *The Evening Chronicle*, we set off on our long journey to London. We met up with Mickey Russen at Scratchwood service station at the end of the motorway and he drove us the rest of the way into the heart of East London.

There was a lot on my mind that night. Funerals are always horrible things to have to go through, but gangland funerals will always lack that certain emotion you are used to. Gangland funerals are foremost a sign of respect by major figures from all over the country. It is a form of etiquette. All cultures have rules; the funeral marks the fact that the person had influence and people want to travel to show their support. There are different levels of intimacy ... I knew Ron well and knew that I was there for my own reasons.

My first job the next day was to write out the card that would accompany the wreath. I wrote: "You always wanted a round-the-world cruise. Now you are free enjoy it, Steve Wraith, Ray Cann, Michael Russen."

Radio Newcastle had asked me to speak to them that morning on their weekly phone-in programme with presenter Mike Parr.

I had done a lot of shows with Mike, so was prepared for his line of questioning. His stance was, "Why mourn the death of a psychotic gangster?" I told him and the listeners back in the North East that Ron had been a friend and that his past did not concern me. I knew him now, not as he was in the Sixties.

Due to the medication and the fact that he had been institutionalised for so long, he was a different man to the one the public had read about. My comments apparently caused uproar with the listeners, and phone-lines were jammed all day with people wishing to voice their concern about that "naive, misled youngster". Radio Newcastle had never had it so good!

The Krays were never going to get good publicity for anything. They are icons of underworld Britain … to mourn Ron, instead of saying "good riddance", the moral majority of listeners felt I didn't know what I was talking about. I knew more about it than most of them, so I did not let it bother me.

We left the flat at 8.45 a.m. Ray drove, while Michael gave directions. I sat at the back with the wreath. As we drove through the streets of East London, I thought about the day ahead and felt honoured to be part of it all. I was surprised at how quiet the roads seemed to be, as it was rush hour in London … then we hit gridlock a quarter of a mile from Bethnal Green Road, where English's was situated.

The roads that had been so good to us looked as if they were going to let us down. Somehow, we managed to push our way through the traffic, and with Mick's local taxi knowledge we reached the funeral parlour with a few minutes to spare.

We pulled up outside, behind a police cordon, and got out to lay our wreath. The first thing that struck me was the number of people gathering to witness another chapter in the Krays' storybook unfolding. It was an amazing sight – like a state funeral.

People were pushing to get a glimpse of anything … reporters and camera crews … police all over the place. It was at this moment I realised that I had finally walked into the books that I had read all those years ago, if that makes sense. I had read every book about the Kray twins and their associates, and now I was part of one. I was not just a bystander; I was a family guest.

The security was impressive. They were massive – all with as much jewellery as Mr. T, all immaculately dressed and intimidating. Leading the operation was Reg's close friend Mr Dave Courtney. As we mingled amongst the who's who of the underworld, we could hear the cameras clicking across the road. Photographers were perched, balanced and clinging on for dear life from different vantage points, all trying to get the best picture for the following day's papers.

I laid the wreath next to Reg's floral tribute, which read, "To the other half of me". As I stood up, I shook hands and embraced Dave. There was no sign of Gary, so as Ray parked the car, Mickey and I nipped to the nearest cafe for a cuppa. Once Ray had parked up, I cleared it with Dave to allow Ray and Mick into the parlour, as we waited outside.

It was impossible to walk anywhere at a normal pace. We just had to stand in line and shuffle in as best we could. I could still not take in the numbers of people that were congregating. The flashguns and the clicking of shutters rattled through the air again as a prison van pulled up outside. It turned into the alley adjacent to the parlour ... all eyes were on it, but no one emerged. God knows how many rolls of film were wasted in those few seconds.

There was confusion until a dark Peugeot pulled up with Reg handcuffed to a well-dressed screw as the passengers. He was led quickly and quietly into English's as the crowd cheered. The authorities obviously wanted to get him in unnoticed, which was an impossible job. Reggie Kray was back in the East of London once more.

We managed to get into the funeral parlour after around fifteen minutes of uncertainty and were shown to the room set aside for friends and relatives. A few familiar faces had already arrived in the shape of Frankie Fraser, Tony Lambrianou, Charlie Richardson and of course Charlie Kray. I also saw Alan and Janet Alsop – we were now good friends after sharing visits to Reg.

I introduced them to Ray and Mickey, before I beckoned one of the funeral directors over. I asked him to tell Reg that I had arrived, and within a few minutes, he re-appeared and took me to see him. I was led down a small corridor to an old oak-panelled door on the left-hand side. He pushed the door open and said, "You can take as long as you like, sir."

My jaw dropped. Instead of seeing Reg, I was now alone in the room with Ron's body in his coffin. I looked back and the door was closed behind me. It was no mistake. He was in a large oak coffin, his hair swept back and immaculate, as usual. He was dressed in a crisp white shirt and silk tie. Even in death, I thought to myself, he looked dignified and dapper – every inch the well-dressed gangster.

I know undertakers are experts at making the dead look good, but all the strain and mental torture that had been etched on Ron's face in his latter days had disappeared without a trace. It was like he had been wearing a mask and now it had been removed. He was free at last; he was completely at peace. I did not feel sad seeing him in the funeral parlour. I felt sad for the fact that he had died in prison. I felt sad for Reg and for Charlie, but in a way happy for Ron.

I put my hand on the coffin, said my own goodbye and left him for the last time. The funeral director had been waiting for me outside and led me back to another door on the opposite side of the corridor. As he opened the door, Charlie Kray spun around, greeting me, "Steve, good to see you, mate, thanks for coming down, it's a long journey." I shook his hand, and he pulled me towards him and embraced me. Standing next to him was Reg, handcuffed to a middle-aged prison officer.

He stepped forward, bringing the officer with him, and put his arm around me as best he could, saying, "Steve, thanks for coming, how are you?" He seemed calm, just as he had on the phone the last time we had spoken, a lot calmer than I thought he would be. English's had put on a lavish buffet for Reg, but food was the last thing on anyone's mind.

Reg then patted me on the head (he was always amused at my lack of hair) and asked, "Who have you come with?" I explained that I had driven down with Ray and met up with Michael, and that we were staying at his place. Quick as a flash, he asked, "What about Bulla Ward? Is Bulla here? Is he coming?"

Bulla and Reg had fallen out in the Sixties. Bulla was a tough bloke and laughed off one of Reg's punches one night in The Regency. There were not many men who could withstand one of his punches, so to save face, Reg had taken out a knife and carved Bulla's face up. He regretted them falling out and had asked me to get him there to make the peace.

To be truthful, with all that was going on, I had forgotten to ask Mickey whether he had managed to get in touch with Reg's old mate, and whether he would be attending the funeral to pay his last respects. Michael claimed to know him and had tried in vain to contact him before the funeral. I had tried as well but to no avail.

Thinking quickly, I replied, "He'll be here, Reg, paying his respects. Reg, I know he will."

Reg smiled, and then asked, "Has he forgiven me?"

I didn't quite know what to say. "Yes, Reg, he's forgiven you." What else could I say on the day of his brother's funeral?

"Good, good. Well, thanks for coming, Steve, I'd like you to go and see Ron now. I'll be in touch. In fact, you ring me later tonight, I'll let the staff know you're going to call, take care and God bless. Thanks again for coming."

He kissed me on both cheeks and embraced me. It was quite a moment, something I will never forget. Charlie repeated the farewell, saying, "I'll see you for a drink later on, Steve."

The same funeral director was waiting for me outside the door and began to lead me down to see Ron's body. "No, it's okay, mate, I've already seen him," I said. He apologised before taking me back to re-join Ray and Michael in the friends and relatives' room. I think they had felt a bit out of place standing alone.

I told them that I had been with Reg and Charlie, and had

been taken to see Ron. It was then that the whole emotion of the day hit me. I had always wanted to see the Kray brothers together, but not like this. I wiped a tear from my eye as we waited for others to pay their final respects to The Colonel and express their sympathies to his brothers.

By now, Dave was close to having a blue fit. "I'm fighting a losing battle. I've got old blokes trying to get in here, saying they are old friends of Ron, Reg, Charlie and any old uncle you can think of. I can't let everyone in, for God's sake." I didn't envy his job one bit, but I knew that if anyone could pull off the biggest organised funeral since Winston Churchill's, then he could.

Once everyone had paid their respects, the wreaths were loaded onto the glass, horse-drawn carriage and into the twenty-two limousines, which were to follow behind in procession. The horses were black and beautifully dressed, with long black plumes protruding from their heads.

We were ushered from the parlour and as we made our way outside, the flashing from the cameras dazzled us once more. There was pandemonium outside. Things were beginning to happen. Dave told me to make sure that I got into a car … it didn't matter which one.

We made our way down to the eighth car; a black, six-seater, top-of-the-range limo. No expense was spared. The cars were immaculate inside and out, and each one was decked in floral tributes (our wreath remained with Reg's tribute alongside Ron's coffin throughout the day, and could be seen clearly in photographs in most national newspapers the next day). Inside our car with me were Ray, Michael and Janet and Alan Alsop. The driver started the engine and with the rest of the procession, we were off on our long journey, first to St Matthew's Church in Bethnal Green, and then on to Chingford Mount Cemetery in Essex to the Kray family plot.

It was an unforgettable journey. We had only to travel approximately three quarters of a mile from the parlour to the church, but it took over forty-five minutes. The crowds of people were ten-deep, all leaning and peering over metal fences, which had been put up by the police.

I stared out at all the people. It was the sort of mania that's normally reserved for rock stars or movie idols ... certainly not the sort of admiration the authorities would expect the public to bestow upon a notorious murderer. Cries of "We love you" and "Good on you, Ronnie" could be heard; while in the distance, the clip-clop of the horses' hooves weaved their way to our first port of call.

I wondered what was going through Reg's mind as we passed along roads and streets that he had not seen for the best part of twenty-five years, and how he would feel as he passed along the street where he and Ron once lived.

As we neared the church, I caught a glimpse of Patsy Palmer (Bianca from the BBC soap *EastEnders*) paying her respects. The East End of London had changed so much since Reg had been taken away from it, and as we finally reached St Matthew's, I promised myself I would ask him how he had felt about what he had seen.

The scene when we reached the church was unbelievable. It was bedlam ... simple as that. Roughly 1,200 people had gathered outside the church gates and many were chanting, "Free Reg Kray. Free Reg Kray!"

I led the occupants of our car towards the church doors. Reg had arrived about two minutes before us and was already inside. At the doors, the orderly queuing system for friends and relatives had been reduced to a free-for-all.

At one stage, it looked like we would not get in. There was a public address system set up for those outside to hear the service, and I did not want to travel all that way to be stuck outside. I noticed the funeral director and luckily, he remembered me ... he ushered the five of us to the front of the crowd and into the church. The pews at the back of the church were all that was left, but I saw Dave and he waved me over.

The coffin was carried into the church by Johnny Nash from

North London, Teddy Dennis from the West, Charlie Kray from the East and Freddie Foreman from the South. Close friend Laurie O'Leary also helped take the coffin in.

Frankie Fraser had originally been asked but felt that his height may be a hindrance. Frank Sinatra's "My Way" played as the coffin was placed alongside Reg. The atmosphere was tense as the service began, the smell of incense hanging heavily in the air. Reggie, Charlie and Dave had masterminded the day's events to Ron's specification, and it was running like clockwork.

Throughout the service, Reg remained handcuffed to the officer. It did not seem to bother him too much. The officer was just there with him as opposed to trying to be heavy-handed.

Every so often, Reg would place his free hand on top of the coffin in a moving display of affection. But why handcuff a man who had no intention of escape? Why humiliate him? Was it a political statement by the Home Office that this man would never be free? Whatever the reasoning, to me it was inhumane. Okay, the officer was just doing a job … if they wanted to, they could have handled the situation differently and let him mourn without being chained to someone.

Sue McGibbon read out messages and telegrams from well-wishers. She also read out a message from Reg. It went, "My brother Ron is now free and at peace. Ron had great humour, a vicious temper, was kind and generous. He did it all his way, but above all he was a man, that's how I will always remember my twin brother Ron."

As the service ended, Ron's coffin was carried out to Whitney Houston's song, "I Will Always Love You". I don't think there was a dry eye to be seen in the rows and rows of hardmen. As Reg left the church, he winked at our group … he was bearing up.

It was bedlam once more as we made our way back to the car. The five of us held onto each other as we made our way through the swaying masses. It was all too easy to get split up as journalists and television and radio interviewers threw questions at us. I was not interested in commenting, not today of all days. I noticed a few others such as Patsy Manning, a close friend of the family, were willing to stop for a chat.

When we eventually made it back to the car, our driver was a little stressed out to say the least. Someone had climbed into our car and refused to move. The driver had tried to explain to him that he was in the wrong car, but he would not have it. After a quiet word, he left to find another car and more people to annoy.

Drama over, the driver started our six-mile journey to Chingford Cemetery ... take two ... enter nutcase door left. The front passenger door was pulled open and in stepped a middle-aged woman, who was madder than a coachload of Hatters at a magic mushroom convention. Her name was Georgina and she was armed with Valium in one pocket and half a bottle of whisky in the other (for Reg, apparently).

She told us a tale of woe – she was supposed to marry Ron before he died and told us a few other things I can't remember. The driver looked back for assistance, but as the procession of cars had already started to move, I told him to drive on. We would have to take our unwanted passenger with us.

As the car pulled away, we all exchanged anxious glances in the back of the car, as Georgina said, "We were going to have kids, you know." This was going to be a long six miles indeed.

This gave me another excuse just to sit back and watch the crowds. Young people, old people ... hundreds upon hundreds had gathered just to catch a glimpse of the brothers. There were many memorable sights throughout the day from that limo rear window, nothing more memorable than the sight that greeted us at the Bow Flyover. Construction work was taking place, yet the whole workforce had downed tools and were standing in a line by the roadside, hard hats off and heads bowed ... it was one hell of a sight. I can only imagine how Reg and Charlie must have felt.

As we reached Chingford, it had taken one and a half hours to travel six miles, though with Georgina in the front, it felt like one and a half days.

The horses pulling Ronnie's hearse had struggled up the steep bank leading to the cemetery gates, and we followed them in. By now, we were almost used to the strobe-effect lighting from the constant photographs, and the pushing and pulling of the crowds. As we followed the road to the family plot, our hitchhiker decided it would be a good idea to walk the rest of the way. There was no argument from any of us.

The surrounding fence to the cemetery had a lot of holes in it and I was shocked to see people, many of them kids, clambering through. If ordinary people had made it to the graveside, we might not gain our place next to the family.

I need not have worried. There were so many people around the grave, but they all kept a respectful distance as Reg first laid flowers on his mother and father's graves, and then his wife's. He paused a little longer there, his face full of sorrow and regret.

Just then, I felt a hand on my shoulder – it was Dave Courtney, looking less flustered than he had been earlier outside the funeral parlour. He asked me to look after Charlie for the rest of the day and to make sure he wasn't hassled by anyone. I told him I'd be honoured.

We made our way to where the family had gathered directly behind Charlie and Reg. There was a tremendous feeling of grief … then looking around, I began to wonder. It seemed a lot of people were there out of curiosity or to somehow enhance their stature from their association. There were 'tourists' – people just there to be a part of it all – staring at Reg all the time, studying his face for reactions and to witness the London gangland boss cry.

As the vicar spoke and Ron's body was finally laid to rest, the cameras flashed en masse for the last time. Ronnie Kray was the centre of the world's attention even in death. He would have loved it.

Reg threw the first piece of soil down onto the coffin and then arose, and then, one by one, we all did the same. Reg then turned, embraced Charlie, shook hands with Freddie Foreman and then out of the blue turned around to me and said, "Thanks for coming, Steve." He stretched out his hand and I grabbed it.

This time, it was my grip that was the strongest. Reg was finally drained of all energy. "I'll be in touch, Reg," I responded. With that, he was led away, pausing to say some more goodbyes.

As Reg left, I stared in disbelief at people, who will remain nameless, photographing the activities at the graveside. Several people who I used to respect lost my admiration that day.

After one last glance at Ron's grave, we all returned to our limos. All the wreaths lined the pathway to the grave, hundreds of them, and we paused to read as many as we could. We finally found our wreath, lying alongside Reg's. To me, it symbolised how close I had become to the Kray family, and I was glad to see it was still next to Reg's.

The driver had been told our destination … The Guvner's public house was the venue for the wake. Without the lovely Georgina, our journey seemed to be quicker and we arrived at the wake within twenty minutes.

There were already quite a few people in there and I could see that it was soon going to be packed out. It was a typical London boozer – dim, cramped, but with wet beer and good conversation. Already, there were people such as Frankie Fraser, Freddie Foreman, Charlie and his son Gary, Tony Lambrianou, Dave Courtney and of course Lenny McLean.

Lenny was still known as The Guvner of London and when I saw him again at the wake, I did not need to introduce myself. Lenny was the sort of bloke who would remember a name and it's always good when that happens. I never got the chance to meet up with Lenny again before his untimely death but followed his acting career with great admiration. The man was a real gent, a legend, and someone who I was proud to call my friend.

Tony Lambrianou was a member of The Firm and was one of the few who stood by the twins, receiving twenty years as his reward. I'd read his book, *Inside the Firm*, and got on well with him. This was the first time I had met Tony … soon after, he introduced me to Freddie Foreman and before long, I was talking with Frankie Fraser, Charlie Kray, Freddie and Tony about Ron and Reg, and their memories of the old days.

Charlie Kray was the perfect host as usual, smiling and chatting to everyone who was there, and thanking them for coming. He told me it had been a great send-off for his brother and that he would have loved it.

As we spoke, the early evening news appeared on the large television screens. A hush fell upon the room as people watched the first pictures from the funeral. The cameras only proved what I had already thought – that Ronnie Kray had received a funeral normally reserved for royalty.

Thinking of Charlie's words … it was true, he would have loved it. It was the best send-off a man could have asked for. There were tributes and messages from rock stars, TV stars and movie icons. The streets were full of mourners and well-wishers, people who were just dumbstruck by the whole thing, all his friends and media people from anywhere you could care to mention. It was the ultimate two-fingered gesture to the authorities, as he had the popularity to bring the nation's capital to a standstill.

As the night progressed, I had my photo taken a few times, but did not really consider it to be appropriate at a wake. Lenny had called me over for one and there were others taken as well. I bumped into Tony Lambrianou again as he was about to leave. We wanted to make sure we kept in touch, so we exchanged numbers and he promised that he would call.

By the time I finished talking, Michael had left, Ray was bored to tears and Georgina had blagged her way in. It was late now, so we had one last drink and decided to return to Newcastle.

We made it back early the next day, and I went straight to bed as soon as I got home. Just as I was drifting off, the phone rang – it was Reg. I was surprised but pleased to hear from him in such a short space of time.

"Hello, Steve, I'm just ringing to thank you for coming down to the funeral. I was in a daze for most of the day to be honest, but I'm pleased it went well. Anyway, was Bulla Ward there? He was, wasn't he?! Bring him to see me, okay? My units are running out, so I'll have to go. God bless."

He did not give me the chance to answer. I decided to leave it at that. He may have known that Bulla wasn't there when I told him ... or knew he wouldn't turn up. He probably decided to leave it till the next day.

I knew Reg had been through a lot lately and I had much sympathy for him. At least to hear him like this on the phone, I knew he was getting back to his old self. I'd smile to myself after such 'conversations' ... we were similar in some respects. We were both stubborn. It was as if we could not let the other have the final word on issues. I think he knew that I would not be enquiring about Bulla again – he just needed to make his point.

Charlie had been moved again, this time to Parkhurst. He had been in Frankland prior to this and was moved because he was suffering from chest pains, and on visits, he had been struggling to catch his breath. He had been happy at Frankland and had made a lot of friends there through me.

The Home Office decided that Parkhurst on the Isle of Wight was the best place for him, as it was near St Mary's Hospital. He was taken down from the high-risk prisoner status, to a Category B prisoner, so that his health could be monitored if need be.

I wrote to Charlie as soon as I heard that he had been moved, just to let him know that I knew his whereabouts and was thinking of him. He phoned me to let me know that he was okay and that he appreciated everything that I had done for him during his stay in Frankland.

He finished by saying that he would be in touch soon and that he would sort out a visiting order for me in the next few weeks. That was the last time that I spoke to him. Charlie's health worsened further ... when the Home Office gave permission for Reg to visit him, I knew that Charlie's days were numbered.

On 4 April 2000, Charles James Kray passed away, with Diane and Reg at his bedside. He had heart problems, which had developed into pneumonia. He was weak and physically frail. He was seventy-three years old.

Reg was devastated; he later told me that he was so overcome with guilt that he begged Charlie for forgiveness on his visit. I called Roberta to pass on my condolences and would have to sort out the arrangements for travelling down to London for what would surely be another big send-off.

Ray Cann and Graham Borthwick telephoned, and along with Ian Freeman, we decided to travel down. I arranged the wreath for the funeral once again through Fitzy and Colly. This time, it was in the shape of a diamond and had the word 'geezer' underneath it. The local papers were on hand to get some shots of us picking the wreath up and ran a story on it. Graham drove us down to Dave Courtney's in Plumstead, South London, the night before.

There was something else on my mind other than the funeral as we made our way down – the woman from Sheffield I'd had a previous relationship with. She was now with someone else, a man I had met many times before and had a lot of respect for. She told her new man that I had beaten and robbed her, that I had called *him* an old dinosaur and that I said he was past his sell-by date.

I had to laugh; this was like schoolyard stuff, but in the whole scheme of things, she was trying to ruin my reputation and get me beaten up in the process. Her new man was an infamous face in London – a hard man with a fierce reputation … it was Roy Shaw. Not the best enemy to have – especially when the animosity from him was based on lies told to him by some mentalist.

Through third parties, I heard that threats were being made, and I took them seriously. I had to. I was concerned that matters were getting out of hand. She was telling all sorts of lies but I was powerless to shut her up. I was not frightened but knew I would have to be a little more cautious on my trips to London, starting with the funeral.

As if there wasn't enough to do and think about on a day like this, now it would be impossible for me to relax. I was concerned about a confrontation at my friend's funeral. I would keep a safe distance from him and hope he would soon see what she was doing.

The funeral had been delayed, but with Reggie making the arrangements, you could guarantee that the day itself would run like clockwork. It was going to be a long day. I only managed a couple of hours sleep the night before at Dave Courtney's, before I was awoken with a cup of tea and a cockney, "Whey aye man ye bugger ye know!"... Dave had been practising his Geordie accent.

Dave explained that the lads were all meeting there at 8.30 a.m. to leave in convoy at 9.30 a.m. He had that sparkle in his eye, so I knew he had something up his sleeve; I was sure we would all know in time. By 9 a.m., the rest of the lads were suited and booted and ready to go.

Dave let us have his white Rolls-Royce for the day with his personalised number plate BADBOY, while he went with Brendan and Seymour in his new Jag. Mad Pete had the privilege of driving Dave's Roller, while Graham, Ray, Ian and I were his passengers.

Nine-thirty struck on a bright spring South London morning, and right on cue, Dave's well-rehearsed plan came into effect. 'The Outlaws' are a motorbike chapter and have bases up and down the country and all over the world. Dave knew a lot of the members of the various chapters and had built up some strong friendships with them, and had arranged for six of their top men to ride as outriders to our convoy of cars, making sure that we all had a safe journey all the way to Bethnal Green and English's Funeral Parlour.

It was a strange feeling this time around for me. Five years previously, when Ron had died, I had been naive and was still quite new to the way of life – still meeting people and still finding my feet, I suppose. Back then, if I'm honest, I was still getting a buzz from it.

Now, though, I felt sadness for Reg. He had seen this happen to both his brothers and each time he was the centre of attention. I never thought this was fair. It was also sad that Charlie had died a prisoner and not a free man. Regardless of his crime and his sentence, being in prison at that age ground him down immediately.

With Charlie, there was still the spectacle of it being a Kray funeral. Charlie was a well-loved and respected bloke; he was also well known for his love of parties and good times ... Champagne Charlie. Again, this funeral would be another event.

Reg's popularity was evident. All the up-and-coming hardmen were there, the top boys from each town and city ... something like this was an opportunity to get their names and faces known. A perfect chance to gain notoriety ... not a criticism. I had been there, done it and printed and sold the T-shirt. I had lived it. I had not only met the three brothers, I had become friends with them and stood by them through the years.

We reached Bethnal Green in good time, with our escorts doing us proud, much to the bemusement of other traffic and the local constabulary. Outside the parlour were a lot of familiar faces, and I introduced Ray, Graham and Ian to Bruce Reynolds, Frankie Fraser, Freddie Foreman, Tony Lambrianou, Charlie Richardson and a few of the other lesser known faces.

Once we had shook hands with the chaps, we put our wreaths in place and went for a drink. I had a tip-off that because of 'that' woman from Sheffield, I would not be welcome at the church. Apparently, she knew the people responsible for security and I would not be allowed in. I told the chaps that I would go to the church alone, but they wouldn't have it. If we were going, then it was all for one and one for all. I appreciated their solidarity.

We finished our drinks and made our way back to our cars, only to be stopped in our tracks by an announcement on a megaphone by the police officer in charge. There was a gas leak on Bethnal Green Road, and he wanted to limit the traffic travelling to the church by car. We would have to walk the half-mile or so there and back. It was a sunny day so there was little or no complaint.

We looked like a mini-army, all suited and booted, walking through the heart of East London with Dave leading the assault with what he refers to as his "Knights of the Round Table".

The Knights, of whom I am proud to be one, our name based on his fascination with King Arthur, are his best friends from different parts of the country. His house is based on Camelot Castle, and he even has the moat and the drawbridge. He has twelve seats at the round table in his dining room.

We had not been walking long and could see the church in our sights when it happened ... taking us all by surprise. He had either been following us or lying in wait for some time, silent ... then he attacked. A Yorkshire Terrier jumped out from nowhere and went straight for Ray, attempting to chew his leg off. It lightened the moment as we made our way through the already swelling crowds.

Dave got us through the gates, and we began to make our way past the flashing lights of the press and up the steps to the church. I saw Rob Davis on the door; I knew him well and had a lot of time for him. He knew about the 'situation' I had found myself in and we were both keen to avoid any fuss. I was there simply to pay my respects.

Reg had not entered the argument one way or another, so Rob was able to make an on-the-spot decision. The church was packed to the rafters and I stood at the back of the church with Dave and Ray, as I had done five years earlier for Ron. Because the church was so packed, and due to the circumstances, I did not get a chance to speak to Reg to let him know that I was there.

He was on his own now and I wanted him to know that I was there and thinking of him. My mind was soon put at ease, though. Ray handed me an order of service and said, "Reg thanks us for coming down." Ray had managed to slip to the front and let him know we were there. Reg shook Ray's hand, hugged him and told him to tell me thanks. I smiled inside. He knew we were there and that meant a lot to me. He knew he had friends there. We may not have been in touch as often now, but he knew. We were still close.

The service was much like his brother's, with the hymns "Morning Has Broken" and "Fight the Good Fight", and there were readings from Sue McGibbon and Freddie Foreman's son, Jamie. He had a lot of supporters.

Charlie's body was carried from the church to the sound of Shirley Bassey's "As Long as He Needs Me", and just like the last time, all eyes were on Reg to study his reactions.

We formed a line of honour outside the church as he was placed back in the traditional black hearse for his journey to the family plot in Chingford, Essex.

We returned to our cars and once our escorts gave us the nod, we were off. Making our own way to Chingford rather than following the procession of cars, we arrived in good time and took our place on a hill overlooking the graveside, waiting for Reg and Roberta to arrive. He'd seen his mother and his two brothers buried while serving his time. At each one of them he'd been handcuffed to an officer ... and each one was getting harder for him to bear. I would have thought this funeral was the one to make a few allowances, but obviously the law is the law.

As Charlie was lowered into the ground, I felt a lump in my throat. I'd had a lot of good laughs with Charlie; as I had said at his trial, he was the perfect host and a gentleman, and I knew I would certainly miss him. I felt close to him because we'd socialised on many occasions. It wasn't just prison visits for a few hours at a time, it was a friendship of talking on the phone and meeting up and going out together ... and he was the best there was for a night out.

Charlie was the type who would do anything for a friend. He had a tremendous lust for life and to see him die in such circumstances left a bitter taste. Everyone was outraged that he was put in prison, but to know just how little time he had left made it worse. Our floral tribute had been the perfect words to describe him: Diamond Geezer.

As the crowds of onlookers dispersed, a man shouted out, "Three cheers for Reggie Kray ... hip, hip ..." The crowd reacted accordingly. With that, Reg shook the hands of those around him, kissed Roberta and was whisked away. That night, we watched the funeral coverage on TV, and then I showed the lads around the West End as Dave and Jenny had a prior engagement at a boxing event with Ian Freeman.

Travelling back the next day, I picked up the papers to see all the coverage of the funeral. As with Ron, it had taken some time for the realisation to sink in. Charles James Kray was dead. When you see it in the papers and on TV like that, that's when you know it happened. On the day, it's just like you are on autopilot, like it is going on but not actually real. When you see yourself and friends in that third-person situation in the media, you *know* you were there and you *know* it did happen.

The headline of one paper proclaimed "And Then There Was One"; the Krays were dying one by one, and now Reg was the last of the family line.

I had to work that night and because of the traffic on the way back, I didn't have time to go home to rest or change clothes. I was shattered. When I finished and could finally get home, I had a message from Reg waiting for me.

"Hello, Steve, Reg Kray speaking. Thank you and thank your friends for taking the time to come down south to Charlie's funeral. You are a good friend. I'll ring another time, God bless."

I played the message over a few times and I admit I shed a few tears. For all his faults, this man had had to cope with his entire family dying whilst he was in prison. He had to deal with the despair, anguish and torment that the death of loved ones brings, but he had to deal with it under different circumstances to most others.

There was the build-up in the newspapers as a Kray death looked imminent. Then he had to make all the arrangements and to deal with the pressures of all the media attention – being in the spotlight throughout the service only to be taken straight back immediately afterwards. Prison can be a lonely enough place, but now he really was alone.

It showed more than anything how strong his character was and I for one hoped that he had enough fight left in him to beat the system, gain parole and spend at least a few years of freedom in the arms of the woman he truly loved.

In the year 2000, Reg had his parole hearing. To be fair, for all Roberta's hard work, I could only see Reg becoming decategorised and not put on a release programme. A lot of stories had circulated about Reg's health, and I'd been asked on numerous occasions by my friends in the media to confirm that he was fit and well.

You can't always believe what you read in the papers, but there had been a lot of coverage over the last year and a half of Reg's frequent trips to the hospital wings at both Blundeston and Wayland, with what was described as an irregular stomach complaint. Some reports suggested ulcers, others a possible cancer.

Reg, although admitting to the pains, assured us all that it was nothing to worry about, and that he had faith in the doctors he'd been dealing with.

I wasn't convinced. In April, at Charlie's funeral, Reg had looked pale, and it was quite noticeable that he had lost weight. A lot of observers put this down to the worry and stress that he'd endured with Charlie's illness and his parole board hearing.

Our worst fears were confirmed when, in September, it was announced that he had been admitted to hospital in Norwich for tests. The reports at first were a little unclear, and then Roberta dropped the bombshell ... Reg had undergone exploratory surgery and a cancer had been detected. He had only weeks to live.

I sat and watched the story break on the lunchtime news and still couldn't believe what I was hearing. As I watched and was taking it in, journalists started phoning me wanting some reaction to the story. I told them I was shell-shocked and that the Home Secretary should show immediate compassion and release Reg so that he could at least taste freedom before he passed away.

Reg's solicitors Mark Goldstein and Trevor Lynn reiterated what I had said when they were interviewed on later bulletins. The Sunday papers carried haunting images of a frail Reggie lying in his hospital bed with tubes leading from his torso, his breathing aided by an oxygen mask. They were sad pictures to have to look at. He was dying and yet he was still considered to be a danger to society.

How could a Home Secretary justifiably keep this man incarcerated? My comments were carried in the *Sunday People*, where I was named as Reg's surrogate son, which I found quite amusing. The pictures of Reg were all over the papers as the exclusive stories began to break. They were a far cry from the Reggie Kray that the public remembered, which is why I thought that they probably helped his cause for support. I'd sent him a card, as had Ray, who was quite keen to visit him. I was not so sure.

I had distanced myself so much from Reg in recent months I felt almost hypocritical, or like a ghoul wanting to see the last dying Kray on his deathbed. I decided against it. It would be good to catch up with Reg and see him one last time. I'd moved on since those early days.

The last time I'd seen him was at Charlie's funeral. I still thought of him as a good friend – it's not that we had a falling out or had decided not to speak; it's just that we had drifted apart over the years. To rekindle what once was just seemed false to me. We had the sort of relationship now where we both knew we supported each other regardless of whether we were in constant contact or not.

I sent him a letter wishing him well and expressing my hope that both he and Roberta could enjoy what little time they had left together. I didn't know what else to say. Have you ever tried to write a letter to someone who is dying? It's not easy. Jack Straw, the Labour Government's Home Secretary, bowed to public pressure and released Reggie on compassionate grounds a few days later. But although a free man, Reggie was confined to a room in the hospital that was even smaller than his prison cell in Wayland.

Basically, the world knew he was dying, and the Government decided to let him die on the outside. The cruel irony is that he could never be free; he couldn't go out and enjoy a walk or do something he'd been longing to do for thirty years.

Reg was delighted at his 'release' and was said to be celebrating with a bottle of Moët and some Henri Winterman cigars. Good on him, he deserved it. I phoned the hospital and left a message for him ... I left my number and hoped now that I could speak to him for the last time.

Not a day passed without a new 'Kray Exclusive' in the newspapers. The tabloids seemed to love the fact that the last of the Krays was dying. It was sensational in their eyes. Reg was a ready-made story they couldn't wait to exploit. It was sick fascination, which I found disturbing.

One paper carried its stories under the subheading "Death of a Gangster" – where is the respect or the dignity in that, I ask you? I suppose a lot of people would say that Reg brought it upon himself by courting the press for years, but everyone should be entitled to privacy in their dying days.

I had still not spoken to Reg by the time he was considered fit enough to leave his sickbed in Norwich Hospital. He was moved to a honeymoon suite in the Townhouse Hotel in Norfolk.

The room, as you would expect, was beautifully decorated, with a four-poster bed and an idyllic view of the river and the surrounding countryside. It had always been Reg's wish to have a house in the country, where he would be able to take long walks and enjoy the simpler things in life. This hotel room would be as close as he would get to realising this dream. It may have come at the wrong time for him, but he was out of prison.

His condition had worsened, and as each day passed, he was visited by many of his old gangland associates, as well as old enemies, to make their peace. Good friend and Kray biographer Laurie O'Leary, Joe Pyle, Freddie Foreman and Frankie Fraser all paid him a visit.

The rumours still circulated ... reports suggested that Reg only had six months to live, but they turned out to be wrong. I tried to contact Reg one last time by leaving a message and my telephone number with the girl on reception at the hotel. She let me down, as the message I learnt later was not passed on, just like my other at the hospital.

Neither Reg nor Roberta were aware that I had tried to contact them. The news the next day came as no great shock or surprise. On Sunday, 1 October 2000, Reg Kray, the last of the notorious Kray brothers, died aged sixty-six. Amongst those at his bedside were Freddie Foreman, Joe Pyle, Johnny Nash and Roberta. Over the next few days, there were yet more rumours, this time surrounding the funeral arrangements.

The lead-up to the funeral was not the set of circumstances Reg would have wanted. The chaps were adamant that Reg's dying wish was that they were pallbearers and that his send-off was to be a mirror image of Ron's. Roberta maintained a dignified silence throughout this period, refusing to be drawn into any dispute. Reg's body was taken back to Bethnal Green in preparation for the funeral, with Wednesday, 11 October to be the day he'd be laid to rest.

The pallbearers were not to be old gangland figures but people who Reg had grown close to through his years of imprisonment. Close friend and former cellmate Bradley Allerdyce, music promoter Bill Curbishley, and Tony Mortimer, singer and songwriter from Nineties teen favourites, boy band East 17. They had already been asked and had agreed to carry the coffin, with others to be confirmed.

There would only be a handful of limos for close friends and the remnants of the family. Others would have to make their own arrangements. This was another direct snub to the old school who still maintained that it wasn't what Reggie wanted. It's something I can't comment on.

From what I understand, Roberta was steering him away from gangland to have the normal life he'd wanted for so many years. In fairness to the chaps, Reg was part of gangland and he always would be. They wanted to give him the best send-off possible. I honestly don't know what Reg had wanted, but it would not have been for his friends and wife to start squabbling. It was appropriate that the wishes of his wife were respected.

I decided to travel down to London on the 6 a.m. train, and

reached King's Cross just after 9 a.m. I made my way to Bethnal Green via the Underground. It's hard to describe my feelings as I travelled. I'd had three hours on the train to do my thinking and I'd done a lot more prior to that. It bothered me that it had to end like this, that I would be attending just like any other civvy. It bothered me that I was not a part of it, not seeing friends and bothered by possible rumours that people may have heard.

Up and out of the station, I strolled past The Blind Beggar. I stopped and paused to look at it for a second ... the place where Ron had shot George Cornell. It felt strange. The first killing that led to their downfall ... the times Ron had described it to me ... it all seemed like a lifetime ago now.

I continued past it and reached Bethnal Green Road just after 10 a.m. I was dressed smart but casual and had decided against a wreath. I simply wanted to pay my respects and be seen at the funeral to show any of the chaps that doubted my side of the story. I popped into a cafe for some much-needed breakfast and flicked through the *East London Advertiser*, which carried an eight-page pull-out on the East End's most notorious family.

From there, it was on to English's Funeral Parlour. It was unusually quiet. The faces I was expecting to see were not there. Roberta seemed to have got her wish; the likes of Freddie Foreman and Tony Lambrianou were conspicuous by their absence. Frankie Fraser was there, as was former train robber Bruce Reynolds with his son Nick; Billy Murray from TV show *The Bill* was the only 'celebrity' on show.

The service was at St Matthew's, as it had been for Reg's brothers. I shook hands with a few of the chaps and watched as Reg's coffin was loaded into the hearse. I had decided to walk alongside Reg to the church, quite an emotional journey as Reg stopped off at 178 Vallance Road for the last time.

Although the crowds were nowhere near the same in numbers as when Ron and Charlie had been buried, they were still big enough to cause a lot of the mourners to be delayed and to miss the start of the service. It seemed to be a different affair than what anyone was expecting. The church was still packed to the rafters as the vicar told of how Reg had turned to God, and the hymns which had been recited at the other two funerals were given an airing again.

There was a feeling of déjà vu ... maybe because it had only been a few months since Charlie had died. There were a lot of strangers in the church, which I put down to the fact that once again the security had failed miserably in getting the right people in. A lot different to how Dave had run things in 1995. Outside the church, I bumped into Bruce and Nick Reynolds again. They were with Andy Jones, curator of the Crime Through Time Museum in Gloucester, and offered me a lift to the cemetery. The lift turned out to be in a beautiful red Bentley, which had had one previous owner ... none other than Mr Terry *Eurovision* Wogan.

The journey to the cemetery was a long one. The police seemed intent on separating the cars and we ended up in a traffic jam and arrived at the cemetery just after the hearse.

Outside the big gates there were people – friends of Reg's – being held back by police officers. Obviously, the police were only acting on instructions, but whose instructions they were remains a mystery to this day. To not let all his friends in seemed a bit harsh to me.

I decided to go it alone and thanked Bruce, Nick and Andy for the lift, and we promised to keep in touch. Both Bruce and Nick were keen to come to Newcastle when they released their books later in the year, and I told them I would be only too pleased to help them with any publicity.

As the gates finally opened, the crowd of mourners surged forward, and I caught a glimpse of a bald head and a cigar ... there was only one person it could be. It was Dave and the boys ... Ray, Ian, Seymour, Brendan, Christian, Wish, Welsh Bernie, Scouse John, Bulldog, Rob, Marcus, Piers and Big John. I shook hands with and embraced all the lads. They were pleased to see I'd not lost my bottle.

We made our way towards the Kray plot, and we waited on the

hillside overlooking the grave. Reg was carried to his final resting place as we gathered. The vicar spoke and the last of the Krays was lowered down into his grave.

With that, Roberta and the other close family said their thanks to those around them and then they were gone. It was all different. I think the lack of 'spectators' was down to the fact that there was not another Kray brother in attendance to look at.

Reggie was always a crowd-puller at the others just because he was Reg Kray and people wanted to say they had seen him. As far as friends go, it was apparent that there had been a falling out of some sort. Some of them had decided to stay clear, which must have been a tough decision to make. Looking around, there were plenty of new faces on the scene just like the last two.

The wake was to be held in the heart of the East End. I decided not to push my luck and instead travelled in style with Dave and the lads in a couple of hired vintage cars back to a boozer in South London to give the last of the Krays a good old send-off.

My mate Gary, who makes cash as a Jaws lookalike from the *Bond* films, made the journey back to Newcastle with me later that night. I finished off my day with a couple of swift ones on Newcastle's Quayside. I'd distanced myself purposefully to avoid a scene at my old friend's funeral. The feud with the gangland figure passed and on a recent trip to London we shook hands and put the past behind us.

My Kray connection had now died along with the last brother. I had my ups and downs with them, just as I would in any friendship, but I know they all died knowing they had me as a friend. That meant a lot to me. The friends I made along the way remain my friends today, and I am privileged to have good memories of all three of the Kray brothers. I was proud to be their Geordie Connection.

There have been a lot of lies circulated over the years about me and Roy Shaw. I always had respect and admiration for Roy, and his relationship with my ex and then a wannabe trying to cause problems between me and Roy meant that at times the waters weren't smooth.

Thanks to my friendship with Joe Pyle Snr and Freddie Foreman, the truth came forward on both occasions. I first met him at a 'white-collar' boxing event in Streatham in the late Nineties. Freddie Foreman was surrounded by autograph hunters and well-wishers, and was taking it all in his stride. He had a neck the size of a bull, hands like proverbial shovels and eyes that could see right through you. For somebody in his sixties, he was still in incredible physical shape. Mistake his politeness as a weakness at your peril.

Royston Henry Shaw was the original Hard Bastard. When they made him, the mould shattered; there would never be another like him. He was an original East Ender, too; born in Stepney in March 1936, he was raised on the same bomb sites as the twins. "I never got in their way and they never got in mine," he said at Reggie's funeral in 2000.

I'm sure anyone reading this will have read *Pretty Boy* and will know his story. Roy was one of the first to have a 'gangster biography' out and became an absolute legend. The problems that were caused between us never came to anything. I certainly didn't hold it against him that he'd been lied to and believed the woman and the wannabe. I mean, how many of us have been in that boat?

I last met Roy in 2010 at a film premier. He remembered me and we talked about the film and exchanged a few opinions on the state of the pro-boxing scene. He wished me well.

The call to say that he had passed away in July 2012 came from his son Gary and was a bit of a shock, but I dropped all engagements to attend his funeral in Essex. The sun came out on the congregation, which was a mix of close family, infamous villains and celebrities. You would expect nothing less.

I'll let Roy have the final word from his interview in Kate Kray's book, *Hard Bastards*:

I don't live in the past, because if you live in the past you die a bit each day. I have no pity or conscience and have been called the devil; maybe I am, but when I die, I know that God will shake my hand and welcome me into heaven with open arms because basically I'm a nice, ruthless bastard.

CHAPTER 8

THE FINAL CURTAIN

I've always wondered how I would sum up my experiences. The Krays played such an important part in my life and writing this has made me realise that they still are a big part. I got to know them while I was growing up, and from knowing them, I grew up with life experiences that I would not have anticipated. I was learning all the time, even though it didn't feel like it, and I suppose my life with them put me on the fast track to adulthood.

The Kray brothers are now gone but never forgotten. I don't think they will ever be forgotten. They will always be remembered by the classic photograph taken by David Bailey. It's one of those iconic images like Che Guevara or Jim Morrison's 'young lion' pose – mysterious and haunting.

They defined an era in Britain – a time of change. I think that change was the most important factor in their rise to fame. If it had not been for a change in the country's economy, the chances are we would never have heard of them and they would just have been another couple of fighters on the cobbles of the East End.

They were around at the right time career-wise – that's the important part. The country was incredibly vulnerable, the city where they lived in particular. The war years meant they could establish themselves, just as all the other criminals were able to, but they had to excel above all the others. It just happened; they weren't waiting to move in. It was fate. The economy changing after the war meant they could achieve a lot more than they could have in poorer times. There were clubs, the gaming industry and fortunes to be made.

In another place, let's say Newcastle, for instance, it may have been different. Newcastle did not undergo the same bombing campaign as London did. Communities up here were still intact and still strong. We were not weakened, and morale was not at an all-time low. It was different in London, especially the East End. I don't think that the statement, "They kept crime off the streets" is strictly true. As mentioned previously, the people in the East End did not have that much to steal. People didn't feel safe; they felt scared.

This book does not set out to glorify violence, gangsterism or anything else the Kray brothers were a part of. They had done all that before I was even born, and those were the crimes they were serving time for when I met them. My interest in them came in my teens, when I was enthralled by their infamy.

My memories of the twins are from their days in prison and, of Charlie, outside as well as inside. I can't try to sell the idea of the twins as a pair of angels who knew they had done wrong and were remorseful about it. We must also bear in mind the memories of some other people's lives that were changed by the Kray brothers ... the people they shot, stabbed, fought with and beat up, the families of the people they killed, those they extorted money from, the people who feared them – people who were just trying to make a living the honest way. They functioned well in their heyday because they were twins. No one had come up against anything like it before, and possibly never will again. They became a classic case study for twin relationships ... another reason why their name will live on.

My experience of the twins was always as separate entities. It was interesting for me because they were similar in many ways, yet different in so many others. I'd never set out to write a book that looked at their lives when they were in their prime and were running the East End side by side with The Firm. That's been done and happened long before I knew them.

Nor would I set out to analyse them as twins and their actions, citing scientific studies and saying why they did what they did

– that's best left to psychologists. My intention in writing this has been to tell a story from a different perspective, make my own observations and share them. I believe I have memories of the three brothers that are worth sharing.

My relationship with Reg was of a father–son nature. We talked about football and women, we argued over money, and nine times out of ten, I did the opposite to what he told me to do. He could be pig-headed at times, but I'll always remember one classic line he came out with. In discussing the duration of his prison sentence, he once said, "I would have spent less time behind bars if I'd killed Mother Teresa."

He was also the king of manipulation. Ron was the one in their heyday who had all the gophers, but behind bars, it was Reg. He could be a nightmare at times, and I don't think he was aware that 'sorry' was a word, never mind what it meant.

Ron and I would chat a lot about the old days and people from his past. I suppose my relationship with him was likened to the role a granddad takes when he tells you about his time as a soldier in the war. Ron certainly took me through his war in graphic detail on some visits. Rather than the beaches of Normandy, Ron's battlefield was the East End of London, where he commanded his troops from Fort Vallance.

My most memorable conversation with Ron has got to be the time he described the killing of George Cornell so vividly. My visits with Ron were good, as they were full of conversation without constant interruptions. He could be volatile. Like Reg, his moods were known to change in an instant. He never had a problem with ordering executions one day and shrugging them off the next. Along with that, Ron had the most wicked sense of humour.

Charlie Kray was like a devilish uncle who wanted to take his young nephew to the West End and show him how to be a ladies' man. I cannot ever remember having a bad night out with Charlie. He was great company and a joy to spend time with. I would say that I miss him the most, because the time we shared wasn't always limited by visiting hours, and the fact that Charlie took the time and effort to visit me in Newcastle. I wonder whether Ron or indeed Reg would have had they been at liberty.

Charlie, too, was an excellent laugh. It was sad to see him deteriorate in the end, and even sadder to see it happen in prison. I would have been interested to see how my relationship would have developed had all three brothers lived for another ten years apiece.

I'd certainly say they succeeded in what they set out to do … they became famous. By whatever means possible, I think in the end, Charlie became a victim of his famous name. That's one of the big regrets I have from my relationship with them – not being present in Birmingham when Charlie was introduced to the Geordie policemen. I would have been able to sniff them out (no pun intended). I'm sure of it.

He would have been sussed out some time earlier after his name kept cropping up in tapped phone conversations, which had led to the convictions of other traffickers. I say victim of his own name, as in sentencing, Kray got twelve years for introducing the people who wanted to do business, and the other two accomplices received nine years and five years for handling the drugs. The drug industry is run by extreme violence and fear, not by a few old men who lived by the old code of never using weapons. Maybe if I'd met up with these 'businessmen' and alerted Charlie, the whole Kray story may have had a somewhat happier ending.

As for getting involved with the twins and the chaps, I don't regret it for one minute. Why should I? I'm a law-abiding citizen. I pay my taxes, have no criminal record and have worked continuously since I left school. I value the experiences I had with the Krays. I think I learnt much from my eleven-year friendship with the brothers. I certainly learnt a lot about them and a lot about what was going on in the underworld. I learnt about business, about trust and how to spot a fake; I also learnt that there are some good and bad people out there, too. In those terms, it's not that different to what I would have learnt growing up on the streets of Felling – but the stakes were a lot higher.

Knowing the Krays was a lesson in friendship. I never anticipated it going as far as it did but was glad it happened. As in any friendship, there were good times and bad, but it was something I had to get used to. I don't really think that the twins had that many genuine friends when it came down to it. I'd say that the ones who stuck by them since the old days were their true friends. There were plenty of people around them who were only too willing to sell stories, photographs, enhance their own reputation by association and take all they could from the Kray name.

Some may say that I'm no different. Everyone is entitled to an opinion. I never planned anything other than meeting the brothers – the rest just happened. The most important thing I learnt through it all was that crime almost certainly doesn't pay. The authorities will always catch up with you. This was true of the Krays and most of the people they surrounded themselves with.

I was unique in that circle as I was never introduced as "Steve, a good burglar from Newcastle" or "Shooter Steve from the Felling". I was just Steve, friend of the twins. I was young and a bit naive, but I'm the person I am today largely through knowing them. It was through them that I drifted towards security work, which is something I have now made a career out of.

In the end, all that the twins had left was the legend. It consumed Reg to the point of him filming a deathbed interview. It was a shock to see how the cancer had reduced this former muscular gangland figure to a frail bag of bones, but the actual show summed the Krays up in one word – money. They loved making it, but the enjoyment was spending it.

I can almost hear the twins now, "A book? Good, good. What's our cut? We'll go seventy-thirty in our favour."

I'm sure they would have approved of it.

The Legend lives on.

CHAPTER 9
LOOKING BACK

It's 28 May 2015. Nine in the morning and I'm boarding the train from Newcastle Central to London King's Cross. I'm on my way to see Freddie Foreman and my closest friend Christian Simpson. Fred is eighty-three now but is still bright as a button and living life to the full. We are working together on a book entitled *The Krays and Freddie Foreman: Read All About It* and, over the last twenty years, we have become good friends. I never imagined twenty-eight years ago, when I picked up my copy of *Profession of Violence*, that I would go on such a journey and become so involved in the continuing story of the Kray twins.

I'm forty-three and it's eighteen years since I finished writing the first draft of this book. So, what has become of the other likely lad ... the naive, fresh-faced Geordie who became besotted with the image of the Kray twins? I guess the good news is that I took Reggie's advice all those years ago in one of the numerous visiting rooms I met him in and steered away from a life of crime. I like to think I took the good things from the Kray brothers' characters – and there were some – and made them a positive for myself.

For example, my first events that I held in the North East were fundraisers for Terry Moran, who Reg had agreed to help after hearing of his horrific accident on Guy Fawkes Night. Charlie Kray hosted the night and Tony Lambrianou was a guest of honour. We raised over £2k for Terry. Nowadays, I run my own event management business – Relentless Promotions – with Danny Cox in Newcastle, and have staged events with names such as Mike Tyson, Anthony Joshua, Joe Calzaghe, Carl Froch,

Jake LaMotta, Bad Manners, Big Country and Alan Shearer. The small events for the twins gave me a good grounding and the knowhow, and I've built on that.

The twins often asked me to contact the press and media on their behalf and put out statements. My infamous stand against then Prime Minister John Major makes me laugh now, but at the time, I was expecting to be whisked away by MI5 as the story spread like wildfire and ended up front-page news in *The Times*.

Again, this taught me a valuable lesson and I learned how important the media could be to me, but how careful you need to be when dealing with them.

I built up some fabulous contacts in the press thanks to the twins, and many remain friends to this day. I admit that I am a self-publicist, another trait that I have inherited from the Krays. In my game, you need to be.

The birth of social media has given me the opportunity to promote myself and events in a way that the twins could only dream of! If Reg was alive today, you can guarantee he would have had me running his Twitter and Facebook accounts.

My journey has not been without its fair share of problems. I don't think a lot of people understood my involvement with the Krays. To the outsider looking in, here was this six-foot tall bald Geordie wearing suits and working for the two most notorious gangsters in the UK, so he must be a villain, right? *Wrong*. You couldn't be further from the truth.

I had no premeditated plans when I wrote to the twins and certainly wasn't looking to become *Gangster No. 1*. Sadly, some people were and, as time went by, jealousy overcame them, and they tried to cause me problems in the London circle. Part of me would love to name names, but why should I give them the glory of being mentioned in another book? Those in the circle and my friends know who those people are and what they did, and I'm happy to say that good prevailed over evil every time.

My relationship with the Krays meant that I had the trust and friendship of not just Freddie Foreman, but also Joe Pyle Snr and

Laurie O'Leary, both trusted confidants of Ron, Reg and Charlie, and they were all good sounding boards when things did not go right or if I needed somebody to help me out.

I look back on how I got involved with the whole London scene and I certainly don't have any regrets. I have met a lot of well-known and influential people, and doors have opened for me in all walks of life. I have been influenced by a lot of the characters that I have met and have listened to a lot of their advice and like to think that I have learned from their mistakes.

With the death of all three Kray brothers, Tony Lambrianou, Joe Pyle Snr, Roy Shaw, Bruce Reynolds and recently Ronnie Biggs, the whole London scene has changed for me personally. I keep in touch with a few people down there these days. Fred Foreman, Christian Simpson, Joe Pyle Jnr, Barry and Cliffy. All good men whom I trust. It's also been an honour for me to finally meet the twins' cousins in recent years, Joe Lee and Rita Smith.

As I've said, with the infamy comes jealously, and if I'm not fending off keyboard warriors on Twitter these days, I'm getting nuisance calls! For every nice person I've met in my life, I've attracted a couple of cranks, but I've learned to live with it. Sadly, there are still a few members of the inner circle of friends and associates who I have no time for.

What I have noticed over the last few years is the increase of wannabes appearing on the scene. There has always been a few of these characters trying to make an impression. People who read the odd hardman book and watch a few unlicensed fights, and then think that they want a piece of the action. They look for a way in by attaching themselves to a well-known face and then try to make themselves useful by running a website about their hero or driving their hero about to the shops or to the opening of an envelope.

These people tend to have low self-esteem and no personality of their own and are born to do what they are told. They are content with living their lives through their association with others. Unfortunately, when they've settled into their new lifestyle, they have tried to cause trouble for the likes of myself and others, by casting doubt over our characters and motives.

I have been a victim of such a character assassination in recent times and only my long-term relationship with the chaps got me through what could have been a tricky situation. I still don't know why I was targeted, but I was not best pleased. Dawn and I received threatening phone calls at home and countless obscene emails. It did not faze me, just angered me.

The emails and calls were easily traced and the whole situation came to a head and was resolved amicably, but things for me will never be the same. There is a lot of jealousy amongst the wannabes and I put this little episode down to that. There are also a few people who aren't what they seem on the surface and are content to leave threatening answer machine messages and texts.

I can think of one person who has also been the focus of a couple of television shows who shall we say is economical with the truth and has written a lot of lies about a crime family in Newcastle. I'm looking forward to righting those wrongs in a book that Stu and I will release later this year, so watch this space.

On the flip side, there have been some great people I have met on this journey and it's time to acknowledge Danny Gordon, Dave MacKay, Matt Leech, Grant Nesbitt, Andy Gravenor, Andy Hollinson, Andy Evans, Wayne Lear, Jeff Mason and Brian Anderson.

Since my book was published, many of those mentioned have passed away and I have attended all their funerals. I miss the likes of Joe Pyle Snr, Eric Mason, Roy Shaw, Bruce Reynolds and Laurie O'Leary, all good men and people I'm proud to have called my friends.

I also lost a good friend in Tony Lambrianou. Christian and I were asked to arrange the security for his funeral. This included looking after Tony's body at English's Funeral Parlour, the request of his brothers Chris and Jimmy. It was a moving experience and another chapter closing on the Kray story. He got the send-off he deserved.

I was also present at Eric Mason's wedding to his true love Trish and asked to be a godfather to one of their children, another proud moment. I briefly managed Charlie Bronson, now known as Charles Salvador. Both Ron and Reg spoke highly of Charlie and on more than one occasion asked me to give him any help and support I could. A good friend of mine, Rod Harrison, runs Charlie's affairs these days and runs a Facebook page called "In Charlie's Corner" – pop on and give it a life. Enough is enough, the man should be released.

As well as running my own business, I have also returned to my first love … acting. After eighteen years on the doors, I decided to leave the security industry and do a degree in Performing Arts after working as an extra on the sets of shows such as *Byker Grove* for six years. With hindsight, I wish I had done this sooner, but I believe your life is mapped out for you and I obviously wasn't ready back then for the challenges that the industry throws at you.

I have had a fair amount of success in the last couple of years, appearing in feature films such as: *Cass*, *In Our Name*, *The Guvnors*, *Mob Handed*, *Scintilla*, *Almost Married* and *Interview with a Hitman*, and have treaded the boards again in pantomime, playing the villain! Well, what did you expect?

I'm currently working on a play entitled "Jump to Cow Heaven", written by Gill Adams. I'm playing Frank Mitchell, an alleged victim of the Krays. Growing my hair for the first time in almost thirty years is the biggest challenge I have faced, believe me!

I'm also working hard to produce a new gangland television series called "Morelands Firm", an idea created by my business partner Danny Cox.

In my personal life, Dawn and I are still together, fifteen years and counting. We are married now and have two beautiful daughters, Rebecca and Isabella. My parents separated, which had a huge effect on me, but they remain friends and that helped the situation. I also lost my grandparents, who I spent a lot of my early life with. They were against my relationship with the Krays, but I know that they would be proud of me now.

We are only a few months into 2015, but I have already been approached to appear in two documentaries on the twins. They would have been eighty-two this October, and the media love an anniversary to churn out stories and anecdotes about days gone by. It's no surprise to me that the legend lives on, and I guess that I am the keeper of the Kray flame in a lot of respects.

I hit a bit of a writing block after finishing the original manuscript of this book in 2000, but have gone on to write the Newcastle Hooligan book *NME: From the Bender Squad to the Gremlins* with Stu and also released *The Krays from the Cradle to the Grave* with Neil Jackson and Wayne Lear, which is a Krays scrapbook; and then there is my first attempt at a kid's book, *The Milk Thief*, which I wrote as a bedtime story for my eldest Rebecca.

As well as the release of this book, I have put together and released *The Sayers: Tried and Tested at the Highest Level* with Stu and another book with Wayne and Neil, and Freddie Foreman, entitled *The Krays and Freddie Foreman: Read All About It*.

On the business front, I have set up and run three successful event management companies and met a lot of my sporting heroes in the process. I have also brought some of the notorious faces to Newcastle for after dinner events, such as Freddie Foreman, Bruce Reynolds, Eddie Richardson, Frankie Fraser and Howard Marks.

I have now taken my first steps into the world of professional boxing. I learned the ropes in the unlicensed game with Spencer Brown, Phil Riley and James Ward, and spent seven years working for the European Boxing Federation. I took out my professional promoter's licence in 2012, thanks to Davey Tweddle putting up a £10k bond, and together with Danny Cox and our company Relentless Promotions, have reignited the passion in the sport in the North East.

We have recently linked up with Eddie Hearn and Matchroom Boxing and hosted a big show on Sky Sports, which featured Anthony Joshua. Our aim is to find the next world champion on Tyneside. I'm sure Reg and Ron would have approved.

I got involved with Ron, Reg and Charlie because I had an interest and was young and naive. I certainly did not sit down as a teenager and forge a plan about how to get into their lives. I read *Profession of Violence* and wanted to meet those people. Nothing more, nothing less.

Nowadays, those people have a game plan and are looking for something out of it. It's quite a dangerous game to play. Some wannabes target caged criminals and offer their services to them. They post things in and publicise their pen pals' plight, and they go on the odd visit to their new chum. They fill their inmate's head full of stories and false hope, and revel in their new-found fame as they ride on the back of another man's pain. Sickening, really.

All told, I am in a happy place these days. I have my health, my house, my family and I'm doing jobs that I enjoy. I'm spinning a lot of plates still and guess that's what I was supposed to do in life. If one of my jobs starts to bring in more money than the others, then I may have to concentrate on one thing, but I don't think that's going to happen unless Mr Scorsese comes calling.

Reading through this book with Stu all these years later has brought back a lot of happy memories. More than ever, I appreciate the time I spent as a friend and confidant of the Kray brothers and yes, I raised a glass to the twins on 24 October 2015, when they would have been eighty-two years old. They are never far away from me.

God bless, Steve.

To contact Steve, please email Gadfly Press at gadflypress@outlook.com

Steve's Facebook page is Steve Wraith's True Crime Inc

If you have enjoyed this book, we would appreciate you leaving a review on Amazon or Goodreads.

Gadfly Press Socials
  Website
  Facebook
  Twitter

OTHER BOOKS BY GADFLY PRESS

By Natalie Welsh:

Escape from Venezuela's Deadliest Prison

By Shaun Attwood:

English Shaun Trilogy
Party Time
Hard Time
Prison Time

War on Drugs Series
Pablo Escobar: Beyond Narcos
American Made: Who Killed Barry Seal?
Pablo Escobar or George HW Bush
The Cali Cartel: Beyond Narcos
Clinton Bush and CIA Conspiracies:
From the Boys on the Tracks to Jeffrey Epstein

Un-Making a Murderer:
The Framing of Steven Avery and Brendan Dassey
The Mafia Philosopher: Two Tonys
Life Lessons

Pablo Escobar's Story (4-book series)

By Natalie Welsh:

Escape from Venezuela's Deadliest Prison

After getting arrested at a Venezuelan airport with a suitcase of cocaine, Natalie was clueless about the danger she was facing. Sentenced to 10 years, she arrived at a prison with armed men on the roof, whom she mistakenly believed were the guards, only to find out they were homicidal gang members. Immediately, she was plunged into a world of unimaginable horror and escalating violence, where murder, rape and all-out gang warfare were carried out with the complicity of corrupt guards. Male prisoners often entered the females' housing area, bringing gunfire with them and leaving corpses behind. After 4.5 years, Natalie risked everything to escape and flee through Colombia, with the help of a guard who had fallen deeply in love with her.

By Shaun Attwood:

Pablo Escobar: Beyond Narcos

War on Drugs Series Book 1

The mind-blowing true story of Pablo Escobar and the Medellín Cartel beyond their portrayal on Netflix.

Colombian drug lord Pablo Escobar was a devoted family man and a psychopathic killer; a terrible enemy, yet a wonderful friend. While donating millions to the poor, he bombed and tortured his enemies – some had their eyeballs removed with hot spoons. Through ruthless cunning and America's insatiable appetite for cocaine, he became a multi-billionaire, who lived in a $100-million house with its own zoo.

Pablo Escobar: Beyond Narcos demolishes the standard good versus evil telling of his story. The authorities were not hunting Pablo down to stop his cocaine business. They were taking over it.

American Made: Who Killed Barry Seal? Pablo Escobar or George HW Bush

War on Drugs Series Book 2

Set in a world where crime and government coexist, *American Made* is the jaw-dropping true story of CIA pilot Barry Seal that the Hollywood movie starring Tom Cruise is afraid to tell.

Barry Seal flew cocaine and weapons worth billions of dollars into and out of America in the 1980s. After he became a government informant, Pablo Escobar's Medellin Cartel offered a million for him alive and half a million dead. But his real trouble began after he threatened to expose the dirty dealings of George HW Bush.

American Made rips the roof off Bush and Clinton's complicity in cocaine trafficking in Mena, Arkansas.

"A conspiracy of the grandest magnitude." Congressman Bill Alexander on the Mena affair.

The Cali Cartel: Beyond Narcos

War on Drugs Series Book 3

An electrifying account of the Cali Cartel beyond its portrayal on Netflix.

From the ashes of Pablo Escobar's empire rose an even bigger and more malevolent cartel. A new breed of sophisticated mobsters became the kings of cocaine. Their leader was Gilberto Rodríguez Orejuela – known as the Chess Player due to his foresight and calculated cunning.

Gilberto and his terrifying brother, Miguel, ran a multi-billion-dollar drug empire like a corporation. They employed a politically astute brand of thuggery and spent $10 million to put a president in power. Although the godfathers from Cali preferred bribery over violence, their many loyal torturers and hit men were never idle.

Clinton Bush and CIA Conspiracies: From the Boys on the Tracks to Jeffrey Epstein

War on Drugs Series Book 4

In the 1980s, George HW Bush imported cocaine to finance an illegal war in Nicaragua. Governor Bill Clinton's Arkansas state police provided security for the drug drops. For assisting the CIA, the Clinton Crime Family was awarded the White House. The #clintonbodycount continues to this day, with the deceased including Jeffrey Epstein.

This book features harrowing true stories that reveal the insanity of the drug war. A mother receives the worst news about her son. A journalist gets a tip that endangers his life. An unemployed man becomes California's biggest crack dealer. A DEA agent in Mexico is sacrificed for going after the big players.

The lives of Linda Ives, Gary Webb, Freeway Rick Ross and Kiki Camarena are shattered by brutal experiences. Not all of them will survive.

Pablo Escobar's Story (4-book series)

"Finally, the definitive book about Escobar, original and up-to-date" – UNILAD

"The most comprehensive account ever written" – True Geordie

Pablo Escobar was a mama's boy who cherished his family and sang in the shower, yet he bombed a passenger plane and formed a death squad that used genital electrocution.

Most Escobar biographies only provide a few pieces of the puzzle, but this action-packed 1000-page book reveals everything about the king of cocaine.

Mostly translated from Spanish, Part 1 contains stories untold in the English-speaking world, including:

The tragic death of his youngest brother Fernando.

The fate of his pregnant mistress.

The shocking details of his affair with a TV celebrity.

The presidential candidate who encouraged him to eliminate their rivals.

The Mafia Philosopher

"A fast-paced true-crime memoir with all of the action of Goodfellas" – UNILAD

"Sopranos v Sons of Anarchy with an Alaskan-snow backdrop" – True Geordie Podcast

Breaking bones, burying bodies and planting bombs became second nature to Two Tonys while working for the Bonanno Crime Family, whose exploits inspired The Godfather.

After a dispute with an outlaw motorcycle club, Two Tonys

left a trail of corpses from Arizona to Alaska. On the run, he was pursued by bikers and a neo-Nazi gang blood-thirsty for revenge, while a homicide detective launched a nationwide manhunt.

As the mist from his smoking gun fades, readers are left with an unexpected portrait of a stoic philosopher with a wealth of charm, a glorious turn of phrase and a fanatical devotion to his daughter.

Party Time

An action-packed roller-coaster account of a life spiralling out of control, featuring wild women, gangsters and a mountain of drugs.

Shaun Attwood arrived in Phoenix, Arizona, a penniless business graduate from a small industrial town in England. Within a decade, he became a stock-market millionaire. But he was leading a double life.

After taking his first Ecstasy pill at a rave in Manchester as a shy student, Shaun became intoxicated by the party lifestyle that would change his fortune. Years later, in the Arizona desert, he became submerged in a criminal underworld, throwing parties for thousands of ravers and running an Ecstasy ring in competition with the Mafia mass murderer Sammy 'The Bull' Gravano.

As greed and excess tore through his life, Shaun had eye-watering encounters with Mafia hit men and crystal-meth addicts, enjoyed extravagant debauchery with superstar DJs and glitter girls, and ingested enough drugs to kill a herd of elephants. This is his story.

Hard Time

"Makes the Shawshank Redemption look like a holiday camp" – NOTW

After a SWAT team smashed down stock-market millionaire Shaun Attwood's door, he found himself inside of Arizona's deadliest jail and locked into a brutal struggle for survival.

Shaun's hope of living the American Dream turned into a nightmare of violence and chaos, when he had a run-in with Sammy the Bull Gravano, an Italian Mafia mass murderer.

In jail, Shaun was forced to endure cockroaches crawling in his ears at night, dead rats in the food and the sound of skulls getting cracked against toilets. He meticulously documented the conditions and smuggled out his message.

Join Shaun on a harrowing voyage into the darkest recesses of human existence.

Hard Time provides a revealing glimpse into the tragedy, brutality, dark comedy and eccentricity of prison life.

Featured worldwide on Nat Geo Channel's Locked-Up/Banged-Up Abroad Raving Arizona.

Prison Time

Sentenced to 9½ years in Arizona's state prison for distributing Ecstasy, Shaun finds himself living among gang members, sexual predators and drug-crazed psychopaths. After being attacked by a Californian biker in for stabbing a girlfriend, Shaun writes about the prisoners who befriend, protect and inspire him. They include T-Bone, a massive African American ex-Marine who risks his life saving vulnerable inmates from rape, and Two Tonys, an old-school Mafia murderer who left the corpses of his rivals from Arizona to Alaska. They teach Shaun how to turn incarceration to his advantage, and to learn from his mistakes.

Shaun is no stranger to love and lust in the heterosexual world, but the tables are turned on him inside. Sexual advances come at him from all directions, some cleverly disguised, others more sinister – making Shaun question his sexual identity.

Resigned to living alongside violent, mentally-ill and drug-addicted inmates, Shaun immerses himself in psychology and philosophy to try to make sense of his past behaviour, and begins applying what he learns as he adapts to prison life. Encouraged by Two Tonys to explore fiction as well, Shaun reads over 1000 books which, with support from a brilliant psychotherapist, Dr Owen, speed along his personal development. As his ability to deflect daily threats improves, Shaun begins to look forward to his release with optimism and a new love waiting for him. Yet the words of Aristotle from one of Shaun's books will prove prophetic: "We cannot learn without pain."

Un-Making a Murderer:
The Framing of Steven Avery and Brendan Dassey

Innocent people do go to jail. Sometimes mistakes are made. But even more terrifying is when the authorities conspire to frame them. That's what happened to Steven Avery and Brendan Dassey, who were convicted of murder and are serving life sentences.

Un-Making a Murderer is an explosive book which uncovers the illegal, devious and covert tactics used by Wisconsin officials, including:

– Concealing Other Suspects

– Paying Expert Witnesses to Lie

– Planting Evidence

– Jury Tampering

The art of framing innocent people has been in practice for centuries and will continue until the perpetrators are held accountable. Turning conventional assumptions and beliefs in the justice system upside down, *Un-Making a Murderer* takes you on that journey.

HARD TIME BY SHAUN ATTWOOD
CHAPTER 1

Sleep deprived and scanning for danger, I enter a dark cell on the second floor of the maximum-security Madison Street jail in Phoenix, Arizona, where guards and gang members are murdering prisoners. Behind me, the metal door slams heavily. Light slants into the cell through oblong gaps in the door, illuminating a prisoner cocooned in a white sheet, snoring lightly on the top bunk about two thirds of the way up the back wall. Relieved there is no immediate threat, I place my mattress on the grimy floor. Desperate to rest, I notice movement on the cement-block walls. *Am I hallucinating?* I blink several times. The walls appear to ripple. Stepping closer, I see the walls are alive with insects. I flinch. So many are swarming, I wonder if they're a colony of ants on the move. To get a better look, I put my eyes right up to them. They are mostly the size of almonds and have antennae. American cockroaches. I've seen them in the holding cells downstairs in smaller numbers, but nothing like this. A chill spread over my body. I back away.

Something alive falls from the ceiling and bounces off the base of my neck. I jump. With my night vision improving, I spot cockroaches weaving in and out of the base of the fluorescent strip light. Every so often one drops onto the concrete and resumes crawling. Examining the bottom bunk, I realise why my cellmate is sleeping at a higher elevation: cockroaches are pouring from gaps in the decrepit wall at the level of my bunk. The area is thick with them. Placing my mattress on the bottom bunk scatters them. I walk towards the toilet, crunching a few under my shower sandals. I urinate and grab the toilet roll. A cockroach darts from the centre of the roll onto my hand, tickling my fingers. My arm jerks as if it has a mind of its own, losing the cockroach and the toilet roll. Using a towel, I wipe the bulk of them off the bottom bunk, stopping only to shake the odd one off my hand. I unroll my mattress. They begin to regroup and inhabit my mattress. My adrenaline is pumping so much, I lose my fatigue.

Nauseated, I sit on a tiny metal stool bolted to the wall. *How will I sleep? How's my cellmate sleeping through the infestation and my arrival?* Copying his technique, I cocoon myself in a sheet and lie down, crushing more cockroaches. The only way they can access me now is through the breathing hole I've left in the sheet by the lower half of my face. Inhaling their strange musty odour, I close my eyes. I can't sleep. I feel them crawling on the sheet around my feet. *Am I imagining things?* Frightened of them infiltrating my breathing hole, I keep opening my eyes. Cramps cause me to rotate onto my other side. Facing the wall, I'm repulsed by so many of them just inches away. I return to my original side.

The sheet traps the heat of the Sonoran Desert to my body, soaking me in sweat. Sweat tickles my body, tricking my mind into thinking the cockroaches are infiltrating and crawling on me. The trapped heat aggravates my bleeding skin infections and bedsores. I want to scratch myself, but I know better. The outer layers of my skin have turned soggy from sweating constantly in this concrete oven. Squirming on the bunk fails to stop the relentless itchiness of my skin. Eventually, I scratch myself. Clumps of moist skin detach under my nails. Every now and then I become so uncomfortable, I must open my cocoon to waft the heat out, which allows the cockroaches in. It takes hours to drift to sleep. I only manage a few hours. I awake stuck to the soaked sheet, disgusted by the cockroach carcasses compressed against the mattress.

The cockroaches plague my new home until dawn appears at the dots in the metal grid over a begrimed strip of four-inch-thick bullet-proof glass at the top of the back wall – the cell's only source of outdoor light. They disappear into the cracks in the walls, like vampire mist retreating from sunlight. But not all of them. There were so many on the night shift that even their vastly reduced number is too many to dispose of. And they act like they know it. They roam around my feet with attitude, as if to make it clear that I'm trespassing on their turf.

My next set of challenges will arise not from the insect world, but from my neighbours. I'm the new arrival, subject to scrutiny about my charges just like when I'd run into the Aryan Brotherhood prison gang on my first day at the medium-security Towers jail a year ago. I wish my cellmate would wake up, brief me on the mood of the locals and introduce me to the head of the white gang. No such luck. Chow is announced over a speaker system in a crackly robotic voice, but he doesn't stir.

I emerge into the day room for breakfast. Prisoners in black-and-white bee-striped uniforms gather under the metal-grid stairs and tip dead cockroaches into a trash bin from plastic peanut-butter containers they'd set as traps during the night. All eyes are on me in the chow line. Watching who sits where, I hold my head up, put on a solid stare and pretend to be as at home in this environment as the cockroaches. It's all an act. I'm lonely and afraid. I loathe having to explain myself to the head of the white race, who I assume is the toughest murderer. I've been in jail long enough to know that taking my breakfast to my cell will imply that I have something to hide.

The gang punishes criminals with certain charges. The most serious are sex offenders, who are KOS: Kill On Sight. Other charges are punishable by SOS – Smash On Sight – such as drive-by shootings because women and kids sometimes get killed. It's called convict justice. Gang members are constantly looking for people to beat up because that's how they earn their reputations and tattoos. The most serious acts of violence earn the highest-ranking tattoos. To be a full gang member requires murder. I've observed the body language and techniques inmates trying to integrate employ. An inmate with a spring in his step and an air of confidence is likely to be accepted. A person who avoids eye contact and fails to introduce himself to the gang is likely to be preyed on. Some of the failed attempts I saw ended up with heads getting cracked against toilets, a sound I've grown familiar with. I've seen prisoners being extracted on stretchers who looked dead – one had yellow fluid leaking from his head. The constant violence gives me nightmares, but the reality is that I put myself in here, so I force myself to accept it as a part of my punishment.

It's time to apply my knowledge. With a self-assured stride, I take my breakfast bag to the table of white inmates covered in neo-Nazi tattoos, allowing them to question me.

"Mind if I sit with you guys?" I ask, glad exhaustion has deepened my voice.

"These seats are taken. But you can stand at the corner of the table."

The man who answered is probably the head of the gang. I size him up. Cropped brown hair. A dangerous glint in Nordic-blue eyes. Tiny pupils that suggest he's on heroin. Weightlifter-type veins bulging from a sturdy neck. Political ink on arms crisscrossed with scars. About the same age as me, thirty-three.

"Thanks. I'm Shaun from England." I volunteer my origin to show I'm different from them but not in a way that might get me smashed.

"I'm Bullet, the head of the whites." He offers me his fist to bump. "Where you roll in from, wood?"

Addressing me as wood is a good sign. It's what white gang members on a friendly basis call each other.

"Towers jail. They increased my bond and re-classified me to maximum security."

"What's your bond at?"

"I've got two $750,000 bonds," I say in a monotone. This is no place to brag about bonds.

"How many people you kill, brother?" His eyes drill into mine, checking whether my body language supports my story. My body language so far is spot on.

"None. I threw rave parties. They got us talking about drugs on wiretaps." Discussing drugs on the phone does not warrant a $1.5 million bond. I know and beat him to his next question. "Here's my charges." I show him my charge sheet, which includes conspiracy and leading a crime syndicate – both from running an Ecstasy ring.

Bullet snatches the paper and scrutinises it. Attempting to pre-empt his verdict, the other whites study his face. On edge, I wait for him to respond. Whatever he says next will determine whether I'll be accepted or victimised.

"Are you some kind of jailhouse attorney?" Bullet asks. "I want someone to read through my case paperwork." During our few minutes of conversation, Bullet has seen through my act and concluded that I'm educated – a possible resource to him.

I appreciate that he'll accept me if I take the time to read his case. "I'm no jailhouse attorney, but I'll look through it and help you however I can."

"Good. I'll stop by your cell later on, wood."

After breakfast, I seal as many of the cracks in the walls as I can with toothpaste. The cell smells minty, but the cockroaches still find their way in. Their day shift appears to be collecting information on the brown paper bags under my bunk, containing a few items of food that I purchased from the commissary; bags that I tied off with rubber bands in the hope of keeping the cockroaches out. Relentlessly, the cockroaches explore the bags for entry points, pausing over and probing the most worn and vulnerable regions. *Will the nightly swarm eat right through the paper?* I read all morning, wondering whether my cellmate has died in his cocoon, his occasional breathing sounds reassuring me.

Bullet stops by late afternoon and drops his case paperwork off. He's been charged with Class 3 felonies and less, not serious crimes, but is facing a double-digit sentence because of his prior convictions and Security Threat Group status in the prison system. The proposed sentencing range seems disproportionate. I'll advise him to reject the plea bargain – on the assumption he already knows to do so, but is just seeking the comfort of a second opinion, like many un-sentenced inmates. When he returns for his paperwork, our conversation disturbs my cellmate – the cocoon shuffles – so we go upstairs to his cell. I tell Bullet what I think. He is excitable, a different man from earlier, his pupils almost non-existent.

"This case ain't shit. But my prosecutor knows I done other shit, all kinds of heavy shit, but can't prove it. I'd do anything to get that sorry bitch off my fucking ass. She's asking for something bad to happen to her. Man, if I ever get bonded out, I'm gonna chop that bitch into pieces. Kill her slowly though. Like to work her over with a blowtorch."

Such talk can get us both charged with conspiring to murder a prosecutor, so I try to steer him elsewhere. "It's crazy how they can catch you doing one thing, yet try to sentence you for all of the things they think you've ever done."

"Done plenty. Shot some dude in the stomach once. Rolled him up in a blanket and threw him in a dumpster."

Discussing past murders is as unsettling as future ones. "So, what's all your tattoos mean, Bullet? Like that eagle on your chest?"

"Why you wanna know?" Bullet's eyes probe mine.

My eyes hold their ground. "Just curious."

"It's a war bird. The AB patch."

"AB patch?"

"What the Aryan Brotherhood gives you when you've put enough work in."

"How long does it take to earn a patch?"

"Depends how quickly you put your work in. You have to earn your lightning bolts first."

"Why you got red and black lightning bolts?"

"You get SS bolts for beating someone down or for being an enforcer for the family. Red lightning bolts for killing someone.

I was sent down as a youngster. They gave me steel and told me who to handle and I handled it. You don't ask questions. You just get blood on your steel. Dudes who get these tats without putting work in are told to cover them up or leave the yard."

"What if they refuse?"

"They're held down and we carve the ink off them."

Imagining them carving a chunk of flesh to remove a tattoo, I cringe. He's really enjoying telling me this now. His volatile nature is clear and frightening. *He's accepted me too much. He's trying to impress me before making demands.*

At night, I'm unable to sleep. Cocooned in heat, surrounded by cockroaches, I hear the swamp-cooler vent – a metal grid at the top of a wall – hissing out tepid air. Giving up on sleep, I put my earphones on and tune into National Public Radio. Listening to a Vivaldi violin concerto, I close my eyes and press my tailbone down to straighten my back as if I'm doing a yogic relaxation. The playful allegro thrills me, lifting my spirits, but the wistful adagio provokes sad emotions and tears. I open my eyes and gaze into the gloom. Due to lack of sleep, I start hallucinating and hearing voices over the music whispering threats. I'm at breaking point. Although I have accepted that I committed crimes and deserve to be punished, no one should have to live like this. I'm furious at myself for making the series of reckless decisions that put me in here and for losing absolutely everything. As violins crescendo in my ears, I remember what my life used to be like.

PRISON TIME BY SHAUN ATTWOOD

CHAPTER 1

"I've got a padlock in a sock. I can smash your brains in while you're asleep. I can kill you whenever I want." My new cellmate sizes me up with no trace of human feeling in his eyes. Muscular and pot-bellied, he's caked in prison ink, including six snakes on his skull, slithering side by side. The top of his right ear is missing in a semi-circle.

The waves of fear are overwhelming. After being in transportation all day, I can feel my bladder hurting. "I'm not looking to cause any trouble. I'm the quietest cellmate you'll ever have. All I do is read and write."

Scowling, he shakes his head. "Why've they put a fish in with me?" He swaggers close enough for me to smell his cigarette breath. "Us convicts don't get along with fresh fish."

"Should I ask to move then?" I say, hoping he'll agree if he hates new prisoners so much.

"No! They'll think I threatened you!"

In the eight by twelve feet slab of space, I swerve around him and place my property box on the top bunk.

He pushes me aside and grabs the box. "You just put that on my artwork! I ought to fucking smash you, fish!"

"Sorry, I didn't see it."

"You need to be more aware of your fucking surroundings! What you in for anyway, fish?"

I explain my charges, Ecstasy dealing and how I spent twenty-six months fighting my case.

"How come the cops were so hard-core after you?" he asks, squinting.

"It was a big case, a multi-million-dollar investigation. They raided over a hundred people and didn't find any drugs. They were pretty pissed off. I'd stopped dealing by the time they caught up with me, but I'd done plenty over the years, so I accept my punishment."

"Throwing raves," he says, staring at the ceiling as if remembering something. "Were you partying with underage girls?" he asks, his voice slow, coaxing.

Being called a sex offender is the worst insult in prison. Into my third year of incarceration, I'm conditioned to react. "What you trying to say?" I yell angrily, brow clenched.

"Were you fucking underage girls?" Flexing his body, he shakes both fists as if about to punch me.

"Hey, I'm no child molester, and I'd prefer you didn't say shit like that!"

"My buddy next door is doing twenty-five to life for murdering a child molester. How do I know Ecstasy dealing ain't your cover story?" He inhales loudly, nostrils flaring.

"You want to see my fucking paperwork?"

A stocky prisoner walks in. Short hair. Dark eyes. Powerful neck. On one arm: a tattoo of a man in handcuffs above the word OMERTA – the Mafia code of silence towards law enforcement. "What the fuck's going on in here, Bud?" asks Junior Bull – the son of "Sammy the Bull" Gravano, the Mafia mass murderer who was my biggest competitor in the Ecstasy market.

Relieved to see a familiar face, I say, "How're you doing?"

Shaking my hand, he says in a New York Italian accent, "I'm doing alright. I read that shit in the newspaper about you starting a blog in Sheriff Joe Arpaio's jail."

"The blog's been bringing media heat on the conditions."

"You know him?" Bud asks.

"Yeah, from Towers jail. He's a good dude. He's in for dealing Ecstasy like me."

"It's a good job you said that 'cause I was about to smash his ass," Bud says.

"It's a good job Wild Man ain't here 'cause you'd a got your ass thrown off the balcony," Junior Bull says.

I laugh. The presence of my best friend, Wild Man, was partly the reason I never took a beating at the county jail, but with Wild Man in a different prison, I feel vulnerable. When Bud casts a death stare on me, my smile fades.

"What the fuck you guys on about?" Bud asks.

"Let's go talk downstairs." Junior Bull leads Bud out.

I rush to a stainless-steel sink/toilet bolted to a cement-block wall by the front of the cell, unbutton my orange jumpsuit and crane my neck to watch the upper-tier walkway in case Bud returns. I bask in relief as my bladder deflates. After flushing, I take stock of my new home, grateful for the slight improvement in the conditions versus what I'd grown accustomed to in Sheriff Joe Arpaio's jail. No cockroaches. No blood stains. A working swamp cooler. Something I've never seen in a cell before: shelves. The steel table bolted to the wall is slightly larger, too. *But how will I concentrate on writing with Bud around?* There's a mixture of smells in the room. Cleaning chemicals. Aftershave. Tobacco. A vinegar-like odour. The slit of a window at the back overlooks gravel in a no-man's-land before the next building with gleaming curls of razor wire around its roof.

From the doorway upstairs, I'm facing two storeys of cells overlooking a day room with shower cubicles at the end of both tiers. At two white plastic circular tables, prisoners are playing dominoes, cards, chess and Scrabble, some concentrating, others yelling obscenities, contributing to a brain-scraping din that I hope to block out by purchasing a Walkman. In a raised box-shaped Plexiglas control tower, two guards are monitoring the prisoners.

Bud returns. My pulse jumps. Not wanting to feel like I'm stuck in a kennel with a rabid dog, I grab a notepad and pen and head for the day room.

Focussed on my body language, not wanting to signal any weakness, I'm striding along the upper tier, head and chest elevated, when two hands appear from a doorway and grab me. I drop the pad. The pen clinks against grid-metal and tumbles to the day room as I'm pulled into a cell reeking of backside sweat and masturbation, a cheese-tinted funk.

"I'm Booga. Let's fuck," says a squat man in urine-stained boxers, with WHITE TRASH tattooed on his torso below a mobile home, and an arm sleeved with the Virgin Mary.

Shocked, I brace to flee or fight to preserve my anal virginity. I can't believe my eyes when he drops his boxers and waggles his penis.

Dancing to music playing through a speaker he has rigged up, Booga smiles in a sexy way. "Come on," he says in a husky voice. "Drop your pants. Let's fuck." He pulls pornography faces. I question his sanity. He moves closer. "If I let you fart in my mouth, can I fart in yours?"

"You can fuck off," I say, springing towards the doorway.

He grabs me. We scuffle. Every time I make progress towards the doorway, he clings to my clothes, dragging me back in. When I feel his penis rub against my leg, my adrenalin kicks in so forcefully I experience a burst of strength and wriggle free. I bolt out as fast as my shower sandals will allow and snatch my pad. Looking over my shoulder, I see him stood calmly in the doorway, smiling. He points at me. "You have to walk past my door every day. We're gonna get together. I'll lick your ass and you can fart in my mouth." Booga blows a kiss and disappears.

I rush downstairs. With my back to a wall, I pause to steady my thoughts and breathing. In survival mode, I think, *What's going to come at me next?* In the hope of reducing my tension, I borrow a pen to do what helps me stay sane: writing. With the details fresh in my mind, I document my journey to the prison for my blog readers, keeping an eye out in case anyone else wants to test the new prisoner. The more I write, the more I fill with a sense of purpose. Jon's Jail Journal is a connection to the outside world that I cherish.

Someone yells, "One time!" The din lowers. A door rumbles open. A guard does a security walk, his every move scrutinised by dozens of scornful eyes staring from cells. When he exits, the din resumes, and the prisoners return to injecting drugs to escape from reality, including the length of their sentences. This continues all day with "Two times!" signifying two approaching guards, and "Three times!" three and so on. Every now and then an announcement by a guard over the speakers briefly lowers the din.

Before lockdown, I join the line for a shower, holding bars of soap in a towel that I aim to swing at the head of the next person to try me. With boisterous inmates a few feet away, yelling at the men in the showers to "Stop jerking off," and "Hurry the fuck up," I get in a cubicle that reeks of bleach and mildew. With every nerve strained, I undress and rinse fast.

At night, despite the desert heat, I cocoon myself in a blanket from head to toe and turn towards the wall, making my face more difficult to strike. I leave a hole for air, but the warm cement block inches from my mouth returns each exhalation to my face as if it's breathing on me, creating a feeling of suffocation. For hours, my heart drums so hard against the thin mattress I feel as if I'm moving even though I'm still. I try to sleep, but my eyes keep springing open and my head turning towards the cell as I try to penetrate the darkness, searching for Bud swinging a padlock in a sock at my head.

ABOUT THE AUTHORS

Steve Wraith

Steve Wraith is an actor, writer and promoter who lives on Tyneside. His previous books include: *The Krays: The Geordie Connection*, *Race for the Premiership*, *The Krays from the Cradle to the Grave*, *NME: From the Bender Squad to the Gremlins*, *The Milk Thief*, *The Sayers: Tried and Tested at the Highest Level* and *The Krays and Freddie Foreman: Read All About It*.

Stuart Wheatman

Stu has written a few books including: *The Machine* and *Cage Fighter* with Ian 'The Machine' Freeman, *The Krays: The Geordie Connection* with Steve Wraith, *King of Clubs* with Terry Turbo, *The Jam Unseen* with Twink and *Slimmer Charlie* with Charlie Walduck.

The authors are researching and writing more true crime ... watch this space.

You can buy them all here www.thekrays.net and www.thesayers.co.uk

Liam Galvin also released a DVD about Steve's story called *The Krays Geordie Connection*.

www.ingramcontent.com/pod-product-compliance
Lightning Source LLC
Chambersburg PA
CBHW071727080526
44588CB00013B/1931